13. Baer, William C.
14. Baker, Curtis R.
15. Baldonado, Secundino
16. Balters, Stephen A. Jr.
17. Bazulto, Salvador
18. Hargett, John Jr.
19. Davis, Richard S. Jr.
20. Bletsch, William P.
21. Blinder, Richard B.
22. Borowsky, Charles George
23. Torello, Carl
24. Anderson, James H.
25. Brockman, Verndean A.
26. Thompson, Charles Michael
27. Broumas, Andre
28. Canas, Roberto L.
29. Bullock, Glen
30. Buckner, Anthony Eugene
31. Bunch, William Lloyd
32. Burnett, Sheldon
33. Choquette, Robert G.
34. Clark, Terry Richard
35. Burns, Darrell Edward
36. Clendenen, Richard
37. Cook, Lewis Collin
38. Buskey, Orrie J.
39. Gambotto, Larry Louis
40. Couch, Leslie
41. Cameron, Virgil
42. Campbell, Keith
43. Derrickson, Thomas G.
44. Caudillo, Joseph
45. Cavender, Jim Ray
46. Chaney, Larry W.
47. Graham, Gilbert James
48. Cruse, Michael L.
49. Eyring, Kenneth R.
50. Clark, Thomas Edward
51. Flores, Raul
52. Cowart, David L.
53. Fuss, Robert E.
54. Long, George Wendell
55. Garcia, Pedro I.
56. Underhill, David Joseph
57. Robertson, Mark J.
58. Glover, Douglas J.
59. Justice, William Paul
60. Delgado, Christopher G.
61. Debernardo, Frank Jr.
62. Gmack, John R.
63. Katzenberger, Raymond L.
64. Brown, Vaughn Lee
65. Dixon, James C.
66. Dixon, Lee C.
67. Ericson, William F. II
68. Kozai, Kenneth B.
69. Lindbloom, Charles
70. Earick, James
71. Elkins, Jerome
72. Turley, Morvan Darrell
73. Lambdin, Daniel Alvey
74. Gage, Norman Glenn
75. Graves, Carter Lee
76. Grace, Larry E.
77. Hauser, Vincent Vanalstyne
78. Chatmon, Nathan Eugene
79. Goodman, James D.
80. Hargrove, Joseph N.
81. Hayes, George F.
82. Youngblood, Charles E.
83. Mullin, Gerald
84. Green, Phillip W. Jr.
85. Stewart, Ulysses
86. Griffis, William A. III
87. Juarez, John Richard
88. Judy, David Lynn
89. Hendricks, Sterling Craig
90. Willis, William Sherrill
91. Hill, Maurice R.
92. Hernandez, Rolando
93. Kawamura, Terry Teruo
94. Kearney, Charles D.
95. King, Patrick Willmer
96. Green, Kenneth Leon
97. Lukert, Edward
98. Margle, Thomas Joseph
99. Masuda, Robert S.
100. Smith, Leslie R.
101. Kincannon, Raymond
102. Murrell, Aaron Crusoe

♦ All They Left Behind ♦
Legacies of the Men and Women on The Wall

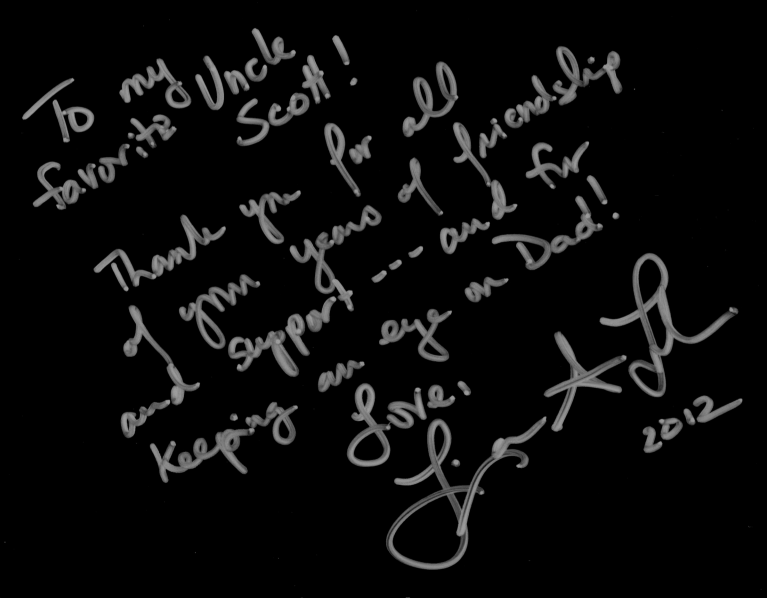

Lisa A. Lark
In Commemoration of the 30th Anniversary of The Wall

1. Goias, Everett William
2. Greene, Joseph
3. Evans, Donald Ward Jr.
4. Di Bartolomeo Ronald
5. Griffin, Harold Dexter
6. Elford, Gary
7. Stringer, Isaac
8. Harmon, Daniel Lee
9. Fischer, Joseph
10. Gerth, Peter H.
11. Freitag, Dieter K.
12. Kelley, Harvey
13. Logan, Bradley J.
14. Ruiz, Jose
15. Sims, Clifford Chester
16. Ellison, Charlie Melvin
17. Matayoshi, Wallace K.
18. Hurry, Samuel G.
19. McGee, Robert L. Jr.
20. Saukaitis, Joseph S.
21. Brower, Ralph Wayne
22. Sargent, Donald
23. Cochrane, John F.
24. Reid, Kenneth Wayne
25. Curttright, Larry Brent
26. Overacker, Earl John
27. Calloway, Ronald D.
28. Faircloth, Henry F.
29. Dalton, Theodore H.
30. Shaw, Joe Carl
31. Omstead, David K.
32. Moore, Ronald A.
33. Smith, Hubert Ray
34. Nelson, Paul Arthur
35. Stemac, Stephen Joseph
36. Carmody, Robert J.
37. Brillo, Albert, Jr.
38. Cabbagestalk, Eugene
39. Snyder, Gerald A.
40. Ammon, William R.
41. Budzinski, Lawrence Joseph
42. Gee, Gregory
43. Gause, Bernard Jr.
44. Ribitsch, Eric
45. Sprewell, John Spurgeon
46. Spitzer, Howard Ray
47. Ramsey, Michael Wayne
48. Balai, Andres
49. Stanton, Scott N.
50. Seagroves, Michael Anthony
51. Shue, Donald
52. Ross, Stanley D.
53. Gallagher, Patrick Joseph
54. Munoz, Jose Jr.
55. Tarango, Magdaleno
56. Williams, Lester Lee
57. Gandolfo, Philip
58. Craig, Edward J.
59. Briscoe, Charles
60. Vasquez, Eddie
61. Herring, Pedro
62. Waters, Samuel E. Jr.
63. Skeen, Richard
64. Winters, Darryl Gordon
65. Graham, Annie R.
66. Sexton, Richard II
67. Zwerlein, Robert
68. Walls, Kenneth Marion
69. Simpson, Douglas Edward
70. Shea, Thomas C.
71. Allen, Lyle Ernest Jr.
72. Alonzo, Manuel B.
73. Slane, William Llewellyn
74. Bennett, Donald Casper
75. Thompson, Dennis Michael
76. Florence, Dexter B.
77. Elwart, Paul
78. Hartwick, Floyd Jr.
79. Elizondo, David
80. Campestre, Albert J.
81. Rodriguez, Israel
82. Blavat, James Norbert
83. Callivas, Gust
84. Aragon, Henry T.
85. Heil, Jackie Phillip
86. Artis, Herbert John
87. Carter, David Edward
88. White, Charles M. Sr.
89. Boone, Dennis Clayton
90. Chamberlain, Robert F.
91. Riles, James C.
92. Houston, Richard P.

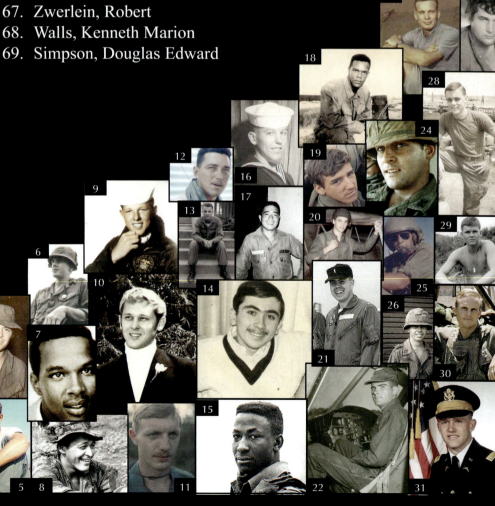

Cover Images

93. Barden, Arnold Jr.
94. Apodaca, Victor Jr.
95. Dickinson, David
96. Adame, Arthur P.
97. Barthelmas, William
98. Clark, Grant
99. Pack, Robert Van
100. Archer, Richard C.
101. Harris, Samuel Gary
102. Collins, Vernel
103. Appleton, John Burdette
104. Collier, James Allen
105. Atteridge, Leon Jr.
106. Parks, Joe
107. Deitrick, George D.
108. Dillard, John A. Jr.
109. Weaver, George R. Jr.
110. Pittman, Robert Edward
111. Chambliss, Roger
112. Castro, Alfonso Roque
113. Eckle, Stephen John

Cover Images

Not Forgotten ♦ Carolyn Marshall

M.T. Publishing Company, Inc.™

P.O. Box 6802, Evansville, Indiana 47719-6802
www.mtpublishing.com

No part of this publication may be translated, reproduced or transmitted in any form or by any means, electronic or mechanical, including photocopying and recording, or by any information storage and retrieval system, without expressed written permission of the copyright owner and M.T. Publishing Company, Inc.

The materials for this book were compiled and produced using available information. Although every reasonable effort has been made to be as accurate as possible about descriptions of events and photos, discrepancies in recorded history and human error are always possible; therefore, neither M.T. Publishing Company, Inc. nor anyone involved with the creation of this book shall be held responsible for any inaccuracies in the content.

Printed in the United States of America.

Copyright © 2012
Vietnam Veterans Memorial Fund
All rights reserved.

Library of Congress Control Number:
2012941596

ISBN: 978-1-934729-91-5

Graphic Design by:
Alena Kiefer,
M.T. Publishing Company, Inc.

Table of Contents

Acknowledgements	6
Foreword	8
Legacies	9
James Gabriel, Jr.	10
Ronald Fegan	11
William Cordero	14
Stephen Phillips	15
Dearborn Soldiers	18
Dennis Stancroff	18
Earl Smith	18
Raymond Borowski	19
David Antol	20
James Davis	20
James Huard	21
Carol Drazba	26
Elizabeth Jones	27
Reuben Garnett, Jr.	28
Fred & Wayne Traylor	30
James Lockridge	32
Eugene Self	34
Charles Meek	37
George Myers & John Schmidt	40
Budd & Charles Hood	42
Matthew Leonard	43
Donald & Cordis White	44
Paul Wolos	45
Xavier Arvizu & Alexandro Nevarez	48
James Watanabe	50
Walter Wright	52
Eleanor Alexander	53
Legacies (cont.)	
Hedwig Orlowski	54
Robert Mason	56
Brian Durr	57
Robert Brett	60
Winford McCosar	62
William & Samuel Nixon	63
Harvey Cooley	64
Pamela Donovan	68
Annie Graham	69
Roger Bartholomew	70
Morton Singer	72
David Land & Ralph Bickford	73
Howard Early	79
Ronald Hacker	80
Samuel Wayne Bell	83
Sharon Lane	84
Michael Painter	85
Douglas Kempf	86
Francis Cortor, Jr.	89
Michael Casey	93
Miguel Keith	97
Barton Creed	98
Alvin Adikai, Jr.	101
Johnny Arthur	102
Robert Brett, Jr.	103
Henry Aderholt	104
Emmet Reid Galbreth II	107
Mary Klinker	108
Bibliography	110
Artwork	112
Index	113

Photo by Bill Shugarts

Acknowledgements

This project began with a question from a student on Memorial Day 2010. A request for more information about a soldier who died in Vietnam soon grew into the search for information about 23 and then 68 and it soon became clear that all of the more than 58,000 names on The Wall deserved to have their stories told and preserved for future generations.

In my quest to tell these stories, I met and spoke with thousands of people who shared their memories, their stories, and their pain with me, a relative stranger. These people lived through the Vietnam years and nearly every one of them lost someone. They opened their scrapbooks, their hearts and, in many cases, their homes to me. Some of them spoke of their experiences for the very first time, and I am forever humbled to be the one they chose to tell. I wish I could tell all of the more than 58,000 stories on The Wall because all of them should be remembered. It is our duty as Americans to know the names on The Wall as the men and women they were, not simply as names carved into black granite. They gave their lives for something larger than themselves, and as those left behind, we must carry on their legacies.

I could not have completed a project of this magnitude alone, and as such I am indebted to many, many people.

The following individuals provided written or oral interviews about specific soldiers or their Vietnam and military experiences: Victor Alvarez, Kay Anason, Stephen Andres, Richard Andrews, Anna Antol, George Archer, Prisylla Arthur-Imel, Brian Atchley, Norm Bailey, Debby Baker, Patricia Barbee, Landis Bargatze, Bud Barnes, Margie Bernal, Jerry E. Brown, Don Buhan, Paul Burton, Andrea Stec Calabrese, Barbara Campbell, Clay Campbell, The Casey Family, Barbara Cehanowicz, Michael Chandler, Ram Chavez, Larry Collette, Mike Collins, Tom and Sue Combs, The Cooley Family, Tony Cordero, Grace Cote, Melissa Brett Coven, Lt. Col. Scott Creed, Philip Cronin, Linda Pinegar Dark, Thelma DeHaven, Robert Demler, Don Dignan, Joseph Drazba, Lynn Duane, Jeannette Early, Judie and Mike Eby, Richard Engelbrecht, Ken Faller, Dr. Susan Ferraris, Dennis Flanigan, Roy Flores, Rich Forman, Norm Friedman, Billie Gabriel, Richard Garcia, India Garnett, Art Garrison, Alan and Lori Gentinne, Ron Gibbons, Laura Davis Gillert, Bonnie Gooch, Robert Goolsby, Joaquin Gracida, Carol Grano, Paul Grice, Fred Hahn, Karen Yuhasz Hahn, John Hannon, Lisa Hanson, Sandy Hargrove, Michael A. Harris, Chuck Healey, Darryl Henley, Ralphina Hernandez, William Higgins, Kim Hoopengarner, Karen Hopkins, Richard Howett, The Huard Family, G. Calvin Hutchinson, Sue Jacklin, Pastor Thomas W. Johnson, Don Kaiser, Joanne Katula, Frank and Sue Kelly, Dr. Dennis Kempf, Janet Klieman, David Klinker, Stephanie Klinker, Ron Kubowicz, E.H. Land, Craig Latham, Jim Laurier, David Lawson, Lou LeGarie, Emme Radcliffe Leslie, Anthony Lockridge, Doris Long, James Machin, William Magri, Tammy McClure Maldonado, Tom Mangan, Virginia Manual, Pete Manuguerra, Greg Marshall, Larry Matthews, John McCorkle, Bunnie McCosar, Colin McGee, Doc McHugh, Jim McIlhenney, John McNown, Gary Meek, Mark Meek, James Meek, Galen Mitchell, Joyce Moore, Hoyt Bruce Moore III, Emily Mora, Bob Morris, Brian Mulcare, Betty Myers, Diane Myers, Bob Neace, Lana Noone, Karen Thall Norton, Page Creed O'Flaherty, Jan Owen, Chuck Payne, Dr. Richard Pellerin, Susan Creed Percy, Nancy Santorum Perhogan, Bill Peterson, Steve Phillips, Marilyn Wright Plise, Ed Pool, Michael Pusillo, Linda Ragle, Major Guy Ravey, Ron Raymond, Jim Reece, Edward Rouse, The Rowley sisters, Dan Ryder, Joaquin Sandoval, Jerry Sandoval, Lt. Col. Teddy H. Sanford Jr., USA (Ret.), Tomeka Saxon, Walter Scoggins, Colleen Shine, Dr. Vera Silberberg, Greg Skilling, Phil Smith, Douglas Smyth, Ruth Sprowls, Homer Steedly Jr., Diane Stephenson, Danny Stewart, Kim Sulek, Brian Sullivan, Gary Tanner, Jill Tarrant, Janice Terry, Joel Thoreson, Craig Tillman, Capt. Robert Treis, USN (Ret.), Victor Unruh, Rachel Vargas, Victor Vilonis, Mary Wade, Diane Walls, Roger Ware, The Watanabe Family, Jerry Wetzel, Glenda Williamson, Bob and Pat Wojciak, Peter and Cathy Wolos, Judy Woodall, the Family of Chip Yokom.

The following people opened their homes to me and spent hours talking about the loved ones that they lost in Vietnam: Darelynn Hacker Clay, Richard Fegan, Tina Fegan Graf, Ron and Elizabeth June, Joseph Land, John Mason, Kristine Meek O'Mara and Frances Cortor Turley.

The following organizations provided invaluable research assistance and direction: American Gold Star Mothers, American Legion Department of Michigan, American Legion Ford Motor Co. Post 173, American Legion Fort Dearborn Post 364, Aultman Hospital, Boston Public Library-Copley Square, Coshocton Public Library-Genealogy Department, City of Dearborn, Michigan and Dearborn Historical Museum, Dearborn Allied War Veterans Council, Gerald R. Ford Presidential Library, Gold Star Wives of America, Lake County Historical Society, Lane Medical Library at Evans Army Community Medical Center, MidAmerica Nazarene University, National Museum of the Marine Corps, New Jersey Vietnam Veterans Memorial Foundation, Sons and Daughters in Touch, Army Art Collection, Vietnam Veterans of America Chapter 154, Vietnam Veterans of America Chapter 267.

Special thanks for the prompt and helpful fulfillment of research requests goes to Del May and his team at the National Personnel Records Center in St. Louis and Duery Felton and the staff of the Vietnam Veterans Memorial Collection. Bill Shugarts, a National Parks Service volunteer, personally created a Wall rubbing for each of the men and women featured in the book.

The staff at the Vietnam Veterans Memorial Fund is without equal in their commitment to America's Vietnam veterans and their families. The team at VVMF, led by Jan Scruggs and Dan Reese, will do whatever necessary to honor and remember those that were lost in Vietnam. I received a great deal of help from Lee Allen, Adam Arbogast, Gjergj Pojani, Jennifer Rowell, Danielle Schirra, JoAnn Waller, and Geoffrey Wiles and was assisted by the rest of the VVMF team.

When I needed captions written, I was fortunate to be able to call on some of the best college students in the country, my former students Cailee Drzinski, Jack Kiraly, Rena Laws, Hayden McDade, Kathleen Peterson, Collette Poisson, Cameron Shane and Samantha Wagner. Thank you for reminding me why I wanted to become a teacher.

I received near constant encouragement over the course of this project. So many people provided motivation, but I call special attention to Hassane Jaafar and the staff and students of Edsel Ford High School. My friends have supported this project from the beginning, and I would like to thank anyone who offered even a small word to me along the way. My eternal love and friendship to all of you, but especially: Kimberly Dieboll; Ann, Heather and Erin Dilly; Alison, Lexi and Maddie Fayz; Jennette Swartout Leal; Alicia Lerman; Jennifer Linting; Anne and Steve O'Connor; Kimberly Spinks Oliver; Lindsay and Natalie Sosnoski; and Jennifer Swartout.

I asked Celia Weyher for some assistance with research on Navy corpsmen. Soon I was asking her to conduct interviews with families and translate medical records. It is amazing that Celia is only recently graduated from high school, as she has the maturity and pride of someone twice her age.

On Memorial Day 2010, Michelle Kerr sang a beautiful song in tribute to Edsel Ford's fallen. The emotion she put into the words she sang led me to select her to help me on this project. For nearly two years she has done everything I've asked and more, working throughout her senior year of high school and her freshman year of college. Michelle has shown me Vietnam through the eyes of the next generation, and has given me inspiration and insight without realizing it.

Margaret Kraft edited every word in this book and helped me tell these important stories. She provided much more than grammar and spelling advice, but helped me understand what the book could be. The fact that she did this work in the time she wasn't teaching English or raising her family is even more astounding. The book is better because she put her pen to it; I am a better teacher because of what I have seen her do and I am a better person because of her friendship and support.

Finally, my family. I don't know what I can say to explain what you mean to me and I know I can never repay all that you have done for me. I will spend the rest of my life trying to show you how much I love you and respect the amazing, wonderful, giving people that you are. I am the person I am because you have loved me.

Christa, thank you for bringing joy to all of our lives. I don't remember a time without your smile around and I hope I never have to.

Bryan, thank you for showing me how to stand up and follow my dreams. The first time I saw you on stage was one of the proudest moments of my life, and your gifts bring tears to my eyes even when I'm supposed to be laughing. I couldn't have asked for a better brother or friend.

Kimberly, thank you for knowing me better than I know myself and for loving me anyway. Thank you for being the best friend I could ever have, and for teaching me how to be brave and honest. My life is less ordinary with you around and I wouldn't have it any other way.

Sebastian, thank you for seeing me as I cannot see myself, and for loving all of my crazy quirks and idiosyncrasies. You are selfless, giving, and kind to me at all times, and I still don't think you realize how much you mean to me.

I am nothing without my mother and father, Carol and Dennis Lark. I can say with certainty that I would not be here today to write this without you. You have believed in me every moment of every day of my life. In my darkest days you never let me give up and because of that I never will. Your words and love are what fills my heart and I am blessed every day to have you as my parents. I love you more than all of the words in the world could help me say.

This book is dedicated to the memory of my Grandpa, Ernest Edward Lark.

POW-MIA ♦ Carolyn Marshall

Foreword

A lesson that those who have ever served in combat have learned time and time again is that our days are numbered. One of the primary goals of our lives should be to prepare for our last day. The legacies we leave are not simply our possessions, but also the ways in which we have done good works and have helped others. Our personal legacy will be determined by the choices that we make. Our values help guide us.

Legacies. That's what this book is about. For 30 years, The Wall has been a stunning reminder of just how many lives were lost during one of our nation's longest and most divisive wars. For me, each of the 58,282 engraved names represents a life lost, a future cut too short…and a legacy that all too often remains unwritten.

Author Ray Bradbury wrote, "Everyone must leave something behind when he dies . . . Something your hand touched some way so your soul has somewhere to go when you die . . . It doesn't matter what you do, so long as you change something from the way it was before you touched it into something that's like you after you take your hands away."

But, there are far too many legacies that are fading into history and too many stories that need to be told. Let's face it, those of us with first-hand knowledge are aging and our numbers are dwindling daily. This confluence of urgency is why the Vietnam Veterans Memorial Fund (VVMF) has produced this book and is exactly why we are working so hard to build The Education Center at The Wall.

In the pages that follow, readers will come face-to-face with just a few of the stories that need telling. By looking at the photos and reading the remembrances, you will come to know these men and women just a little better. You will see glimpses of who they were and what their lives meant to those who loved and still miss them. These pages show their photographs and tell stories of not only how they met their fate, but also how they lived their lives. You will be reminded that the legacies left behind are so much more than names on The Wall.

With this effort, Lisa Lark has once again proven herself to be an accomplished historian and a valued friend. This 2011 recipient of VVMF's "Hometown Heroes Award" continues her exceptional dedication to gathering information, remembrances and photographs of those whose names are on the Vietnam Veterans Memorial. She originally set out to collect photographs of the 23 fallen service members from Edsel Ford High School in Dearborn, Michigan, where she teaches. What began as a class project turned into an effort to collect all the photographs from her hometown, and eventually seek to compile all 2,663 photographs from the state of Michigan. Her dedication has been a source of inspiration for many and continues to rally support across the country.

Enjoy this book and look forward with us to the day, very soon, when we will celebrate the opening of the Education Center. Like The Wall itself, this will be a fascinating location for us to connect with those individuals who died wearing their nation's uniform throughout our history, ensuring that their sacrifices will always be treasured…and that their names, their lives and their legacies will never be forgotten.

◆ Jan C. Scruggs,
Founder and President
Vietnam Veterans Memorial Fund

Laying of Eight Wreaths, Memorial Day 2012 ◆ Bill Shugarts

Legacies

Leaving the Perimeter ♦ Richard Yaco
Courtesy of the National Museum of Marine Corps,
Art Collection, Triangle, Va.

JAMES GABRIEL Jr.

Specialist 5th Class, Army • 3/22/38–4/8/62 • Panel 1E, Row 8

Many Americans got their first introduction to the Army's Special Forces through the 1966 song "Ballad of the Green Berets" by Staff Sgt. Barry Sadler. The song's stirring lyrics tell of the dedication and bravery of the men who wore the Green Beret. What many don't realize about the song, which reached number one on the Billboard charts in March of 1966, is that there is another verse. In the verse, which did not make the final version of the song, Sadler reveals his inspiration for the powerful song. The verse, written by Sadler and his co-writer Robin Moore is as follows:

"Remember Gabriel died on Asia's shore
To a wife and child he'll return no more
They heard this man say
I would give my life for the Green Beret."

James Gabriel Jr. was born on March 22, 1938 to James Gabriel and his wife, Juliette. James Jr. was called Kimo by his family, which meant James in the native language of Hawaiians. He was the oldest of nine children in the Gabriel family and grew up in Honolulu, Hawaii. The family also spent time with their grandmother in the countryside of Wailua. In his free time, James loved to swim. He was very musical and loved to play Hawaiian music on his ukulele. He also held a second-degree black belt. James was an intelligent young man, making excellent grades while in school. He was well-liked at Farrington High School and graduated in 1956. While at Farrington, James was involved with the Junior Reserve Officer Training Corps (JROTC). It was in the JROTC that his love for the military first began to blossom. He became an officer and thrived on the discipline and routine. Classmates remembered his uniform always perfectly starched and his shoes polished to a mirror's shine.

James in jump school, Ft. Bragg, 1957. Photo courtesy of Billie Gabriel.

It was this love for the military and a love for the United States that motivated James to enlist in the Army in 1958. He was the first of his family to serve, and his family was proud of him. After his basic training, he attended jump school at Fort Bragg, N.C. and then served with A Company of the 307th Airborne Engineers, 82nd Airborne. Larry Falcone served with James, who his Army comrades called Gabe, and remembers him well. "He was the most polished trooper in our outfit. Always smiling, he led us with the confidence of a combat veteran." After Fort Bragg, James served in Okinawa for a time. It was there that he met his wife, Nobue Morimoto, whom he married in 1960.

James joined the Special Forces in 1961 after earning the coveted Green Beret. He arrived in Vietnam and was assigned to A-1/213 1st Special Forces Group. His frequent letters home to his mother reveal a soldier who was proud to be serving his country but who missed the comforts of home, particularly Juliette's coconut cookies.

Army Specialist 5th Class James Gabriel Jr., U.S. Army. Photo courtesy of Billie Gabriel.

One of the responsibilities of the 1st Special Forces group was to train soldiers in Vietnamese villages to defend themselves from the guerilla tactics of the Viet Cong (VC) and their sympathizers. James and three other Special Forces soldiers were on a three-week field mission training a group of approximately 30 Vietnamese villagers near the village of An Chau. On the third night of their exercise, James and his team heard movement in the jungle around them. During the night, a group of VC attacked the Special Forces group but were pushed back. But in the morning, James' group was attacked again and this time they were surrounded by enemy forces. In the fire fight that ensued, James called for reinforcements and ammunition and was hit three times by enemy gunfire.

By the time reinforcements made their way from Danang, it was too late. The Americans arrived near An Chau to find the bodies of James and Staff Sgt. Wayne Marchand. The men's hands were tied behind their backs and they had been shot in the back of the head.

James was the first native Hawaiian to lose his life in Vietnam, and many believe him and Marchand to be the first two Special Forces soldiers killed in the Vietnam War. His son, James Gabriel III would be born just five months after James' death.

The 5th Special Forces group, housed at Fort Campbell, Ky., named their parade field in honor of James in 2010. In preparing to attend the ceremonies, James' sister Billie read some of the letters that Kimo had sent home to his mother. Billie was only 11 when her oldest brother died. She remembered being pulled out of school by her father and the quiet ride home to her devastated mother. She read all of the letters that Juliette had kept in a shoebox after Kimo's death. "I wanted to know what was in his heart—in his mind," Billie said. "I could really feel his youth and at the same time I could feel the strength of a man." ♦

RONALD J FEGAN

Ensign, Navy • 2/11/41–4/9/65 • Panel 1E, Row 103

The profession of combat aviator is a dangerous one, and the field is filled with men and women who love the feeling of flight and the power of the aircraft. From the earliest days of American military aircraft, being a military aviator has required years of arduous training, extreme focus and a love for the adrenaline and risk that come with strapping oneself into an airplane and taking flight.

Ronald Fegan loved the feeling that came with flying, particularly the feeling that came with flying fast. He'd always had an interest in planes and would often spend hours with his father watching the planes take off and land at the nearby airport. He would learn to fly and he would be a pilot. Ronnie wanted to fly the fastest planes in the world and he wanted to fly them for the rest of his life.

Born in 1941 in Brockport, N.Y., Ronald Fegan was the middle of five children born to Walter and Velma Fegan. The family grew up in the Brockport area and Walter and Velma separated in 1955. Growing up, Ronnie and his older brother, Richard, shared a bedroom and most of the time, they even shared a bed. They never had heat in the upstairs part of the house on Drake Rd. in Clarkson, so Ronnie and Rich would often put on all of the clothes in their closet to keep warm. Clarkson, just east of Rochester in upstate New York, was prone to cold, windy winters. These nights would have Ronnie and Richard scrambling for every piece of clothing that they could find to keep from freezing, and Richard's best efforts to stay warm were often thwarted by Ronnie's desire to keep the windows open.

Ronnie and his siblings attended Brockport Central School and Brockport High School. Ronnie was a fine but unmotivated student, and he was interested in mechanics and automobiles while he was growing up. He worked at an area Ford dealership and saved money to go to college and study engineering. After graduating high school in 1959, Ronnie enrolled at the State University of New York (SUNY), Agricultural and Technical Institute in nearby Alfred, in September of 1959. His goal was an associate degree in applied sciences, with a focus on farm power and machinery. Around this same time, Ronnie began spending time with Harold Redinger, his brother Richard's father-in-law. Harold had a small Aeronca Chief that he flew out of a small airport on Sweden Walker Rd. in Brockport. It was at this small airport, flying in Harold's small, two-seat Aeronca that Ronnie learned to fly. The plane was designed for flight training and could get up to 100 miles per hour. Ronnie was on his way to becoming a pilot.

Ronnie's senior portrait from Brockport High School. Photo courtesy of the Fegan family.

Ensign Ronald Fegan, U.S. Navy. Photo courtesy of the Fegan family.

After completing his associate degree at SUNY Alfred in June of 1961, Ronnie headed down to the University of Georgia to continue his education. He enrolled in the fall quarter of 1961, with a major in agricultural economics. He completed five terms of coursework at UGA and graduated with a bachelor's degree in 1963. Although there was much Ronnie could have done with his degree, he still carried his dream of becoming a pilot. On July 1, 1963, Ronnie made his way to Buffalo and enlisted in the U.S. Navy. He wasn't simply going to be a pilot; he was going to be a naval aviator.

The training that Ronnie would undergo to achieve his dream of flying military airplanes would test his intellectual and psychological limits and would begin almost immediately after enlisting. After signing up for six years of service to the Navy, Ronnie was assigned to Officer Candidate School (OCS) at the U.S. Naval Base Station, Newport, R.I. Ronnie had always been small, but he was strong, and his physical performance in OCS supported that. Ronnie was determined, though, and highly motivated to succeed at OCS. Though he measured just 5 foot 6 inches and barely 140 pounds at OCS, he was in excellent physical condition and a medical report in August 1963

An illustration of the F-4B that Terence Murphy and Ronald Fegan were flying when they disappeared on April 9, 1965. Illustration by Jim Laurier.

deemed him "physically qualified and aeronautically adapted for duty involving flying."

His next duty station was Naval Air Station Pensacola, Fla. While at Pensacola, he underwent basic ground and air training that all prospective naval aviators received. He received instruction in Pensacola from December 2, 1963 until April 1964 and was rated excellent in his officer's fitness report. Ronnie would then report to U.S. Naval Air Technical Training Center in Glynco, Ga. It was here that he began receiving instruction as a radar intercept officer (RIO) in the F-4 Phantom. The McDonnell F-4 Phantom II was a two-seat military aircraft that weighed more than 33 tons and could travel twice the speed of sound. Designed to fill multiple roles, the Phantom could be used in air-to-air combat or could drop a bomb payload on ground targets. The Phantom featured high-end computer electronics to guide the plane and its weapons systems, and enabled pilots to aim for targets that were out of their range of vision. This would allow American pilots to attack targets from a much greater distance.

By this point, Ronnie loved what he was doing in the Navy and was considering making the Navy his career. His training at Glynco taught him to be the RIO, or "back-seater" of the F-4. The F-4 was set up for a two-man system, with the pilot in front responsible for the directionality of the plane, and the RIO in the back operating the air-to-air weapons systems. Ronnie once again completed the course with excellent ratings and was sent to Fighter Squadron 21 to be trained as replacement personnel for the Pacific Fleet Attack Carrier Striking Force. He would be with Fighter Squadron 21 from July 1964 until mid-February 1965. His performance review for this time period was particularly impressive. His commanding officer said that, "Ensign Fegan has performed all of his duties in an excellent manner. He has demonstrated superior knowledge of the F-4 weapon system and is highly motivated as a radar observer for carrier based all weather air intercept operations." He then headed to Fighter Squadron (VF) 121 where he would continue training, this time with a focus on carrier take-offs and landings. In a letter to his brother Richard, Ronnie described his responsibilities on those training runs: "My job as RIO is to monitor approach path, keep the F-4 at the correct airspeed, altitude and handle the communications." This letter, sent in February 1965, told his brother of his next posting: the USS Ranger.

A Forrestal class aircraft carrier, the USS Ranger was commissioned by the U.S. Navy in 1957. More than 1,000 feet long, the Ranger arrived in the waters off Vietnam in 1964 after the Gulf of Tonkin incident. Ensign Ronald Fegan arrived on the USS Ranger on February 15, 1965. At that point, Ronnie told his brother that "The F-4s are not bombing yet, but are used to cover bombers from MiGs. I guess I might see a little action out there but they are not using the F-4 for bombing or strafing missions." Ronnie told his brother he planned to be back in the U.S. in April and would be in Norfolk, Va. in September.

Once on board the Ranger, Ronnie was assigned to VF-96 as the back-seater for Lieutenant Junior Grade (Lt. j.g.)

Ronnie and one of the planes that so fascinated him.
Photo courtesy of the Fegan family.

Terence Murphy of New York. Murphy, a 1961 graduate of the United States Naval Academy, was already on the Ranger when Fegan arrived. Murphy was a strong pilot and flew without fear. He, along with other members of VF-96, had already flown combat missions in Vietnam since arriving in the area in 1964. On April 9, 1965, Murphy and Fegan were in one of four F-4 Phantoms launching off of the Ranger as part of a mission in the Hanoi area. Fegan and Murphy were flying as *Showtime 611* that morning. Just as Fegan had said in his February letter to his brother, Richard, the F-4s would be used to try and draw enemy MiGs away from the target area and over the Navy ships in the Gulf of Tonkin. At around 8:15 a.m., just 15 minutes after leaving the Ranger, the F-4s from VF-96 were picked up by North Vietnamese and Chinese radar. According to statements made by Li Dayun, a pilot in the Chinese Naval Air Force, "Our flight was alerted to intercept four U.S. aircraft which had intruded over Chinese air space." The Chinese airspace that Li refers to is the area surrounding Hainan Island, China's southernmost province. Hainan Island, surrounded by the Gulf of Tonkin and the South China Sea, was Chinese territory, and the American pilots had been briefed to stay away from it. The Chinese pilots took off at 8:21 a.m. and headed north toward the American planes.

In the 17 minutes after the initial engagement, the Chinese and American fighters scrambled to determine both where they were and what, if any, action they were allowed to take. Neither country's planes were allowed to fire freely; they had to request and receive permission to fire. For the Americans, a great deal of confusion arose from the fact that the F-4s were scrambling to keep up with one another and to stay in formation, and the

American planes were performing repeated evasive maneuvers in and out of the clouds. The actual events of the 17 minutes after engaging with the Chinese are not clear, as the American participants and the Chinese have multiple stories of the events of that morning. But one thing is certain: after the firefight ended, *Showtime 611* did not return to the USS Ranger. Murphy and Fegan were nowhere to be found.

Some accounts have Murphy and Fegan shooting down one of the Chinese fighters before being shot down themselves by the Chinese, while other accounts (including those by the Chinese pilot Li Dayun) say that *Showtime 611* was shot down by an errant missile fired from another American plane. Regardless, when the other three F-4s returned to the Ranger, Fegan and Murphy were not with them. The ship made several attempts to contact *Showtime 611*, but the calls were not answered. The Ranger contacted Da Nang airbase, but Murphy and Fegan had not changed course and made a landing there, either. As best as can be determined by interviewing both Chinese and American participants in the battle, as well as Chinese witnesses on the ground, Murphy and Fegan went down near Hainan Island, and crashed into the waters of the Gulf of Tonkin. Neither the wreckage of the plane nor the remains of Murphy or Fegan have ever been found.

In Brockport, Ronnie's family was first notified that he was missing. They received the message on April 9 and were told only that he and his pilot were missing while on a mission from the Ranger. They were told that searches were ongoing in the area and that the weather was good in the area. This left the Fegans hopeful that Ronnie might be found alive. On April 14, however, they received word that the five-day search of the area had turned up no trace of the two men or their plane. By the 14th of May, the Navy had determined that the two men had not survived the crash and declared them dead.

Although the Fegan family did not have Ronnie's remains, they still had a memorial service for him in Brockport. In a testament to the brotherhood of naval aviators, four F-4 Phantoms, just like the one Ronnie had been in when he died, landed at Monroe-Rochester Airport on May 21. In the F-4s were members of VF-96, including some of the men who had flown with Murphy and Fegan on the morning of April 9. At the memorial service, one of the VF-96 men told Richard that his brother "was a hero."

It has been more than 45 years since *Showtime 611* fell from the sky over the Gulf of Tonkin, and the Fegan family has never fully recovered from their loss. "You always want their body back and we really have no hope of that," said Richard. "My brother died doing what he loved, but he didn't expect to die." Though he was declared dead in 1965, the U.S. government still searches for the remains of Fegan and Murphy. On what would have been Ronnie's 71st birthday, his sister Tina reflected on the family's long search for closure: "My mother and father didn't talk a lot about Ronnie, they wouldn't share those feelings. They always wondered what really happened to him. Near the end of my mother's life, she had a dream where Ronnie told her he was all right and that she shouldn't worry about him. That brought her some peace, I think." Tina herself treasures the memories of her brother, and while she realistically knows he is gone, she still thinks about the possibilities for miracles that the world holds. The circumstances of her brother's death have held so many mysteries for so long, and there have been so many conflicting stories that she is never quite sure what to believe. When asked if she believed that her brother might have survived the crash, she looks up sadly and smiles. "I did have hope he'd come home. Still do, actually." ♦

Another of Ronnie's loves: a fast car.
Photo courtesy of the Fegan family.

Photo of Ronnie's post at Vietnam Veterans
Memorial of Greater Rochester.
Photo by Sebastián E. Encina.

WILLIAM E. CORDERO

Major, Air Force • 7/20/35–6/22/65 • Panel 2E, Row 15

Bill Cordero's family had been in California for 10 generations. Corderos had been granted land from Spain, had helped build the missions that dot the California landscape and had fought to preserve the Union at President Lincoln's urging. When Bill Cordero was commissioned an officer in the U.S. Air Force in 1957, his family name already had a legacy of honor. By the time Bill Cordero would lose his life eight years later, the Cordero name would be further linked with honor, service and sacrifice.

Bill Cordero was born in 1935 in Santa Barbara, Calif. Bill was outgoing and friendly, with a dry sense of humor. The son of a blacksmith with an eighth-grade education, Bill admired his father's work ethic but wanted more. After graduating from what was then called Santa Barbara Catholic High School, Bill became the first of his extended family to attend college. He enrolled in Loyola University in Los Angeles and became involved in the Air Force Reserve Officer Training Corps (ROTC) program. He had natural leadership ability and soon decided to make the Air Force his career. He saw himself becoming a general, and after retiring, coming back to the city he loved. Someday, he knew he would be the mayor of Santa Barbara. He had a gift for bringing people together. His sister Dorothy said, "He could go into a group that was angry and turn the anger around so that all emerged happy. He was a diplomat."

While at Loyola, Bill met Kathleen Carroll at an ROTC dance. The two married in 1957, the same year that Bill received his commission. As Bill's pilot training took them across the country, their family grew to include four sons and a daughter. As the U.S. became more involved in Southeast Asia, Bill embraced the role that he would play. Bill headed to Vietnam in November 1963, where he would fly B-26 bombers as part of the Air Commandos. In the book *Dreams Unfulfilled*, Bill's son Tony describes his father's life as an Air Commando: "They were living on a jungle air strip, 8,000 miles from home, flying ancient planes that were literally falling apart on them." Regardless of the conditions or the equipment, Bill and the Air Commandos did their jobs.

The following August, Kathleen and the children joined Bill in Asia. The family was stationed at Clark Air Force Base in the Philippines, where Bill would be based between two-week bombing runs to Saigon. He would fly B-57s to Tan Son Nhut Air Base and then would leave for runs into North Vietnam. Bill kept up this routine into 1965. On Father's Day weekend, Bill was back at Tan Son Nhut, assigned to fly with the 8th Bombardment Squadron. That night he would fly as a navigator in a B-57B, call sign *Jade 22*, piloted by Maj. Charles Lovelace from North Carolina. The flight was to be a flare mission, with *Jade 22* being tasked with providing illumination for other aircraft over North Vietnam. The mission on June 21st was the first time that Cordero and Lovelace had flown together. They would not return.

Maj. William Cordero, U.S. Air Force.

The reasons for the crash are unknown. They were declared missing in action (MIA) in 1965. In 1969, a team of Special Forces came upon the plane's wreckage just across the border into Laos. They also found a small amount of human remains, too small for identification. The remains were buried in one grave at Arlington National Cemetery, with a headstone bearing the names of Cordero and Lovelace.

In 1994, the wreckage of Cordero and Lovelace's plane was rediscovered in Laos, and today the families wait until the site can be excavated and both men may finally come home. ♦

SHEPHEN H PHILLIPS

Sergeant, Army • 3/13/42–7/18/65 • Panel 2E, Row 39

The lasting, public tribute to the sacrifice of Sgt. Stephen Phillips in Vietnam is carved on Panel 2E, Row 39 of the Vietnam Veterans Memorial in Washington, D.C. Standing in front of The Wall, however, a visitor will not see the name of the six-year Army veteran. A look up at Panel 2E reveals the name Shephen H. Phillips. The lasting, public memorial to this husband and father from Springfield, Mo. is spelled wrong.

The Memorial was dedicated on Veterans Day, 1982. In time, it would come to be known as simply The Wall. The Vietnam Veterans Memorial Fund used casualty lists provided by the Department of Defense to compile the names of those dead and missing in action in Vietnam. These would be the 57,939 names carved into granite. Somehow, mistakes were made. The names of some who served so nobly were carved incorrectly in granite. Regardless of how their names are spelled, their legacies persist.

In the early 1940s, Springfield, Missouri was a city of more than 60,000 people. Located in southwestern Missouri on the Springfield plateau of the Ozarks, it was one of the larger cities in Missouri. Stephen Hiett Phillips was born there in March of 1942, the only child of Wood and Opal Phillips. His father was called Jack by all of his friends, and Jack, like his wife (who went by Arlene), had lived in the Springfield area for most of his life. Jack Phillips enlisted in the U.S. Army in the spring of 1944 and was in Europe not long after. He was part of the Army unit that helped liberate the Dachau concentration camp in southern Germany in late April 1945.

When Jack Phillips returned from Europe, the young family settled in to their life in the Springfield area. Stephen enjoyed playing baseball and was particularly fond of hunting and fishing with his father. The family lived on North Hayes St. in Springfield, a home in a nice neighborhood near Downtown Airport. As a high school student, Stephen was unmotivated and uninterested in education, and he dropped out during his junior year. On October 2, 1959, Stephen joined the Army.

Stephen was assigned to Basic Training at Fort Hood, Texas and arrived there on October 26, 1959. He would stay at Fort Hood until March 1960, receiving his Advanced Individual Training there as well. His first post in the Army was with C Company, 1st Armored Rifle Battalion, 48th Infantry. He was stationed in Worms, in what was then West Germany. During his years in Germany, he was not the most motivated soldier. His family says, "He liked to raise some hell and was busted a few times." Stephen's service record while in Germany supports

Stephen while he was stationed in Germany in the early 1960s. Photo courtesy of Steve Phillips.

Sgt. Stephen Hiett Phillips, U.S. Army. Photo courtesy of Steve Phillips.

that. Between July 1960 and November of 1961, Stephen was promoted and demoted an equal number of times, bouncing between the ranks of private 1, private 2, and private first class. In November 1961, Stephen was transferred to B Company of the 1st Armed Rifle Battalion, but was still unable to move up in the ranks. He served as a gunner with B Company, received a promotion to private first class in January 1962 and was busted down to private by the time he left Germany in the spring of 1963. Those who served with him said, "He loved life."

His time in Germany over, Stephen was sent to Fort Riley, Kan. to serve with E Company, 2nd Battalion, 12th Infantry. Once back in the states, Stephen's military career turned around and he quickly began rising through the ranks. He served as the senior rifleman with E Company for seven months and was promoted back up to private first class shortly after arriving with the company. He served with E Company until January 1964, before being transferred to Headquarters Company where he would begin serving as a team leader. By June 1964, Stephen was a sergeant with 2nd Battalion, 12th Infantry. He celebrated his promotion with a party at the Non-Commissioned Officers Club on Custer Hill at Fort Riley.

While at Fort Riley, Stephen met and married Neoma Jean Phillips, whom friends called Jeannie. By this time, Stephen had decided to make the Army his career. In 1964, he volunteered to go to Vietnam. Stephen understood the risks of going into combat, but it was something that he had always known was possible. By the end of 1964, Stephen was preparing to go to Vietnam. Casualties in Southeast Asia had increased, but U.S. troop losses in Vietnam were still relatively low. More than 200 American troops had been killed by the end of 1964.

Before leaving for Vietnam, Stephen wanted to make sure that his wife was settled back in Springfield. She would live in a house on North Hayes, just a few houses away from her in-laws. She would need their support while Stephen was in Vietnam; she was pregnant with their first child and was due to give birth while he was away. The motto of his division, the 18th Infantry Division, was "In all things prepared." Before he left, Stephen wanted to make sure that everything was prepared for his expected child. "He didn't pretend that Vietnam was a safe place, but he was willing to go," said his mother.

Phillips and the rest of the 2nd Battalion, 18th Infantry left San Francisco for Vietnam on June 26, 1965 as a part of the 2nd Brigade, 1st Infantry Division. The 1st Infantry Division, known as "The Big Red One," was a highly decorated division that had seen combat in every U.S. action since World War I. They were traveling on the USS Gordon, a transport ship that would make many trips from the West Coast to get U.S. troops to Vietnam. The 2nd Battalion disembarked at Vung Tau on July 16, 1965. The area would become a popular in-country rest and recuperation (R&R) stop for U.S. troops, but in 1965 it was still a primary unloading area for ground troops. The 2nd Battalion was to head northwest toward Bien Hoa to establish a base camp. They boarded C-130 airplanes to make the 85 kilometer trip to Bien Hoa.

The battalion was to set up near Route 1, in an area near the village of Ho Nai called "Catholic Village." William Miller, a soldier who served with Stephen, recalls that, "The area was totally unprepared and consisted of thick undergrowth and jungle. On the first evening, July 17, we were positioned as a reserve platoon. Our battalion was provided with little or nothing in the way of defensive supplies, such as barbed wire, mines, trip flares, etcetera." Fortunately, no contact was made with the enemy on that first night.

The next day, the company commander wanted to deploy rifle companies around the outer perimeters. Miller received orders to send out a two-man listening post to the front of the perimeter. "I knew it was a risky proposition considering the terrain," Miller said. He asked for volunteers. The first man to volunteer was Phillips. He and another soldier took a field phone and headed out into the jungle. As dusk fell, Phillips was able to establish the listening post.

Around 9:30, Phillips called in to report movement in his area. Miller asked if he was able to pull back, but got no response. "Just as I asked if they could get out of there, the sky opened up with a tremendous downpour. The monsoon had arrived," said Miller. Shots rang out just after the rains came and Miller received word that both Phillips and his partner had been hit. Miller left his position and ran to where the two men had set up their listening post. When he arrived, Phillips was already dead. He was 23 years old. Phillips had been shot in the back

Stephen and his family: His father, Jack, wife, Jeannie, and mother, Arlene. Photo courtesy of Steve Phillips.

while attempting to return from the listening post. He had been in Vietnam for less than a week. When Jeannie Phillips received word of her husband's death, she was in her third trimester of pregnancy. Her son, Steve Harden Phillips, was born 43 days after his father's death.

Jeannie buried her husband at the Springfield National Cemetery. His headstone reads "Stephen H. Phillips, SGT, US Army, VIETNAM." The funeral featured an honor guard from Fort Leonard Wood in Missouri. Stephen's father, Jack, sobbed as the flag from his only child's casket was presented to his daughter-in-law Jeannie.

Steve Phillips was raised by his mother, and his father's parents. Steve knew who his father was and how he had died, but the family never spoke much about him while Steve was growing up. The loss had been devastating to Jeannie, Jack and Arlene, and they tried to protect Steve from the pain of that loss. Steve grew up to look remarkably like his father, and as his father and grandfather before him, would serve his country in the U.S. Army. He served for 21 years and retired a sergeant first class.

In the early 1990s, a friend of his went to Washington, D.C. and made a rubbing of Phillips' name on The Wall. It was then that Steve Phillips discovered that his father's name, although spelled correctly on his headstone, was spelled incorrectly on The Wall. He began making phone calls, but didn't get very far. He was in the midst of his Army career and was about to have his own son, so getting his father's name corrected fell by the wayside. He worked on fixing the misspelling on and off for the next nine years, but in time he began to think that maybe the error could not be corrected and he eventually gave up.

Just after the new year in 2012, Steve's sister-in-law Michelle was standing in line at a convenience store in Fair Grove, Ark. She glanced at the day's *Springfield News-Leader* and saw the name Stephen H. Phillips printed across the front page. She got in touch with Steve and he was shocked to learn that he was not the only one who had discovered the misspelling of his father's name on The Wall. He was even more shocked to realize that he was not the only one who cared that it was wrong.

Stephen while he was stationed in Germany in the early 1960s. Photo courtesy of Steve Phillips.

Sgt. Stephen Hiett Phillips, U.S. Army. Photo courtesy of Steve Phillips.

Larry Thompson and Pete Neumann did not know Phillips, nor did they know his son, Steve. Their only connection to Phillips was having served in the same regiment in Vietnam. The pair believed the spelling mistake originated in the Combat Area Casualties file of 1967, which explained why the name on Phillips' headstone was spelled correctly. Neumann believed that Phillips deserved to have his name spelled correctly on The Wall and that his family deserved that honor as well. The Springfield paper ran the story about the misspelling and not only did it catch the family's attention, but also helped facilitate contact with the VVMF. The misspelling, carved in granite nearly 30 years earlier, would not be easy to fix. But, a correction was made on the VVMF's Website, where visitors can search for information about those who died in Vietnam. The mistake was also corrected in the printed directories at The Wall.

The misspelling of his father's name can never be removed from The Wall, as doing so would damage the entire panel. Steve Phillips will have to decide if he can live with the mistake and the corrections that have been made, or if he wants his father's correct name added to The Wall in a different location. While the corrected "STEPHEN H PHILLIPS" would be added to the same panel, there is no guarantee it would be near where it currently is. Steve Phillips is still not sure what he is going to do. "Part of me wants my dad's name to be near those that died when he did," Steve said. "I think he would want that."

It is important to remember that, like all other documents that tell the story of the United States, the personnel records of those that served in the military were created by humans. Humans, as we all know, are fallible creatures, and sometime between 1959 and 1967, the first name of that Army sergeant from Springfield was written down as Shephen rather than Stephen. That one letter may have changed how his name appears on The Wall, but it does not change what he did that night in Bien Hoa. ♦

Jeannie Phillips receives the flag from her husband's casket in 1965. Photo courtesy of Steve Phillips.

DEARBORN

They were just normal American boys, living normal American lives. Alan Hosnedle was a star swimmer. Phil Gandolfo played saxophone and might have run into Jamie Hath at the music store down on Telegraph. Jamie played upright bass in a local band called Kit Redding and the Imperials. While he was in high school, Michael Troyan thought he might like to be a priest someday. Mark Robertson made the Dearborn All-City Football team in 1966. John Wells wanted to be a Michigan State Police Officer.

Cities and towns all over the United States lost sons and daughters, mothers and fathers, and sisters and brothers. The names of these towns read as an atlas of America, with losses being felt from sea to shining sea. Los Angeles, Calif. lost 539 soldiers. Rutland, Vt. lost five. Dallas, Texas lost 261. Aliquippa, Pa. lost 14.

Somewhere between Aliquippa and Los Angeles is Dearborn, Mich. Fifty-seven sons of Dearborn, the hometown of Henry Ford, gave their lives in service to their country during the Vietnam War. These boys were children of the '50s, coming of age in a city that, despite being one of Michigan's largest, still behaved as a small town. Residents of Dearborn didn't always lock their doors in the 1950s, and these boys could be found in her parks and pools and river. Some carried the names of America's long history of immigration, names that sang of far-away lands: Bonnici, Gambotto, Nozewski. Others carried strong, solid English names that could have been brought over on the Mayflower: Smith, Davis, Clark. They were athletes and Boy Scouts, altar boys and paper boys. They left behind mothers and fathers, sisters and brothers, children and siblings. They left behind the stories of lives that were shortened by a war that, though they didn't understand, they gave their lives in.

Dennis Stancroff was the first of the Dearborn boys to lose his life in Vietnam. Dennis, a 1963 graduate of Edsel Ford High School, had enlisted in the Marine Corps with his friends George Siegwald and George Roehler. He did his boot camp training at Marine Corps Recruit Depot San Diego, and he wrote home often, both to his parents and to his high school sweetheart, Nanette Brancheau. Even though Nan was attending school in Monroe and Dennis was in Dearborn, they were very close. In November 1965, Dennis was sent to Vietnam to serve with the 3rd Marine Division. Passing through Okinawa, Japan, on his way to Vietnam, Dennis made the decision to marry Nan and bought her a ring. But he never got the chance to send Nan that ring. He was killed in action on Christmas Eve, 1965. He was on patrol near Da Nang when the company was ambushed by North Vietnamese troops. He was 20 years old, just one week shy of 21. "He was a brave boy," his mother told the *Dearborn Guide* in 1965. "He's gone now and I guess we'll have to go on without him."

Lance Cpl. Dennis Stancroff. Edsel Ford High School Yearbook, 1964.

Dearborn was a very patriotic town, with a large wooden memorial board in front of City Hall that listed all of the men from Dearborn who gave their lives in service to their country. The city hosted large Memorial Day parades that drew thousands of citizens to watch bands, veterans and civic groups make their way down Michigan Avenue. Dan Ryder, who grew up in Dearborn in the 1950s said, "We grew up with American flags all over. Our grandfathers served, our fathers served, our uncles served. It seems like everyone knew someone in their family that had fought in World War II or Korea."

Mayor Orville Hubbard was presiding over a Dearborn that would reach its population high in the 1960s; the 1960 census put Dearborn's population at 112,007. Hubbard was a Marine and a patriot who loved America. He requested that all Dearborn businesses recognize the sacrifice of Dearborn's soldiers lost in Vietnam by flying their flags at half-staff from the day that word of the loss was received until the soldier had been buried. All Dearborn government offices would also fly their flags at half-staff until the fallen man was laid to rest. This was only one of the policies that Hubbard would institute in the early years of the war and maintain until the last Dearborn service member came home.

Shortly before Hubbard instituted flag policies for Dearborn's fallen service members, Earl Smith arrived in Vietnam. Smith, a medical aidman assigned to 2nd Battalion, 18th Infantry, had been in Vietnam since late March. Earl had left Edsel Ford High School his senior year and entered the Army in January 1965. After medic training at Fort Sam Houston, Earl was sent to Germany for on–the–job training at a military hospital. He told a friend in a letter that he was putting in for transfer to Vietnam. After arriving, he told a friend of an ambush that he had responded to in late May. A squad had been ambushed and he was the only medical aidman that was able to respond. "The squad had seven wounded, bad wounds. It took me half an hour to reach them, my weapon was all shot up. The bullets were really thick." On June 30, 1966, a patrol from Earl's company was ambushed while attempting to deploy an Armored Vehicle Launch Bridge (AVLB) over a destroyed bridge. When he reached the ambushed patrol, Earl immediately began treating the wounded. The Bronze Star citation that Earl's family received shows how he responded to the

Pfc. Earl Smith, U.S. Army medical aidman.

Lance Corporal Dennis Stancroff, Marine • 12/31/44–12/24/65

18 Dearborn Soldiers

Private First Class Earl Smith, Army • 10/18/46–06/30/66

*Earl Smith
Edsel Ford High School
Yearbook, 1965.*

scene he came upon that day in Srok Dong: "Moving from man to man in total darkness, he expertly and rapidly applied first aid to his wounded comrades while ignoring the heavy volume of fire of the Viet Cong. On several occasions, he struck matches in order to determine the best means of treating the wounded, although light made himself a target for the insurgent riflemen." While he was treating the wounded members of his company, Earl was killed by Viet Cong small arms fire. He was 19 years old. In his last letter home to his parents, he talked about why he wanted to do the job of a medic. "That's the reason I came over here in the first place: to be a medic and do something important for once in my life."

It wasn't just young Dearborn boys that were serving and dying in Vietnam; the career soldiers were also over there risking their lives. In May 1967, Raymond Borowski was serving with the 1st Battalion of the 8th Infantry. "Doc" to his fellow soldiers, Borowski was on his 3rd enlistment in the Army. He was well-respected by his fellow soldiers and, because he was 32, served as a mentor to the other medics assigned to the 1/8th Infantry. Borowski had a wife and four young children back in Dearborn and he longed to get back to them. Still, he believed in taking care of his men. He wrote to his mother-in-law that some told him he didn't have to be in the field. "Some people tell me I'm sort of crazy. I could be working in the aid station. I would just as soon be out here with the boys, where I can be of some help when they need me. I don't want to be here, Ma. But I sure am not going to run away from my duties."

Sgt. Raymond Borowski.

Sgt. Raymond Borowski in Vietnam.

In May 1967, the 1/8th was engaged with enemy forces in the "Nine Days of May" battles that took place on May 18–26, near the Cambodian border. On the night of May 20, A, B and C Companies of the 1/8 had established a defensive position on a hill and at approximately 8:30 p.m. the position came under mortar attack. The attack had been going on for more than two hours when Doc was moving a wounded man to the safety of a bunker. As he moved the wounded man, Borowski was hit with shrapnel from a mortar. He somehow managed to get the wounded man to the bunker and collapsed in pain. Doc insisted that every other man be treated for his wounds before he'd allow himself to be treated. The next morning, the medevac chopper was finally able to get to the area, but was not able to land due to heavy small arms and live rounds of mortar fire. The chopper lowered a lift basket down and Doc Borowski was loaded into it. Tragically, when he was being raised up to the chopper there was a malfunction and the basket tumbled to the ground. Borowski did not survive the fall.

Before he died, Borowski was preparing to be picked up by the medevac chopper when he removed his St. Christopher's medal and gave it to the soldier who had stayed with him during the long, painful night. A medal bearing the image of St. Christopher, the patron saint of travelers, was often worn by soldiers for protection from harm. Though seriously wounded, Borowski's thoughts were still with his soldiers and he must have thought that another soldier needed the Patron Saint of Safe Passages more than he did. Forty-two years later, Lou Macellari returned that St. Christopher's medal to Patricia Paprocki, Borowski's widow.

Margaret Garrison had been the Selective Service Systems clerk in Dearborn for as long as anyone could remember. Since the late 1940s, hers had been a name that potential servicemen in Dearborn knew well. When young men in Dearborn became eligible for military service, Garrison signed their draft cards. She was just the clerk of the draft board and had very little control over the decisions regarding deferments and classifications. It was her name, however, on the draft cards, so it was often Garrison that bore the brunt of the anger directed at the draft board. During the height of the war, when Dearborn was sending dozens of young men to Vietnam each month via the draft, Garrison and her family regularly received threats. On one occasion, she was at a Dearborn stoplight when a car pulled alongside of her. The driver pointed a gun at her. Garrison, accustomed to threats by this time, calmly drove away. The threats, the name calling, the phone calls and letters were part of her job. She didn't enjoy sending these young men off to war, and certainly did not enjoy signing the draft cards for her own two sons and watching them go off to Vietnam with the rest of her Dearborn boys.

One of the Dearborn boys who carried a draft card bearing Garrison's signature was David Antol. He was a happy young man who loved the outdoors. He was the oldest child and only son of Anna and Stephen Antol, and along with his younger sister, Patricia, they formed a very close-knit family. His friends describe him as being kind

*Pfc. David Antol,
U.S. Army.*

Sergeant Raymond Borowski, Army • 04/05/35–05/20/67

Private First Class David Antol, US Army
12/29/46–12/20/67

Pfc. David Antol poses in front of one of the 189th AHC's helicopters. Vietnam, 1967. Photo courtesy of the Antol family.

Spc. James Davis.

and good-natured and as someone who would always stick up for the little guy. While growing up, David would take on any neighborhood job he could find to earn money for hunting and fishing equipment and parts for his motorscooter. His friends considered him a class clown and he always made everyone laugh. His smile was infectious. He graduated from Edsel Ford High School in June 1965. Afterwards, he worked at Great Lakes Steel and attended Henry Ford Community College. He hoped to become either a forest ranger or a pipefitter after he finished his education. David was drafted into the Army in 1966, and although he was proud to serve, something changed in him when he was in the Army. While home on leave after basic training at Fort Knox, Ky., he didn't smile as much. His mother also thought it was strange that he didn't want to see any of his friends, and that even the family's pet poodle didn't seem to know him. The small dog, who had adored David before he left for the Army, would not go near him anymore.

David was sent to Vietnam in May 1967 and was assigned to the 189th Assault Helicopter Company (AHC). He was a crew chief on helicopters, responsible for the daily maintenance and performance of the chopper he was assigned to. He had received the Air Medal with two Oak Leaf clusters for flying 75 hours in combat. Having survived all of those combat hours, it was an accident that would cost David his life. On December 20, 1967, just nine days before his 21st birthday, David was flying as a crew chief on a UH-1 Huey with the call sign *Ghostrider 154*. The chopper was on a resupply mission dropping water, tools and food down to troops of the 3/8th clearing an area below. While airborne, a lieutenant colonel on the flight borrowed David's helmet so that he could communicate with the aircraft commander. Without his helmet, David couldn't pass on that they were dangerously close to the trees. The Huey's tail rotor struck a tree and the chopper crashed to the ground below. David, the lieutenant colonel and two others were killed in the crash. Witnesses reported that the crash burned for hours and the search for survivors was made difficult by the heat of the flames. It was not until December 31st that the Antols were notified by the Army that David was dead, having suffered chest and head injuries and severe burns over his entire body. David's parents and sister were never able to recover from his death; when he died, they died. To this day, his mother still lives in the home on Linden Street in Dearborn where David grew up. A portrait of David hangs on the wall; his bright, beaming smile fills the room.

Dearborn was tired of burying so many young men; it seemed like flags were always at half-staff in 1967 and 1968. By the time the presidential election of 1968 rolled around, Dearborn had lost 34 boys in Vietnam. "We're sick and tired of hearing about friends' sons dying. We're sick and tired of saying goodbye to neighborhood boys who have played at our house since they were tiny," Mrs. Biggers, one mother from Dearborn, told the *Dearborn Press* on October 28, 1968.

James Davis shouldn't have even been in Vietnam that day. He should have been back home in Dearborn with his ailing wife, Lena, trying to figure out what was causing her loss of vision. James and Lena had been married only a few months when he received his draft notice in January 1969. James had been enrolled in a Ford Motor Company apprenticeship program, but was drafted when he completed the program early. He finished his basic training and was sent to Vietnam in July 1969. While James was serving with the First Battalion of the 506th Infantry Regiment of the 101st Airborne, his wife was staying with her parents on the east side of Dearborn. Lena began having trouble with her eyesight and by September 1969 was struggling to see. Her condition became so bad she had to quit her job. After keeping the news from her husband for a while, she eventually told James and he began the process to be transferred back to the states to care for his wife. James refused to request a discharge, but instead asked the Army for an emergency leave to return and take care of her. Doctors in Dearborn prepared medical reports and sent them to the Army, but James was only granted R&R leave to Hawaii. At least that would give him some time with Lena and his parents to try and figure out what they should do.

Instead of being with Lena in Dearborn, he was sitting at Firebase (FB) Granite in Thua Thien waiting for the chopper to take him to the air base. James sat at FB Granite and waited as the transport choppers were delayed because of foggy weather. In the early morning hours of March 20, 1969, FB Granite was attacked. The attack, what the Army called "a coordinated mortar and sapper attack," lasted nearly an hour. During the attack, James moved from his position to assist the men receiving the most fire. He had pulled one wounded man to safety and was

James Davis' Senior portrait from Cherry Hill High School. Photo courtesy of the Davis family.

Specialist James Davis, Army • 03/08/47–03/20/70

heading towards another when he was struck by enemy fire. He was awarded a Silver Star on March 20, for the actions that had cost him his life. James was 23 years old when he died at FB Granite alongside 11 others. Army officials went to his wife's home in Dearborn, only to discover that Lena was on her way to Hawaii to meet her husband. Pan Am airline officials pulled Lena and James' parents off the airplane, where Army officials were waiting to notify them of James' death in Vietnam. Six months after James' death, his wife Lena would find the cause of her vision loss – multiple sclerosis.

As the 1970s dawned, Dearborn had buried 48 of her sons. The City Council now had a moment of silence at the end of every meeting in honor of those serving. For his part, Mayor Hubbard was at every funeral possible and when he could not attend, he made sure that the family was taken care of.

Cyndie Cain, widow of Capt. James Huard, holds his flight helmet. It was returned to her in 2010 by a Vietnamese citizen who saw the crash site. Photo courtesy of the Huard family.

Capt. James Huard. Photo courtesy of the Huard family.

James Huard, Dearborn High School Yearbook 1963.

Air Force pilot Jim Huard was serving as forward air controller based out of Ubon, Thailand in 1972. Flying an F-4, Huard had been in Vietnam since October of 1971. Considered a gifted pilot by those who flew with him, Huard was fulfilling his lifelong dream of flying airplanes. After graduating from Central Michigan University in 1968, Jim was back in Dearborn teaching mathematics when he told his wife, Cyndie, that he wanted to join the Air Force and learn to fly. Before he left for Vietnam, Jim sat down with Cyndie and they discussed the challenges that lay ahead. Cyndie trusted Jim implicitly, even when he told her that he didn't think he would be coming back from his tour in Vietnam. He shared this only with Cyndie, and they prayed together and trusted in their faith to get them through Jim's tour. Jim tried to prepare his wife for life without him, asking her to remarry if she could, so that his boys would have a father.

"Jim didn't like being away from his family, but he believed what he was doing would make the world a better place for his sons to grow up," said Cyndie. In late June 1972, a bullet entered the cockpit and grazed Jim's neck. After landing the plane, he called his wife to tell her of his close call and to let her know he was running out of time. "He truly believed he wasn't coming home from Vietnam," said Cyndie, "and he was trying to prepare me." On July 12, 1972. Huard and his weapons officer, Capt. Samuel O'Donnell from Pennsylvania, took off in their F-4E, call sign *Wolf 08*. They were headed into North Vietnam on an armed reconnaissance mission to locate troops and supplies in the area of the Rao Nay River. Huard's last radio communication was at 7:30 a.m., asking for his assignment. Neither Huard nor O'Donnell were heard from again. When *Wolf 08* didn't return to Ubon by 9:00 a.m., they were declared overdue. Numerous aerial searches of the area revealed no sign of Huard or O'Donnell and one year later the Air Force declared the two men killed in action.

Just as her husband asked, Cyndie Huard moved away from her family in Dearborn and started a new life in Florida. "I never believed Jim was alive, because he had told me all along that he wouldn't make it," said Cyndie. "He told me that if he was ever declared missing that I should know he was dead. He was emphatic that he would never be taken prisoner." It was not until 1988 that remains were discovered in the area where Huard and O'Donnell went missing. It took another nine years before the remains could be identified. By comparing DNA from his mother, the remains were found to be those of Jim Huard. He was buried at Arlington National Cemetery in May 1997.

In 2009, Jim's son, Peter Rogers, received a call from a Vietnamese refugee. He had a relative in Vietnam who claimed he was a member of the North Vietnamese Army unit that had shot *Wolf 08* down. The relative claimed he had been a doctor in the unit and had been one of the first to the scene of the crash. Remarkably, this man had saved Huard's helmet. In October of 2010, Cyndie received a package from Vietnam. It contained the helmet that her husband had been wearing when his plane disappeared 37 years earlier.

In all, 57 men from Dearborn died in Vietnam: 46 Army soldiers, three Airmen, three sailors and five Marines. They ranged in age from 18 to 32. Two of them did not return home until more than 20 years after they arrived in Vietnam. ♦

James Huard Memorial at Dearborn High School. Photo courtesy of Vietnam Veterans of America # 267.

Captain James Huard, Air Force • 03/17/46–07/12/72

Dearborn Soldiers

Richard Anderson   *Robert Bonnici*   *David Brannon*   *James Brock*

David Brown   *Jerry Clark*   *John Cochrane*   *Thomas Daily*

Randy Dillinder   *Paul Elwart*   *James Fleming*   *Roger Foxworth*

Henry Fugett   *Larry Gambotto*   *Philip Gandolfo*   *Thomas Gentinne*

Charles Hanselman   *James Hath*   *James Hintz*   *Alan Hosnedle*   *Rudolph Jackymack*

Dearborn Soldiers

Charles Karr

David Kowitz

Bradley Logan

Cecil McCann

Robert McKenna

Thomas Naughton, Jr

Michael Niezgoda

Robert Nozewski

Richard Paton

James Patterson

Michael Patterson

William Pearce, IV

Wilbert Pennell

Mark Robertson

Donald Rowley

David Smith

James Stubblefield

David Terwilliger

Charles Trescott

Michael Troyan

John Wells

*Not Pictured:
Tommie Ray Angel,
Jay Cee Dyer,
Franklyn Germany,
Douglas McIlroy,
James Morrow,
Ralph Mueller,
Mark Pietrzyk,
and Ronald Smith.*

24 *Photos by Bill Shugarts*

Vietnam Veterans Memorial — partial list of names:

RAYMOND S FORD · JOHN V KE... · LARRY D ... · VERNON ...
RICHARD P LANCASTER Jr · CHARLIE K SCATES · MARSHALL R HIRSCH · RICHARD H CAS...
PEDRO SANTOS-PINEDO · JOHN A GIROD Jr · WILLIAM T CALLERY · LEO F KR...
VERNON G CHASE · JOHN A GIROD Jr · ROBERT L BEATON · CALVIN R HEBERT Jr ·
CLINTON R ANDERSON · GARY W GARIS · CALVIN R HEBERT Jr · MICHAEL J NEM...
JAMES L FAIN · LYNDSEY F FONGER · MICHAEL W McDONALD · CHARLES A SC...
ROBERT L MACK · RALPH A MAXHAM Jr · WILLIAM B PARNELL · RICARDO J PEREZ
ADAN MONSIVAIS OLVERA · WILLIAM B PARNELL · DONALD B ADAMSON · WILLIAM O ALLEN
DAVID W UTLEY · CLARENCE WILLIAMS · DONALD B ADAMSON · ARLEN J DUCKETT ·
HARMON C BURD · WILLIAM H COBURN · CHARLES R DALE · MATTHEW HOUGH ·
CHARLES E DYSON Jr · RODGER L EGOLF · DOVE ELHONDAH · WINSTON MORRIS · ISAIAH MULWEE ·
DALMER D JUREK · BURTON C MONTROSS · WINSTON MORRIS · JACK RABINOVITZ · RICHA...
PATRICK C NEVIN · TOMMY L NICHOLAS · W H NORMAN · JACK RABINOVITZ · MARSHALL R SMITH
KENNETH A REYNOLDS · FRANKIE SANCHEZ · JIMMY C SEXTON · MARVIN J WILSO...
WILLIAM J STEPHENSON · PAUL J STOCHAJ · WILLIAM B WATSON Jr · HARVEY L BOWEN ·
JIMMY E BOAN · JAMES R BOLAND · FELIPE BONILLA-VIERA · JIMMIE LEE FOSTER · FLEM...
WILLIE A COOPER · JAMES B W DETRIXHE · JAMES R FOLEY · JIMMIE LEE FOSTER · RAYMOND H HETRIC...
GENTRY GRAHAM · FLOYD S HARMON · THOMAS E HARTUNG · RAYMOND H HETRIC...
JOE C LILE II · ROBERT K LOWE · LARRY LEE KEENER · ROBERT D MERRELL · GEORGE A M...
THOMAS J OGLETHORPE · ROBERT D PERDUE · ALLEN L PIERCE · DONALD C PIPER ·
JOSEPH L ROBINSON · CHARLES C WHITFIELD · BENNIE LEE SIMMONS · FREDERICK A ...
ALBERT R WHITE · O'DELL ROBINSON · TOMMIE LEE WILLIAMS · JESSE J BOLTON · FRAN...
JOHN B CAUSEY · PHILLIP A LOTTA · NICHOLES SOCHACKI · JAMES M TERMINI · CLYDE ...
GEORGE W WOODALL · DOUGLAS D ALLEY · SIMMIE BELLAMY Jr · ELMER E BERRY · TH...
JAMES T BROWN · RONALD C CAVINEE · IRVIN CLARKE Jr · CHARLIES E DANIELS · JOHN ...
LAMAR D FREDERICK · JOHN P GILLIAM · JACK L HIMES · ROBERT L HOSKINS Jr · DANIE...
ERNEST A LAROCHE · CLARENCE MITCHELL · DONALD S NEWTON · ROBERT D WILLIA...
WILLIAM M TARBELL · ROBERT L TERRY · BILLIE N PLUM · FRANCIS D WILLS · WILLIAM ...
DAVID L DANOWSKI · EDWARD S GRAVES · PAUL E HELSEL Jr · RICK E KOPKA · LAWRE...
JOSEPH J REILLY · DONALD W SMITH · JAMES M SPENCE · ROGER D BULIFANT · HENRY ...
WARREN L CHRISTENSEN · LESTER H CLEGG · PETER W FIELDS · WILLIAM FUCHS Jr · FRA...
PATRICK J KELLY Jr · JAMES F HUBISZ · ARTHUR J JACKSON · WILLIAM FUCHS Jr · FRA...
RICHARD R HERCHKORN · JAMES B LAIRD · RAYMOND E MEYERS · MARSHALL JESSIE · CHARLES ...
LARRY E MacDONALD · EDWARD J McCARTHY · BRENT A McCLELLAN · KENNETH D MIDDL...
DANNY JAY McGRIFF · ANDY McGUIRE Jr · JAMES R McLEMORE · GEORGE P McC...
JAMES G PATZWALL · ARTHUR C PEDERSON · MICHAEL D PLISKA · JOSE TORRES · RICHA...
JOHN H ROBERTS · LESTER A ROGERS · CHARLES W SIMS · DARRELL T RAY · ALB...
CARTER L WILLIAMS Jr · RICHARD F NUGENT · CLARK N WOODWORTH · MIGUEL E ...
LEONARD J BOCEK · WILLIAM M CHRISTENSEN · CLARK N WOODWORTH Jr · MIGUEL E ...
ROBERT LOPEZ · BRUCE L MAROSITES · WILLIAM P FORAN · CHARLIE ...
THOMAS J FEARS · CARLOS R HATCHER · JOHN W WILLIAMS · DONALD · WILLIAM D FRA...
PAUL A MEINERS · KARL E WORST · MARSHALL M HOLT Jr · DONALD · WILLIAM D FRA...
WILLIAM JONES Jr · LOOMIS OGLESBY III · CHARLES F COINER · ROBERT F FIELDER · JACK M HOPKINS ·
RICHARD G ALLEN · STEPHEN P ALSTED · CHARLES W RADER · ROBERT F FIELDER · PAUL F GR...
ALLEN C BAILEY · ISIAH BAKER III · STUART M ANDREWS · DENNIS L TALKINGTON ·
NORMAN J BUELL · JAMES E BUSH · DANIEL P BIRCH · RAYMOND · HERIBERTO ARMENTA ·
JOHN F CONLON III · RICHARD P CORSON · RUPERT S CARVEN III · PHILLIP H CLARK · WILLIA...
JOHN J EDWARDS · REUBEN L GARNETT · BRUCE DAVIS · PHILLIP H CLARK · WILLIA...
WOODROW W HAM Jr · REUBEN L GARNETT · ANDREW L HASTINGS · STANLEY T DEMBOSKI · LESTER L...
KLAUS J HERMS · JOSEPH S HERRON · JOHN H HARDEN · RONALD S DEMBOSKI · LESTER L...
LAWRENCE E JOHNSON · WILLIAM JOHNSON · JOHN H HARDEN · RONALD S DEMBOSKI · LESTER L...
WILBUR G KIRCHOFF · WILLIAM JOHNSON · JOHNNY RAY HOLLOWAY · MICHAEL W GODE...
ALBERTO A LUCERO · FRANZ J KOLBECK · HARVEY W JONES · HENRY J HOOPER ·
HENRY D ODOM · DONALD R LUMLEY · ROBERT B LABBE · ARNOLD L ...
CRESENCIO P SANCHEZ · SAMUEL G ORLANDO · DIEGO MERCADO · JACK W LINDSEY · VINFORD L ...
ROBERT L SMITH · DONNELL D McMILLIN · PAUL G PARSONS · VINFORD L ...
THOMAS WARDROP III · DWIGHT D TOLLEFSON · JAMES R SCOTT · JACKIE D REYNOLDS ·
CHARLES E ANDERSON · DAVID B WARREN · DELBERT L TRUBE Jr · MICHAEL ...
ANIBAL F AVILES · JOHN H BELL · LESTER A WESIGHAN · MICHAEL ...
ROBERT BROWN Jr · LEWIS D BELL · RAY MAX BARNWELL · ROSCOE A HA...
LELAND F DIXON · ALBERT CABANAYAN · MICHAEL L BIANCHINI · CHARLES V...
GARY W EMMETT · HENRY L FOSTER · ROBERT ...
RICHARD N GEREAU · THOMAS ... · ROBERT ...

25

CAROL A E DRAZBA

Second Lieutenant, Army • 12/11/43–2/18/66 • Panel 5E, Row 46

A young Carol Drazba, before her time in Vietnam.

Carol Ann Elizabeth Drazba was a very bright young woman who loved life. She scored straight A's at Dunmore High School and dreamed of one day working as a nurse. She was enthusiastic and happy, whether roller skating with friends or attending school dances. Growing up in Dunmore, Pa. with her parents, brother and sister, Carol was always smiling. Her interest in nursing came from a desire to help people. She attended nursing school at State Hospital School of Nursing in Scranton and enlisted in the Army in 1963.

According to her sister, Joanne, Carol joined for both the challenge and for monetary assistance. After graduating from nursing school and passing her certification tests, Carol was commissioned as a second lieutenant in the U.S. Army. Her first assignment was at a hospital at Fort Huachaca, Ariz. Carol was an operating room nurse, a highly demanding and stressful position that required long hours on her feet and focused attention. She was very good at her job. While at Fort Huachaca in 1965, Carol encountered many pilots returning from tours in Vietnam. They spoke of the worsening situation and the need for nurses and doctors. Carol, who always wanted to challenge herself and improve her skills, saw an opportunity to do more. "She was excited to serve and wanted to help the G.I.s," remembered Joanne. Carol volunteered for duty in Vietnam and was sent to Fort Lewis, Wash. for additional training. She was assigned to the 51st Field Hospital and would sail to Vietnam in October 1965.

The 51st Field Hospital would be established in Tan Son Nhut Airbase at the very end of October, 1965. A 19–day cruise across the Pacific on the USNS Upshur took the 51st to Vietnam. Carol would once again serve as a surgical nurse. She worked long hours and many consecutive days treating the wounds of the men being brought in from combat. In letters home to her family, Carol didn't speak much about the war. She rarely had a break, but in February 1966 told her friend, Marianna Fisher, also a nurse in Vietnam, that she was excited about a two-day leave that she had coming up. She planned on making her way to Dalat, a mountain resort area 80 miles northwest of Saigon.

On February 18, 1966, Carol boarded an Army UH-1B helicopter from the 197th Assault Helicopter Company at the Tan Son Nhut Airbase. The destination was Dalat, and onboard the Huey was a crew of four with three passengers, including Carol and another nurse from the 51st Field Hospital, Elizabeth Jones. About 10 minutes into the flight, the helicopter struck a tension wire strung across a river near Bien Hoa. The helicopter crashed, killing all seven people. Drazba and Jones became the first two American military women killed in Vietnam. Carol's friend Marianna Fisher, whom she had known since childhood and had joined the Army with, would escort her body home from Vietnam.

Back in Pennsylvania, the Drazba family was stunned at Carol's death. "She was so full of life and took such an interest in it, we never thought of anything like this happening," said her sister, Joanne. Marcella Drazba and her surviving children, Joseph and Joanne, would bury Carol in Sacred Heart Cemetery, where she would rest next to her father, Joseph, who had died in 1963. ♦

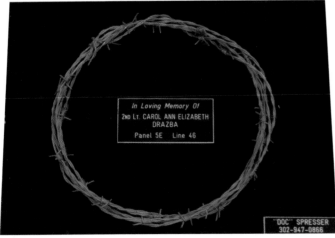

This handmade piece was left in Carol's honor at The Wall, along with one for each of the eight women who lost their lives in Vietnam. From the Vietnam Veterans Memorial Collection. Photo by Sebastián E. Encina.

2nd Lt. Carol Ann Elizabeth Drazba, U.S. Army.

ELIZABETH A JONES

Second Lieutenant, Army • 9/12/43–2/18/66 • Panel 5E, Row 47

2nd Lt. Elizabeth Jones on board the USNS Upshur with Army Chaplain Frederick Hanley.
Photo courtesy of Pastor Tom Johnson.

Betty Jones was in the prime of her life. The young woman from Allendale, S.C. loved her job as a nurse and always had a smile on her face. She made friends wherever she went and was highly respected by her colleagues. A neighbor remembers her as "vivacious…she had a wonderful and wholesale zest for life."

And then she was gone.

Elizabeth Ann Jones grew up in rural South Carolina, the daughter of George and Mabel Jones. She was called Betty by her family and spent many hours riding horses on a farm near the family's home. She found joy in helping others and decided that nursing would be the best way to make a living doing what she loved. She enrolled in nursing school and in her second year enlisted in the Army. "She loved the Army," her mother said. Betty was commissioned a second lieutenant. After a one-year posting at Fort Jackson, S.C., Betty volunteered to go to Vietnam. Her brother had already served, so when Betty told her mother of her new assignment her mother was not worried. "I wasn't scared," said Mabel Jones. "My son had been over there for a year and he said not many had died." After a brief period of training at Fort Lewis, Wash., Betty boarded the USNS Upshur for the trip to Vietnam where she would work at 51st Field Hospital in Tan Son Nhut.

While aboard the ship, she met Tom Johnson, a chaplain's assistant who had been assigned to a post at the 3rd Field Hospital in Saigon. Johnson had a projectionist's license, so even though he was an enlisted man, he spent many hours on the officer's deck. He remembers Betty's smile vividly. "She was always friendly and talked to me, an enlisted man, while most officers would not interact with enlisted men socially." She was a genuine and down to earth young woman and Johnson said, "You could not help liking her."

Betty's arrival in Vietnam quickly made her realize that more men were dying than during her brother's time there. Her mother told a newspaper in 1989 that the young age of the soldiers and how badly they were suffering was difficult for Betty to handle. "It upset her terribly about the young boys that were wounded." Betty soon found a routine in caring for the patients and was quickly well-respected by her colleagues. She was a hard worker, conscientious in her duties and tried to gain experience while she was in Vietnam.

While she was in Vietnam, Betty also found love. She had written to her family that she had become engaged to a lieutenant colonel from Georgia, and Mabel Jones remembers the joy that began to come through in her daughter's letters. She wrote her grandmother about her fiancé and how happy she was. After about four months service at the 51st Field Hospital, Betty managed to get a two-day leave. On February 18, 1966 she was on an Army Huey helicopter with fellow nurse Carol Drazba and Capt. Thomas Stasko, a doctor at the hospital. The helicopter struck a high tension wire over a river and crashed. All onboard were killed. Betty's fiancé, Lt. Col. Charles M. Honour, was one of the four crew members of the helicopter that day.

"I remember clearly when I heard of her death," said Tom Johnson. "My first reaction was disbelief. We were in Saigon, we were in a 'safe' area. Throughout the day, word spread rapidly throughout the whole hospital–always in a whisper."

The staff of the 3rd Field Hospital where Betty, Drazba and Stasko worked held a memorial for them on February 18. The service, conducted by Chaplain Frederick Hanley, was held in the courtyard of the hospital. As Hanley began the service, clouds rolled overhead and it began to rain. The mourners stayed in their seats throughout the downfall. The rain stopped at nearly the same moment that the service ended.

Devastated by the loss, Mabel Jones could find solace only in the joy that came through in her daughter. "What else could you want other than for your daughter to be happy?" ♦

A memorial bracelet left at The Wall in Elizabeth's honor. From the Vietnam Veterans Memorial Collection.
Photo by Sebastián E. Encina.

REUBEN L GARNETT Jr.

Specialist 4th Class, Army • 7/22/42–3/4/66 • Panel 5E, Row 102

Reuben Garnett Jr. did nothing halfway. He gave everything he had to everything he did and he gave everything in him to those he loved. Reuben was the oldest of four children born to Bertha and Reuben Garnett. There was something special in him right from the beginning.

Reuben's family lived with his grandmother on Fourth Street in Steelton, Pa. when Reuben Sr. was away serving as a chaplain's assistant. India Garnett remembers her brother as the center of attention even at a young age, "My grandmother's neighborhood was filled with ethnically diverse people who had come to work in the steel mills. There were no limitations there; we saw no color."

It was in this accepting environment that Reuben learned to love people for who they were. He had friends of all races and was devoted to them as though they were a part of his family. He and his sister India were like twins, having been born only one year apart and 10 years before their other two sisters. The Garnett children all looked alike, but in different sizes. Reuben was by far the biggest at a towering 6 foot 3 inches.

After Reuben Sr. got out of the Army, he took a job as a warehouseman at nearby Olmstead Air Force Base. Bertha Garnett also worked there in the data processing division. Reuben Sr. felt limited by the job at Olmstead, as he spoke seven languages but could not find work anywhere else. The family made their home at 306 Ridge St. in Steelton, a city on the eastern side of the Susquehanna River. Although some publications indicated Reuben was from a lower-income area of Philadelphia, this was not the case.

Reuben loved learning and loved to read. He was an excellent, inquisitive student who wanted to know more about the world. He was extremely likeable and was the sort of dependable young man that teachers love to have in their classroom. Reuben had many friends in school and often came to the aid of other students. India recalls a time when a classmate was being bullied by a group of boys, and Reuben came to the boy's aid. He made sure the bullies understood that the young man, who was on crutches because of a disability, was not to be bothered again. It was clear that Reuben meant what he said and the bullies were not a problem again. Despite his strength and size, Reuben never put anyone down and respected everyone.

While in high school at Steelton-Highspire High School, Reuben continued to get good grades. Although he loved learning, Reuben wanted to see the world, so he dropped out of high school in 1960 and enlisted in the Army. He did his training at Fort Knox, Ky. and was trained as a light weapons infantryman. He finished his high school education while at Fort Knox and planned to go to college after he served his time in the Army. He loved the military and the opportunities it presented him, and quickly formed strong bonds with the men he was serving with. By the mid-1960s he had risen to the rank of specialist. He received his assignment for Vietnam and returned home to Steelton on leave. The day he left, he and India had a conversation on the steps. "He made me promise to care for our mother and sisters while he was gone. It was a strange morning. I was aware that he was letting me know that he knew that his return was not guaranteed." There was no dancing or jokes or laughter that day, just reflection and conversations about the family. The Garnett family was very worried for Reuben, but they respected his decision and supported him.

Specialist 4th Class Reuben Garnett, U.S. Army. Airborne Jump School photo.

Reuben headed to Vietnam as a part of A Company, 1st Battalion, 327th Infantry July 1965. Galen Mitchell, who his comrades in the 1/327th would come to call Sweet Daddy Grace, served with Reuben. "Reuben made a massive and everlasting impression on everyone he met, which wasn't influenced by his great size but by his character, charisma, presence and an infectious smile that I still see to this day. I was so captured by that smile, along with his charisma, that it made the situation more tolerable by allowing me to escape from the realities of war." Reuben was a good soldier and though he didn't like war, he put all of his heart into it. In a letter to *The Harrisburg Patriot Evening News* in 1966, he wrote: "I am from Steelton and I am proud to serve in the forces which guard our country and our way of life and protect fellow Pennsylvanians like you. May God bless and protect you all."

The well-being of his fellow soldiers was constantly on his mind, as evidenced by a letter to the editor that he sent to *Evening News* in 1965, shortly after arriving in Vietnam. In the letter, Reuben reminded readers that their sons were in Vietnam fighting a war, and that mail from home meant everything. "So when I get mail I want my buddy next to me to get some also, even if I have to write to them myself." Just as he did his family, Reuben loved his Screaming Eagle brothers fiercely and with everything he had.

A Company was operating in Phu Yen Province in March 1966, in an area near Tuy Hoa that contained many rice paddies. On March 4, Reuben's platoon was among several that were near the small village of My Phu. The 1/327th had been in contact with North Vietnamese Army soldiers during the previous days, and as they moved, they once again began receiving fire. What began as occasional fire from the NVA soon quickened, and before long Reuben and his company were engaged in an all-out battle.

Reuben was a member of 2nd Platoon, which was led by 1st Lt. Harry Godwin. As Godwin's radio telephone operator (RTO), Reuben would have been directly next to Godwin. The two had become close since Reuben had been assigned RTO. The 2nd Platoon charged across a 75-yard long rice paddy that

Left:
Reuben among the villagers of Vietnam.
Photo courtesy of 101st Infantry, 327th Infantry Regiment and Galen Mitchell.

Right:
Sweet Daddy Grace in Vietnam.
Photo courtesy of 101st Infantry, 327th Infantry Regiment and Galen Mitchell.

gave them no cover; it was an all-out sprint to the other side. The platoon, that had started the day with 35 members, was down to eight men as they approached the midpoint of the paddy. Godwin was hit and fell wounded. Like he always had, Reuben went to the aid of a friend in need and ran to Godwin's side. As he attempted to carry his friend to safety, Reuben was hit by small arms fire, likely from the same gun that shot Godwin.

Due to the ferocity of the fire fight, 1/327th couldn't get to the wounded and dead immediately, so it is not known how long Godwin and Reuben lived in that rice paddy. When their bodies were finally recovered, the two men were holding hands. ♦

Day in Nam
© Roland Castanie

Specialist, Army • 11/5/46–5/11/66 • Panel 7E, Row 50

Wayne and Fred Traylor grew up as many brothers in rural areas did, spending a lot of time together outside. The boys, along with their sisters, Peggy and Glenda, were raised first in Woodland and then in Heflin, Ala. Both small towns were in sparsely populated areas of eastern Alabama. Wayne was the oldest, born in 1946 to Howard and Velma Traylor. Fred came next in 1949, followed by sisters Glenda and Peggy. After their mother died in 1959, the Traylor children came to rely on each other even more, particularly while Howard was working at the Anniston Army Depot.

Both boys loved to hunt and fish, spending many hours outdoors. Fred was much taller than his older brother, standing 6 foot 2 inches to Wayne's 5 foot 8 inches. Fred was taller than everyone in the family, so much so that the family nicknamed him Lurch, after the butler on the TV show *The Addams Family*. Fred loved music and could often be found playing his favorite Beatles and Elvis Presley songs on his guitar, either by himself or with his band. He hoped to make music his career some day.

Wayne didn't have the same focus as his brother and dropped out of school in the 10th grade. He had struggled in school and wanted something more than what he thought he could find in Alabama. He knew he wanted to see the world, so he followed in the footsteps of his father and several uncles, and joined the Army in 1963 when he was 17 years old. His family was proud of him for joining up and taking steps to improve his life.

Wayne completed his Army training at Fort Benning in 1964 and was sent to Forts Polk and Campbell for additional training in his military occupational specialty of 63H2P, tracked vehicle mechanic, in 1965. He also took the basic airborne course that would allow him to serve in airborne units. Wayne liked being in the Army and the job he was doing. He spoke of perhaps making the Army his career. His first overseas assignment was to Vietnam.

Wayne was assigned to the 1st Brigade of the 101st Airborne Division when he arrived in Vietnam and served with them from July to November 1965. In his letters home to his family, he expressed the difficult living conditions, specifically mentioning the horrible weather. Still, he was focused on doing his job and committed to serving his country. In November 1965, Wayne was sent to A Company, 2nd Battalion of the 502nd Infantry. His rank was specialist, and he was about halfway through his tour in Vietnam. In early May 1966, the 2nd/502nd moved to Bu Gia Map, a former Special Forces camp in Phuoc Long Province. Located about 90 miles northeast of Saigon, the camp had been abandoned in 1965 because of imminent enemy invasion.

On May 12, 1966, Fred, Peggy and Glenda Traylor were at home while their father was working. A car pulled up and several soldiers knocked on the door. At the same time, another car of Army officers was contacting Howard Traylor at his job at the Anniston Army Depot. Specialist Wayne Traylor had died the previous day at Bu Gia Map. He had been killed by enemy small arms fire. He was 19.

After Wayne's death, the Traylor family struggled to go on. After graduating from Cleburne County High School, Fred decided that he had to do something more, something to make Wayne's death easier to handle. According to his sister Glenda, the main reason that Fred wanted to join the military was to get revenge for Wayne's death. The family was devastated when Fred informed them that he was going to join the U.S. Marine Corps.

Fred Traylor at An Hoa. Photo courtesy of Walter Scoggins.

Fred did his boot camp training at Parris Island, S.C. in September 1967. After Wayne's death in Vietnam, Fred was classified as a sole surviving son, a designation that would prevent him from seeing combat. However, during boot camp Fred made the decision to sign a waiver allowing him to serve in a combat unit. He was

Corporal, Marine Corps • 1/12/49–6/17/69 • Panel 22W, Row 71

Spc. Wayne Traylor.
Photo courtesy of Glenda Williamson.

Cpl. Fred Traylor.
Photo courtesy of Glenda Williamson.

then sent to Camp Lejeune, N.C. and Camp Pendleton, Calif. for additional training in preparation for being sent to Vietnam as a field artillery control man. As the training progressed, Fred's family was increasingly worried. "We were fearful that he wouldn't come home," Glenda said. After long discussions with his family, Fred decided it would be best if he didn't serve in combat. He requested to rescind the waiver he had signed. The request was denied and Fred arrived in Vietnam in June 1968.

While in Vietnam, Fred was homesick and worried about his fate. "He was a tough kid, but he was concerned for his life as he knew he had a good chance of not coming home. However, he was loyal to the men he served with and he wanted to do his job," remembered Glenda. Fred was assigned to the headquarters battery of the 12th Marine Regiment at Dong Ha. He worked at a fire direction center at the base, which was large and relatively secure. His battery mate Walter Scoggins remembered serving with Fred at Dong Ha: "He was a good artillery man and a good friend. He didn't hide the fact that his brother had died in Vietnam, but he didn't wear it on his sleeve, either." While in Vietnam, Fred received additional training at the Naval Gunfire School and was soon transferred out into the field as a gunfire spotter. Walter immediately saw the change in his friend. "One day out of nowhere he stopped in unexpectedly. He was transformed–salty and grungy and a corporal now. He had become a grunt, no longer a soft artillery man like me."

On June 17, 1969, shortly before the end of his tour, Fred was on a search and destroy mission in the area of Dong Ha. The Marines soon found themselves receiving heavy fire and pinned down by enemy forces. Fred's Bronze Star citation affirms the actions of the day: "Fearlessly volunteering to assist in evacuating his companions from positions dangerously exposed to enemy fire, Corporal Traylor began maneuvering across the hazardous terrains toward the wounded Marines when he was mortally wounded by the detonation of a mortar round." Fred Traylor was 20.

Back in Heflin, Glenda Traylor was home alone when she heard a car pull up in the driveway. The family was anxiously awaiting Fred's homecoming as his tour was almost up. "I saw two soldiers get out. I began crying because this was the second time this had happened. I screamed at them when they asked to talk to my parents." The family reeled from this second loss and Howard Traylor would never really recover. He retired from Anniston Army Depot shortly after Wayne's death and struggled with the loss of his sons until 1973 when he took his own life.

"Peggy and I lost both of our brothers and our parents by the time we were 22. The pain of our loss is still strong in my heart, but we are survivors." ♦

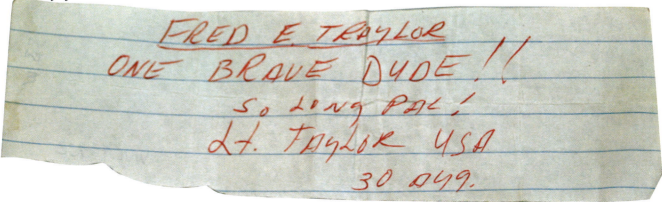

Note for Fred Traylor left at The Wall in D.C.
From the Vietnam Veterans Memorial Collection. Photo by Sebastián E. Encina.

JAMES T LOCKRIDGE

Corporal, Army • 11/28/41–6/12/66 • Panel 8E, Row 42

When families send their sons and daughters, brothers and sisters and husbands and wives off to war, there is typically a great deal of worry. Worry about their loved one being so far from home and being surrounded by the dangers of bullets and rockets and booby traps. The family of James Thomas Lockridge had the same worries when their son begged them to allow him to sign up for the Army. They feared they would lose him.

James was called either JT or Thomas by his family and he wanted nothing more than to be in the Army. His brother, Anthony, remembers that JT always wanted to be a soldier. While at Carver Smith High School in Tennessee, the only thing he wanted to do was enlist so that he could follow his dream. His parents, Raymond and Annie Lockridge, were reluctant. The country had been at war for much of the 1940s and 1950s, and the Lockridges did not relish the idea of their son being put in harm's way.

Cpl. James Lockridge and his wife Hui Cha after their marriage.
Photo courtesy of Anthony Lockridge.

JT was persistent and his begging eventually wore his parents down. He enlisted in the Army in May 1959; the first step in his dream of becoming a career soldier. He completed training at Fort Jackson, S.C. and Fort Campbell, Ky. before being assigned to a post in Korea from 1961 to 1963. While there, he fell in love with and married a local woman, Hui Cha. They had two children. By 1965, JT was in Vietnam.

He was assigned to 2nd Battalion of the 503rd Infantry Division of the 173rd Airborne Brigade. While serving, the unit saw a great deal of combat, and as a sergeant, JT was concerned about the number of young men that he saw dying. Anthony Lockridge recalls his brother's emotions coming through in letters home. "It bothered him about losing his friends, and about how the new soldiers were dying as soon as they got there. It was hard for him because he felt they were not allowed to do what they needed to do to win the war."

Hon Cong Mountain Signal Complex
Photo courtesy
of Victor Alvarez

In mid-June, the worst fears of the Lockridge family were confirmed: JT had been killed in action in Vietnam. They had received little information, only that JT was gone. As the family pressed the Army for details about JT's death, it became clear that everything was not as it seemed. A friend who was with JT when he died contacted them and the truth began to come out. JT had not died in combat. He had been murdered.

The details provided by the young man who was with JT when he died were eventually confirmed by the Army and told a strange tale. A new lieutenant joined JT's company and they were on a patrol when the lieutenant gave an order that JT disagreed with. The lieutenant wanted to send a group of newly arrived soldiers to a position and JT felt that it would put the soldiers in extreme danger. He tried to offer an alternative solution, but the discussion soon elevated to violence and JT threw a punch that broke the lieutenant's jaw. Consequently, JT was demoted from sergeant to corporal. About a week later, JT was at a combination bar/laundromat enjoying a beer while waiting for his clothes to dry. As the music played, he stood up and began to dance. As JT enjoyed his time on the dance floor, two South Vietnamese soldiers approached him. One of them shot him in the chest. JT's friend rushed him to the hospital, but it was too late. JT was dead at the age of 24. The Army lists his cause of death as intentional homicide. The two soldiers who shot him were never located. ♦

EUGENE L. SELF

Quartermaster 3rd Class, Navy • 6/02/46–10/18/66 • Panel 11E, Row 88

Gene was a happy young man with many friends. Photo courtesy of Sue Jacklin Self.

Carteret, N.J. was a typical American town in the early 1960s. About 25 miles southwest of the bustle of Manhattan, Carteret had a small town feel to it, a place where everyone in the neighborhood knew each other and kept an eye on each other. The town, comprised mostly of single-family homes, had a bowling alley and a small strip mall, but didn't have a movie theater. Most of the teenagers hung out at an area luncheonette where they talked and listened to music. Gene Self would often be among them, talking and laughing with one of his many friends, or with complete strangers who would soon find themselves entertained by the gentle giant that was Eugene Lawrence Self.

Born in New York City in 1946, Gene Self was the oldest child of Mason and Bernice Self. The family lived in Brooklyn for many of Gene's younger years before moving to Carteret in 1957 when Mason took a job in the area. Mason was a machinist and Bernice was a credit manager for the Yellow Pages. The couple, along with Gene and his sister, Susan, lived an idyllic life surrounded by friends. His family sometimes called him "Baby Huey" because, as Susan said, "Baby Huey was a gigantic baby duck with a funny personality, just like Gene."

The family was an engaging one and to be friends with Gene or Susan meant you were a member of the family. "I was always welcomed in their home. They had a city vibe that I'd never experienced and Gene's family included his friends in their conversations and family activities," remembered Andrea Stec-Calabrese, a longtime girlfriend of Gene's. Even among such a friendly family, Gene's personality stood out nearly as much as he did.

Gene stood 6 feet, 6 inches tall and had a personality to match. Though typically called Gene, a few friends called him "Moose" because, according to his friend William Nigro, "He was a big guy, but also had a big heart." Gene had an adventurous spirit and would talk to just about anyone. He was well-liked by classmates and was able to straddle the line between high school social groups, fitting in with the "greasers" as well as the college-bound. He made friends everywhere he went.

Gene's senior portrait from Carteret High School, Class of 1964. Photo courtesy of Sue Jacklin Self.

After graduating from Carteret High School in 1964, Gene joined the Navy to help pay for college. He was very patriotic, and although America's involvement in Southeast Asia was just beginning, Gene believed in what the U.S. was doing there. The Self family believed in military service, with Mason having served in the Coast Guard during World War II. Gene did his recruit training at the U.S. Naval Training Center, Great Lakes, Ill. from July through October 1965, and was assigned to duty on the USS Bexar upon completion of his training. His father had been diagnosed with colon cancer and a hereditary kidney disease and his disease had worsened. As the only son, Gene could have applied for a hardship discharge or transfer because of his father's illness, but he refused to even discuss it. The Bexar was transporting troops to Vietnam during the six months that Gene was on board and he spent enough time in Vietnam to know that he wanted to do more. After three months at U.S. Naval Airbase at Coro, Calif., Gene volunteered to go back to Vietnam. He was assigned to Patrol Craft, Fast (PCF) Division 101 stationed at An Thoi, where he would work on a swift boat.

The official name for a swift boat was PCF. Gene was assigned to PCF 9, a 50-foot boat with a crew of six. As a Quartermaster, 3rd Class, Gene had many duties on board PCF 9. He kept logs and records, conducted weather operations and assisted deck officers and navigators. The swift boats' responsibility at that time was to patrol the coastlines. According to Doug Smyth, who served in PCF 101 with Gene, "He (Gene) made several patrols a week patrolling the coastlines and stopping any craft, looking for contraband." The swift boats were also armed and would sometimes be used to support the missions of ground troops in the area.

On the morning of October 18, 1966, PCF 9 was one of several PCFs that was supporting a U.S. Special Forces mission. The ship was in position one-half mile east of Phu Quoc Island in the Gulf of Thailand. PCF 9 was providing fire support for the ground troops and had just fired a white phosphorous (WP) round from their 81mm gun. White phosphorus rounds provided huge puffs of white smoke when they exploded and were often used for marking locations or to provide cover for soldiers in the area. Immediately after the WP round was fired, the command was given for PCF 9 to fire an explosion round. The mortars used to fire both the WP round and the explosive

Gene leading the riderless horse in the Carteret Memorial Day Parade in May 1965. Gene was in the U.S. Navy Reserve at the time. Photo courtesy of Sue Jacklin Self.

round worked with a trigger, allowing the gunner to fire the round rather than firing with a firing pin. After the explosive round was loaded, it detonated inside the mortar tube, causing an explosion that destroyed the mortar and launched the nearby .50 caliber machine gun over the side of the ship. The explosion on PCF 9 could be seen by PCF Division 101 ships up to four miles away.

Killed in the explosion were Boatwain's Mate 2nd Class Hubert Tuck, Jr. of Lenoir City, Tenn., Ensign 2nd Class (EN2) Gale Hays of Falling Rock, W. Va., and Quartermaster 3rd Class (QM3) Eugene Self of Carteret, N.J. Tuck was 29, Hays was 34, and Gene Self was only 20. His death was mourned by comrades in Vietnam and friends in New Jersey alike. Doug Smyth was tasked with the difficult job of sending his friend's personal effects home to his family and Gene's death affected him deeply. "Bottom line, he was a good man who did not deserve what happened to him. A life cut way too short."

Mason Self's illness progressed rapidly after his son's death, and he lived less than eight months after the family buried Gene at Beth Moses Cemetery in Farmingdale, N.Y. Mason Self succumbed to his illness in June 1967.

Decades after her brother's death, Susan Self visited Washington, D.C. with her husband and her two children. Susan had always told her children about their Uncle Gene and all he had accomplished in his short life. They also knew about his "Baby Huey" nickname. "When we visited The Wall, my children wanted to leave something. While in a store we saw this duck. It wasn't Baby Huey, but my daughter thought it was a good representation. We left if by Gene's panel with a note."

The note ended "Someday we'll all meet again." ♦

Gene's sister, Sue, and her children left this at The Wall in D.C. One of Gene's nicknames was Baby Huey. From the Vietnam Veterans Memorial Collection. Photo by Sebastián E. Encina.

Self 35

Photos by Bill Shugarts

CHARLES E. MEEK

Lance Corporal, Marine Corps • 3/12/47–11/12/66 • Panel 12E, Row 63

Chuck's boot camp photo from Marine Corps Recruit Depot, San Diego. Photo courtesy of Kristine Meek O'Mara.

11,791 days. From the fall of 1966 to the late winter of 1999, there were 11,791 days. 11,791 days, 11,791 visits to the son who gave his life in Vietnam.

Ed Meek visited his son Charles' grave every day for more than 32 years, regardless of weather or health or what was going on in the world. At first, Ed made the drive from his home in Macomb County down Groesbeck Highway to Mt. Olivet cemetery on the east side of Detroit, where Charles lay buried next to his mother, June. Then, in 1975, Ed moved his wife and his son to Resurrection Cemetery in Clinton Township so that they would be closer to him. Every day, Ed Meek made his way to the graveside of his oldest child, lost in the early years of the war in Vietnam. For more than 32 years, Ed made sure that his beloved son would not be forgotten.

Charles Edward Meek was the oldest child of Ed Meek and his wife, June, born in 1947 in Macomb County, Mich. When Chuck was seven, his mother died of heat stroke and the family moved to St. Clair Shores, where Chuck and his siblings would grow up. Set along Lake St. Clair, east of Detroit and the wealth of the Grosse Pointes, St. Clair Shores was a working class community when the Meek family moved there in the mid-1950s.

Ed Meek sold paper for Beecher, Peck & Lewis, and his second wife was a secretary when the family settled at Yale Street, down the block from Wheat Elementary and around the block from Lakeview High School. Chuck, his younger sister Kristine and their younger brother Gary lived on this tree-lined street filled with single-story brick ranch houses until the mid-1960s.

The Meeks lived a typical suburban life and Chuck participated in many school and neighborhood activities. In elementary school he had a paper route for the *South Macomb News* and he played football for Ottawa Junior High. As a youngster, he played second base for the Little Jets. A good, but not great student, Chuck was happy and kind, a young man who was always laughing. His classmates saw him as easy-going and friendly, someone who was liked and respected by just about everyone. While at Lakeview, Chuck began dating his classmate Sandy Martin, and the couple grew closer as their high school years went on. As Chuck grew older, his interests moved from sports to cars, and as a teen he spent much of his time with his red 1959 Chevy convertible.

When his Lakeview class graduated in 1965, Chuck felt drawn to military service. Chuck and his father began looking at the branches of the military to determine the best fit to shape Chuck's future. "He thought the Marines best suited him," said his father in a 1966 newspaper article. Ed Meek was no stranger to military service, having been a staff sergeant in World War II. He was not surprised when his oldest son expressed a desire to join up. Ed was proud of his son's desire to serve his country and contribute to the greater good of the nation and Chuck strongly believed in America's mission in Vietnam. Although the war in Southeast Asia was just beginning, Chuck told Kristine that he felt he needed to be there. "He felt very passionate about what we as a country were doing over there and felt strongly about helping the people of Vietnam." Chuck enlisted in the Marine Corps on the buddy system with his friend, Dennis Flanigan, and reported to Marine Corps Recruit Depot (MCRD) in San Diego in September 1965 for the beginning of his four year enlistment. He was 18.

Eighty-four days. Once arriving in San Diego, Chuck and Dennis spent 12 weeks going through the process of becoming Marines. A demanding and arduous process for even the most physically fit, boot camp at San Diego was designed to make its attendees earn the title of Marine and prepare them for what lay ahead. For many of the recruits at MCRD San Diego in September 1965, including recruit Chuck, what lay ahead was Vietnam.

After additional individual training at Camp Pendleton, Calif. from November 1965 to January 1966, Chuck proposed to his high school sweetheart, Sandy, and the two enjoyed leave in California, taking in the fun of Disneyland before Chuck's deployment to the escalating war in Vietnam in early 1966. She was the last of Chuck's family to see him alive.

Chuck receiving his diploma from Lakeview High School in 1965. Photo courtesy of Kristine Meek O'Mara.

Chuck's senior portrait from the St. Clair Shores Lakeview High School 1965 Yearbook. Photo courtesy of Kristine Meek O'Mara.

When he arrived in Vietnam, Chuck was assigned to India Company, 3rd Battalion of the 1st Marines. He joined a Marine division that established its headquarters near Chu Lai in March 1966. When Chuck joined the 3/1, they were in the area near Da Nang, on the eastern side of the country about 85 miles from the 17th parallel and the Demilitarized Zone. As the long, hot Vietnam summer went on, Chuck was part of the escalating ground war in Vietnam. Chuck eventually trained to be a radio telephone operator, or RTO, for India Company, learning from a Marine who was due to depart Vietnam in early November. The RTO carried a 25 pound radio on his back, in addition to his standard Marine rifleman equipment. He was responsible for ensuring that officers could communicate with each other and with headquarters, and for carrying signaling flares and grenades that would make sure that the men could be located by air. The RTO was a critical part of the squad and was usually with the platoon commander and squad leader, often making the RTO an enemy target.

In 1966, the 3rd Platoon was set up at the village of An Trach, in Quang Nam province in South Vietnam. The perimeter surrounded parts of An Trach and villagers lived inside the perimeter with the 3rd Platoon. They had several Vietnamese boys working with them as interpreters and guides. Once the perimeter was established, it served as a base for the ambushes and patrols that the 3rd Platoon would carry out. They had been in An Trach for about five months when, in the early morning and late afternoon of November 11, the defensive positions on the northern perimeter received significant small arms fire. After this attack, the platoon was on alert until sunrise. The night was a particularly dark one, with overcast skies and poor visibility in the area, and because of the earlier attacks on the perimeter there was no illumination. Around 2 a.m. on November 12, a group of about 25 Viet Cong soldiers, led by a few sappers, attacked India Company's position. Sappers were individuals or small groups of soldiers that would be sent into fixed enemy positions to attack using stealth and surprise. Almost simultaneously, six of 3rd Platoon's positions were attacked: the command post, the corpsman quarters and four gun positions. This ambush engaged the men of 3rd Platoon and H&S Company in a firefight that lasted nearly 30 minutes, and although the men fought bravely, the VC's small arms fire, demolition charges and grenades would prove to be too much. One of the radios in the command post had been blown 75 meters from its position when it was found the next morning and it took nearly 30 minutes for India Company's commanding officer to make contact with the 3rd Platoon. The first message received from An Trach came from a private first class in the .81mm mortar section who was able to call in, "We have been hit! All the tents are down!" In the darkness of that morning, 14 Marines and one Navy corpsman lost their lives. Chuck Meek was among the dead. He was 19. He had been in Vietnam for 245 days and was due to return home from Vietnam in January. He planned to marry Sandy and to begin their life together. Instead, Sandy would place their already purchased wedding rings into Chuck's casket to be buried with him.

Chuck in Vietnam where he was stationed with 3rd Platoon. Army of the Republic of Vietnam troops that sometimes served with India Company. Photo courtesy of Kristine Meek O'Mara.

After Chuck's death, his father strove to have his son's memory, service and sacrifice remembered by his community. Almost immediately it became clear that Chuck would be remembered. Once news of his death began to spread, the St. Clair Shores and Lakeview High School communities responded. Chuck's former Lakeview classmates raised $550 for a school memorial in Chuck's honor and the school hosted a memorial program shortly after his death. Ed, who had been moved by a World War I memorial in his own hometown, wanted his son's memorial to "remind younger boys that this country stands for something–and that freedom costs something."

Affected tremendously by the loss of his oldest child, Ed began his daily ritual of visiting his son's grave. As the years passed and the war in Vietnam escalated, Ed continued to honor his son and watched as more and more Americans lost their lives in a war that he began to see as "an unpopular" one. He became frustrated as the war raged on and eventually ended with the fall of Saigon. The war ended 3,091 days after Chuck died.

Every Marine is first a rifleman. Cpl. Chuck Meek in Vietnam. Photo courtesy of Kristine Meek O'Mara.

In September of 1974, President Gerald Ford granted conditional amnesty to those who had evaded the draft or deserted their duty. Though the program required service to the community as a condition of the amnesty, Ed was outraged. He had given five years of his own service in one war and lost his son to another. He believed service to one's country in a time of war was a responsibility of citizenship and could not bear that those who had fled their duty were being forgiven. He packed up the flag that had covered his beloved Chuck's casket and sent it to Ford as a sign of his protest. According to the White House, this was not the only flag received from the families of soldiers killed in Vietnam. In a credit to his respect for the families of veterans, Ford returned nearly every single one.

In a noble gesture, Ford not only responded to Ed's letter, but also attempted to explain the reasoning behind his actions and invited the Meek family to the White House. On May 19, 1975, Ed, his daughter, Kristine, and son, Gary, flew to Washington and met with Ford. The President greeted them in the Green Room and Ed once again received his son's flag from the government. When he gave Ed the flag that had once draped his son's casket, Ford said, "We have been keeping this honored flag for you and I am honored to return it."

Ed wrote another letter to the President for the hospitality shown to his family during their visit. In it he shared his hopes for his son's memory:

"My son can today be justly proud as can each of the 55,000 men who gave their lives in Vietnam. Our hearts and lives will always contain an emptiness that can never be filled, but at some time and day they will take an honored place in the world to come and then we will fully understand."

Like so many other mothers and fathers of the Vietnam era and the parents of those fallen in America's earlier wars, Ed wanted to believe his son's death meant something. He believed his son should be remembered for the man he was and the life he lived. Ed died in 1999 – 11,791 days after Chuck's tragic death in Vietnam. But his son's memory and legacy live on in those who knew him. Some of Chuck's Lakeview classmates gather every year and Chuck is often the topic of conversation. They remember his laugh, his smile and his ability to bring joy into the lives of those around him.

Chuck has been gone for more than 16,000 days, but he has most definitely been remembered. His name is on The Wall in Washington and on the multiple traveling memorials that cross the nation every year, and his name is on the monument in front of the St. Clair Shores Library. His friends have told stories of Chuck to their children and his name will be remembered as those children age. In the years since Ed's death, Chuck's grave, now near both his parents, has been visited regularly by his sister, Kristine, and is never without an American flag. Every day, that flag is there, a testament to both a son's service and a father's dedication to his son's memory. ♦

Chuck with his fiancée, Sandra Martin, on leave in California. Photo courtesy of Kristine Meek O'Mara.

Ed Meek, Kristine Meek O'Mara and President Gerald Ford in May 1975. President Ford was returning the flag from Chuck's casket that Ed had sent in protest of the pardoning of draft evaders. Photo courtesy of Kristine Meek O'Mara.

GEORGE A MYERS

Lance Corporal, Marine Corps • 8/17/47–11/25/66 • Panel 12E, Row 117

Artie in uniform before leaving for Vietnam. Photo courtesy of Mary Wade and Betty Myers.

Artie at Christmas 1963 at the age of 16. Photo courtesy of Mary Wade and Betty Myers.

Johnny while at basic training at Fort Hood, Texas in 1966. Photo courtesy of Mary Wade and Betty Myers.

George Arthur Myers and John George Schmidt were cousins, born eight days apart in August 1947. The family called George "Artie" and John "Johnny." They were both named for their grandfather George Myers Sr. The boys grew up together and came from a large extended family; Johnny's mother, Theresa, and Artie's father, George, were brother and sister. The Myers and Schmidt families spent lots of time together, enjoying picnics and parties at the homes of various relatives in the St. Louis area where they all lived. As they grew older, both Johnny and Artie joined Boy Scouts and Little League.

Though the boys spent time together and with their families, as they aged their interests began to vary. Artie developed a love for woodworking and thought he might pursue a career in medicine, while Johnny stayed active in the Boy Scouts, and though his dream was to play baseball for the St. Louis Cardinals, he thought he might become a police officer.

Johnny and Artie lived in different areas of St. Louis, so they attended different high schools. Johnny went to Central High School and Artie to Maplewood Richmond Heights. Both boys graduated in 1965. Their futures would take them on different paths, but send them to the same place – Vietnam.

After graduating from high school with straight As, Johnny enlisted in the U.S. Marine Corps. He wanted to serve his country and to follow in the footsteps of his grandfather, father and mother. George Myers Sr. had fought with St. Louis' 138th Infantry Regiment during World War I, and George Myers Jr. served in the Army in World War II. Frances Myers had been an Army nurse during World War II. Artie entered Marine Corps Recruit Depot, San Diego in November 1965, and after completing training there, went to Camp Pendleton. In January 1966, he left for Vietnam. Assigned to the 2nd Battalion, 7th Marines, Artie was proud to be a Marine. Although he was scared while in Vietnam, he was also more than willing to do what was necessary. His actions in combat earned him a Purple Heart for wounds he received on June 13, 1966. At that time, he had been transferred to D Company, 1st Battalion, 7th Marines. He would stay with this battalion for the rest of his tour in Vietnam, but moved between B and D Companies.

Meanwhile, back in St. Louis, Johnny had also determined what he wanted to do with his life. "He liked to do things for people," remembered his mother, Theresa. "I think that's why he wanted to be a policeman." He was a cadet at the St. Louis Police Academy in May 1966 when his father, John, suddenly passed away. Johnny and his father had been very close and Johnny was devastated by the loss of a man who was just as much a friend as a father. Johnny, his mother and his sister, Mary, buried John E. Schmidt on May 13, 1966. When the family returned home from the cemetery, Johnny found his induction notice in the mailbox. Unlike his cousin Artie, Johnny had no interest in military service. He would have much rather stayed at home in St. Louis, especially once his father was gone. Johnny wanted to become a police officer, marry his girlfriend, Judy Kampworth, and take care of his mother and sister. But, Johnny was a conscientious young man and believed in doing his duty. He went to his Army basic training at Fort Hood, Texas in October 1966.

While Johnny was just learning to become a soldier, Artie was fighting in the jungles of Vietnam. On November 25, 1966, Artie would earn his second Purple Heart. His company was on an operation near Quang Ngai when they engaged in a firefight with enemy troops. Artie sustained a gunshot wound and was killed. He was 19.

After Artie's death, the family became even more worried about Johnny. He may not have wanted to serve, but once he was in the Army, he was dedicated to doing his job. In letters home, he expressed more concern for his mother and sister than he did for himself, even though he knew he would eventually head to Vietnam. In a letter to his mother in April 1967, he expressed surprise that

JOHN G SCHMIDT

Specialist 4th Class, Army • 8/25/47–1/17/68 • Panel 34E, Row 64

Johnny in his room at basic training, Fort Hood, Texas 1966. Photo courtesy of Mary Wade and Betty Myers.

it had already been a year since his father had died. He missed his father desperately. "I know in my heart if there is such a place as Heaven and Hell and the good people go to Heaven, Dad is in Heaven because people don't come any better than him." In October 1967, nearly one year after Artie's death, Johnny was sent to Vietnam.

Johnny was assigned as a light weapons infantryman with A Company, 1st Battalion, 52nd Infantry. The unit had suffered heavy casualties and was frequently ambushed by enemy troops. Still, in his letters home, Johnny tried to remain upbeat. But at one point, he told his mother that mortar attacks were frequent and that "there isn't a soul out here who doesn't get scared." He spoke often of the jungle heat, the mosquitoes that "could almost pick you up and carry you off," and the poor living conditions of the Vietnamese people. Johnny told his girlfriend Judy that he often thought of her at night and that he dreamed of the memories they would make together.

Johnny had been in Vietnam for three months when, on January 17, 1968, his company was on a search and destroy mission near An Thinh. As they neared the village, they suddenly began taking heavy fire. Johnny was one of two men sent out by the platoon commander to secure an area around a hedgerow when they became the target of heavy machine-gun fire. Johnny was wounded twice in the initial burst of fire but kept his wits and notified the platoon commander of the machine gun location. As his fellow troops advanced, they became the target of the machine gun's fire. Johnny began crawling toward the enemy position, and while taking fire, threw two grenades at the machine gun nest. His actions allowed the rest of the platoon to eventually reach and overtake the machine gun position. Johnny succumbed to his wounds and was awarded the Silver Star for his actions. He was 20.

Lance Cpl. George Arthur Myers and Spc. John George Schmidt are buried in St. Louis, Mo. ♦

John Schmidt and George "Artie" Myers together at a family gathering in 1948. Photo courtesy of Mary Wade and Betty Myers.

John Schmidt and a fellow soldier at Fort Hood.

John Schmidt.

BUDD E HOOD

Specialist 4th Class, Army • 6/27/45–2/28/67 • Panel 15E, Row 118

Spc. 4th Class Budd Hood, U.S. Army.

Pfc. Charles Hood, U.S. Marine Corps.

There were three Hood brothers: Budd, Charles and Ronald. Between the years of 1958 and 1969, all three of them were in the military. Their younger sisters, Bobbette and Valerie didn't want any of them to go. Ron would serve first, finishing up his service in 1965. Budd, Butch to his family, joined the Army in 1965. Charles, who the family called Chuck, joined the Marine Corps in 1969. By the end of the decade, only one of the three Hood brothers would be alive.

The family lived in Painesville, Ohio near Lake Erie. They were a patriotic group and believed strongly in serving their country. Though their mother worried about them, her brother had served in World War II and made it home all right. She was confident that her boys would finish their service safely.

Ron did make it home safely, serving seven years in the military before he got out in 1965. Shortly before he finished, his younger brother Butch enlisted. Butch was sent to basic training at Fort Knox, Ky. in January 1965. He stayed there until April, when he went to Fort Gordon, Ga. for advanced individual training in his military operational specialty of light weapons infantry. Unlike his brother, Butch would not stay stateside during his service. He was then assigned to two different divisions in Europe, first serving as an assistant gunner and then as an infantryman. From Europe, Butch was sent to Vietnam in February 1967 and was assigned to B Company, 1st Battalion, 16th Infantry, a part of the 1st Infantry Division. He arrived to the company on February 15.

On the morning of February 28, B Company was commanded by Capt. Donald Ulm. The company left their position around 8:00 a.m. on a search and destroy mission, heading east toward the Prek Klok river. The terrain that covered the mile and a half to the river was dense, tangled jungle, and the company's progress was very slow. They'd moved barely one–half mile in two hours when one of the platoons began taking fire. The initial bursts of small arms fire led them to believe the enemy forces were small, but the observation of three enemy machine guns indicated a much larger force. The fire, coming from both the south and the east, soon included extremely accurate sniper fire from the tree line. Soon, B Company was pinned down and nearly surrounded. Casualties mounted until another company was able to reach them and provide cover. The fighting continued until 3 p.m. It was not until 9:30 p.m. that Ulm was able to get his men to the landing zone for evacuation. More than two dozen men were wounded in what would be called the Battle of Prek Klok I and 25 men lost their lives. One of the dead was Spc. Budd Edward Hood. He was 21 years old and had been in Vietnam for only 21 days.

When the news of Butch's death made it to Painesville, Chuck was living with Ron. Chuck was very angry about the death and felt that he had to do something. "He wanted to avenge Butch's death, so he enlisted. I tried to stop him, but he went anyway. We all wanted him to stay home." Ron tried to enlist with his brother, but no service would take him and he was forced to stand by and watch his youngest brother join the Marine Corps.

Chuck did his Marine Corps boot camp at Parris Island, S.C. in the early part of 1969 and then went to Camp Lejeune, N.C. for training as an assaultman. By the first of August, he was in Vietnam.

Assigned to B Company, 1st Battalion, 7th Marines, Chuck served as an infantry assaultman. His job was to provide rocket fire and demolitions to support rifle squads and platoons on patrol. He was with B Company near Hill 10, Da Nang on August 12, 1969. In the early morning hours, the company was preparing to leave its defensive position when it came under enemy attack. One of the D Company listening posts was attacked and became pinned down. B Company and the rest of D Company headed out to get them, and both companies were attacked by a large, coordinated enemy force. The attacks lasted from the early morning of August 12 until the early morning of August 14, and resulted in the deaths of 18 Marines, including Pfc. Charles Alan Hood. He was 20.

Ron is the last of the three Hood brothers. He thinks of his brothers often and wonders what would have become of their lives. "I wish I could have taken their place." ♦

CHARLES A HOOD

Private First Class, Marine Corps • 7/2/49–8/12/69 • Panel 19W, Row 15

MATTHEW LEONARD

Sergeant First Class, Army • 11/26/29–2/28/67 • Panel 15E, Row 119

Sgt. 1st Class Matthew Leonard lived through the Korean War, bravely serving his country in combat far from home. He had always wanted to be a soldier and by the late 1960s had spent all of his adult life in the Army. The strong Alabama native wore his uniform whenever he could, even when he was home on leave. His wife, Lois, said he preferred being in his uniform rather than in civilian clothes. "All of the little boys in the neighborhood loved when he came home," she remembered. "They'd be in the backyard with sticks on their shoulders and he'd be drilling them." By the time the Vietnam War was rising in intensity in 1967, Matthew was training soldiers at Fort Leonard Wood, Mo. That duty, was not enough for the veteran and he told his wife that he felt compelled to volunteer for duty in Vietnam.

Matthew met his wife, Lois, when they were adolescents, she in sixth grade and he in the eighth. They fell for each other almost immediately. He was a Boy Scout and even way back then his love for uniforms was obvious; he would walk the halls of the school in his Boy Scout uniform. Lois remembers him as handsome and well-mannered. He was liked by both teachers and students and was very conscientious about his appearance. They married in November 1950 and he left for the Korean War shortly after. His time in Korea taught him much about himself and the military and Matthew was more sure than ever that he wanted to spend his life as a soldier. He and Lois had five children, two sons and three daughters; and Lois understood that he loved the Army just as much as he loved his family. "I know he was doing something that he loved to do," she told the *Tuscaloosa News* in 2011. "That was his life and mine, too. He made it mine. I was glad he was doing something he loved to do."

His position as an instructor at Fort Leonard Wood was a safe one during the Vietnam War, and his wife was angry when she heard that he had volunteered for a tour of Vietnam. But she understood that Matthew felt that was where he was needed. "He said there were too many young soldiers going over there and dying. He felt like he could go over there and help them because he had already been through one war." Lois became even more upset when her husband told her, as well as some of his friends, that he didn't believe he would make it back from Vietnam. He prepared her for what would happen if he did not make it back and promised to do everything he could to make it back alive.

He arrived in Vietnam in August 1966 and was assigned as a platoon sergeant with B Company of 1st Battalion, 16th Infantry. He was the senior enlisted man in his platoon and was responsible for assisting the platoon leader and making sure that the men of the platoon were ready for combat. His personality served him well in this leadership role and the troops responded to him.

On February 28, 1967, Matthew's platoon was near Prek Klok in the Quang Tri province. As they moved through the jungle, the platoon was ambushed by North Vietnamese Army (NVA) forces using hand grenades and automatic weapons. In the firefight, the platoon leaders were injured. Matthew's experience in the Korean War and his training enabled him to lead his men in a charge against the enemy. He formed a perimeter of defense

Sgt. 1st Class Matthew Leonard, U.S. Army.

and redistributed the ammunition of the wounded men to those in key positions. One of the men wounded in the initial assault was outside the perimeter and Matthew left his position to get him. He was able to bring the man to safety, but was wounded in his left hand. He refused treatment knowing he was now in charge of the platoon. The NVA forces were camouflaged in the dense jungle, so Matthew was constantly moving to instruct his men where to fire and when to engage. As the battle continued, the enemy machine gun began to sweep the area, and while returning fire the platoon's machine gun jammed. Matthew again left his position to clear the jam and assist with returning fire. Shortly after, he sensed an opportunity and charged the NVA machine gun position and was able to capture the gun and defeat the crew even though he had been shot several times. With multiple wounds on his body, he continued to fire. He died propped up against a tree, still firing his weapon at the NVA forces. Inspired by his actions, the remaining members of his platoon held off the enemy until reinforcements could arrive.

For his actions on February 28, 1967, Matthew was awarded the Congressional Medal of Honor. He is one of only 3,458 recipients of the nation's highest military decoration and one of only 248 recipients during the Vietnam War. The 37-year-old left behind his wife of 17 years and their five children. Though the family was proud of Matthew's actions in Vietnam, they were not a replacement for the husband and father that they loved. Although her husband had tried to prepare her for the possibility of his death, Lois was devastated by his passing. "He tried to prepare me for it, but you can't be prepared for something like that. I still think about it. It still hurts." ♦

DONALD E. WHITE

Private First Class, Army • 1/24/46–3/5/67 • Panel 16E, Row 25

Pfc. Donald Eugene White, U.S. Army.

Donnie White was the seventh of the 10 children of Cordis and Lucille White. Ray was the eighth. The family lived in Barton County, Mo. where Cordis worked as a farmer and on the highways, and Lucille was a cook at a local motel. Of the 10 children, only seven survived into adolescence. Donnie and Ray were two of six boys and they had one sister. Two of Cordis and Lucille's children had died in childbirth, and the oldest, Lila, had passed away at 18 months. Donnie was born in 1946. Ray in 1948.

By the time that Donnie and Ray reached Lamar High School, they had seen their father and five older brothers set examples of hard-working lives. Donnie got there first and was very popular among his classmates and teachers. He was a star football player who many said was the best Lamar had seen in years. He also demonstrated his skills on the track team, where he set the school record in the shot put. In his spare time, Donnie liked to hunt. He graduated from Lamar in 1966 and almost immediately was drafted into the Army.

Donnie was first sent to basic training at Fort Leonard Wood, Mo. and then to Fort Polk, La. for his advanced individual training where he was trained as an infantryman. He left for Vietnam on November 25, 1966 from Fort Ord, Calif. When he arrived in Vietnam, Donnie was assigned to A Troop, 3rd Squadron, 4th Cavalry of the 25th Infantry Division. His unit was serving in Hua Nghia Province in South Vietnam in the spring of 1967. By that time, Donnie was the driver of an armored personnel carrier (APC) for A Troop. On the morning of March 5, the APC was part of a convoy when it hit a mine in the road and exploded. He was 21.

About a year after Donnie's death, his younger brother Ray was finishing up his own time at Lamar. Ray's given name was Cordis, after his father, but he had always been called Ray. He followed Donnie through school, and after his graduation would follow him into the Army. Ray was also drafted right out of high school. Ray was more introspective than Donnie, preferring puzzles and drawing to sports. Ray had married the former Verna Parnell in January 1968 and the two had been married for just over a year when Ray was sent to Vietnam in May 1969.

In Vietnam, Ray was assigned to the famed 1st Cavalry division. Serving with C Troop, 1st Squadron, 9th Cavalry, he was a radio operator. His tour of duty in Vietnam began on May 2, 1969 and he had been in country for four months when another soldier went on R&R to Australia in September. Ray filled in for the soldier, Thomas Criser. Criser was the RTO for the platoon leader of Blue Troop, answering to Blue-India on radio transmissions. Ray was the RTO on September 18 when Blue Troop went on a helicopter mission to assist a long-range reconnaissance patrol soldier. Ray was killed by small arms fire on that mission and received a Bronze Star medal for his actions.

Both Donnie and Ray died for their country in Vietnam at the age of 21. They are both buried at Memory Gardens Cemetery in Lamar, Mo. ♦

*Spc. 4th Class
Cordis Ray White, U.S. Army.*

CORDIS R. WHITE

Specialist 4th Class, Army • 3/18/48–9/18/69 • Panel 18W, Row 112

PAUL H WOLOS

Private First Class, Marine Corps ♦ 7/22/47–4/28/67 ♦ Panel 18E, Row 112

Paul during his boot camp training at Marine Corps Recruit Depot, San Diego. Photo courtesy of Peter and Cathy Wolos.

Paul's senior portrait, 1965. Photo courtesy of Peter and Cathy Wolos.

Peter and Paul Wolos. Photo courtesy of Peter and Cathy Wolos.

From his earliest days, Paul Wolos was full of life. The middle child and oldest son of Michael and Nellie Wolos, Paul had an older sister, Margaret, and younger brother, Peter. During Paul's childhood, the Wolos family moved around, as Michael was a career man in the Canadian Army. Paul was born in Port Arthur, a city in northern Ontario that would eventually become part of Thunder Bay. The family moved to Manitoba in 1959 and lived in the city of Brandon. Located along the Assiniboine River in southwestern Manitoba, Brandon was a city of nearly 30,000 when the Wolos family moved into a middle-class area with lots of families. There were many children in the neighborhood and lots of space to capture Paul's attention. Though one of the larger cities in Manitoba, Brandon was surrounded by agriculture during the years of Paul's adolescence. The wooded areas and farmlands near his home made Brandon the perfect place for Paul to grow up.

Paul loved the outdoors. Peter recalls a boy who would do anything to be outside hunting and fishing. The family would often stay at their uncle's farm near Togo, Saskatchewan. A creative thinker, Paul used his intelligence to his benefit, like the time he wanted to hunt ducks and geese. Shooting the waterfowl wasn't the problem, as Paul could shoot just about anything. The problem was that he didn't have a shotgun. He did, however, have a violin. A gift from his mother, the violin simply didn't fit with Paul's interests, and he managed to trade the instrument for the shotgun that he needed. Far from being upset at her son's actions, Nellie was pleased; Paul was now bringing home ducks and geese on a regular basis, and these became regular family meals.

Deer were no match for Paul either. He'd learned to follow the animals while hunting prairie rabbits with a native Canadian friend and he would go great distances to bag the deer. Peter remembers a time when Paul was gone an entire Canadian winter day. He had gone so far to shoot the deer that he had to drag it 12 miles back home. "Paul was strong and determined and he would have never left that deer behind just because he was tired." He was usually successful in bringing an animal home. When he set his mind to something, he did not stop until he had achieved his goal.

At age 13, Paul joined the Royal Canadian Sea Cadets (RCSC). A national program for Canadian youths aged 13-18 that is sponsored by the Canadian Forces, the RCSC was founded in 1895 in Great Britain as the Navy League. Paul thrived in the organization, and it was here that his leadership skills really began to be noticed. He was a strong member of the company of Her Majesty's Canadian Ship Swiftsure based in Brandon. Serving throughout his years at Vincent Massey High School, he had risen to the rank of Petty Officer Second Class by the time he was in his 12th grade year. It was then that Paul was given the opportunity of a lifetime.

In 1965, Paul was one of three RCSC cadets selected to go on a three month Pacific cruise on a Canadian Navy vessel. Cadets from all over Canada were selected based upon their service, leadership and their qualifications for a career in the Canadian Navy. Paul would serve on HMCS Beacon Hill during the spring of 1965. The Beacon Hill was a river class frigate that was serving as a training ship for the new Canadian sailors. Paul's cruise would take him to Japan, Hawaii, Alaska and the Philippines. He was tasked with the various jobs performed by Canadian sailors and got three months of first-hand experience of what life was like in the military. He loved it.

Paul had always been a great student, at one point earning the highest mark for math in his grade. His three months at sea left him wanting more than high school could provide, and after missing school while on the HMCS Beacon Hill, he didn't go back to Vincent Massey. He wanted to join the military.

Throughout Canada, there were men who believed in fighting to stop the spread of Communism, including those who sought the training and skills that could not be provided to them in the Canadian Armed Forces. Estimates are that more than 30,000 Canadians went south and joined one of the branches of the U.S. military. While serving on the HMCS Beacon Hill during her Pacific cruise, Paul was able to see the Canadian Armed Forces in action, but he also participated in exercises with the U.S. military. When he returned home from sea, he told his brother that he had been impressed by the American forces, and that he had seen the results of their better training and equipment. Just as in everything else he did, Paul wanted to be the best. To him, being the best meant being a U.S. Marine.

Being from a military family, Paul understood the risk he was taking by joining the Marines during a war. He knew that he would most likely see combat in Vietnam, but that was what he wanted. Just as Paul knew the risks, so did his parents. His father was a career officer in the Canadian Navy, and had fought in both World War II and Korea. He knew what his son was about to undertake and tried his best to offer instruction on what he should do to stay as safe as possible. Despite their fears, neither Michael nor Nellie attempted to dissuade Paul from enlisting. They knew he was a determined young man who would do whatever he set his mind to. Paul enlisted in the U.S. Marine Corps in September 1966 and was sent to Marine Corps Recruit Depot, San Diego for boot camp.

Just as he had in sports and in the RCSC, Paul excelled in his Marine Corps training. His test scores and marksmanship ratings were high, and he rose to the rank of private first class soon after boot camp while he was receiving individual training at Camp Pendleton, Calif. He had been assigned the military occupational specialty of rifleman. Paul left for Vietnam on March 27, 1967 and arrived there on April 1. He would be assigned to K Company, 3rd Battalion, 5th Marines.

K Company moved frequently, and had no base camp, so they often slept in foxholes and scavenged food from the surrounding jungle. His comrades in K Company took to him immediately, responding to both his dedicated work ethic and his commitment to the Marine Corps. According to Norm Bailey, who served with Paul, "He never professed himself to be an American, but he was very proud to be a Marine." He quickly earned the respect of his commanding officer, then 2nd Lt. Joaquin Gracida. "From the beginning he was very conscientious, the kind of serious young man that I looked at and hoped my son would grow up to be." As a Canadian, Paul could opt out of combat duties and be sent to a unit that was not in the field. According to Gracida, Paul's response was that he was a Marine and that he had volunteered to serve in combat alongside his fellow Marines. Paul was not afraid to do the work required of a Marine in combat and although he missed his family, he told them in a letter home that "Whatever happens to me, remember that this is what I wanted to do and this is where I wanted to be." Paul wanted to be in Vietnam, and once he got there he had no regrets. He was not a Canadian fighting alongside Americans, he was a Marine fighting alongside his brothers.

Paul as a drum major in the Royal Canadian Sea Cadets. Photo courtesy of Peter and Cathy Wolos.

The Wolos family at Kakabeka Falls, Ontario. Front row: Paul and Peter. Back row: Mike, wearing his Canadian Army uniform, Margaret in her Girl Guide uniform, and Nellie. Photo courtesy of Peter and Cathy Wolos.

Paul had only been in Vietnam for a few weeks when K Company began participating in Operation Union I. On the night of April 27, 1967, they had been chasing the enemy for five straight days in the vicinity of Quang Tin, South Vietnam. That night found them engaged in the task of securing a minefield when a member of Paul's platoon stepped on a mine and the platoon took several casualties. A medevac chopper was called in to remove the casualties and Paul assisted getting the wounded men onto the chopper. He was returning to his foxhole around midnight when he stepped on a Bouncing Betty mine. The Bouncing Betty was a particularly harmful mine, as it would shoot 3 to 4 feet in the air when it was tripped and detonate again when it was in midair. This type of mine sprayed shrapnel all around when it exploded, and according to Marine Corps records, Paul was hit with the shrapnel from this mine on his lower extremities, his chest and his back. His wounds were very severe, but Paul was alive.

Gracida had Paul wrapped in a blanket so that he wouldn't go into shock while the corpsman was working on him. As he lay in extreme pain, the corpsman recalls hearing Paul say, "Mom, I'm okay." Paul clearly needed to be evacuated for additional treatment, but the enemy was still firing. Each time the helicopter tried to land it was pushed back by the enemy fire. The helicopter took a big risk by landing with its lights off so that it could evacuate Paul and the other wounded Marines to a field hospital.

Paul Wolos made it to the field hospital. He died in transport. He was 19 and had been in Vietnam for 27 days.

Back in Brandon, Paul's mother had a dream. The same night that Paul was securing the minefield, Nellie dreamt that her son had died. She saw him lying dead, but heard him saying the same words in her dream that the corpsman had heard him say in the jungles of Vietnam, "Mom, I'm okay."

Peter remembered his brother and missed him every day. As he grew older and had his own children, Paul's photo was always in a place of honor in their home. He was always spoken of with pride and with a bit of sadness. Peter often told his children about the adventures he and his older brother used to have.

What Peter didn't realize was that he was not the only one who carried memories of his Paul. Even though Paul served with K Company for less than a month, he left an indelible mark on those with whom he served.

In 2011, the Marines of the 3rd Battalion, 5th Marines held a reunion in South Carolina. At this reunion, their honored family was the Wolos family. None of the Marines had forgotten this brave Canadian who crossed the border and died for a country that was not his own. Forty-four years after his death, Paul's family would meet the men who shared his final days. Perhaps the most comforting piece of information was knowing that Paul did not die alone. Even though he was mortally wounded and in extreme pain, it comforted Peter to know that Paul was not by himself during his final moments. Paul had been surrounded by his platoon, other members of K Company and even the battalion commander. He had died surrounded by his brother Marines.

Paul was one of 103 Canadian men to lose their lives in Vietnam and seven are still listed as missing in action. ♦

The American, Canadian, and Marine Corps flags adorn Paul's gravestone in Thunder Bay, Ontario. Photo courtesy of Peter and Cathy Wolos.

Wall from 3 Servicemen ♦ Leroy Lawson

XAVIER AMADO ARVIZU

Specialist 4th Class, Army • 7/6/47–2/24/69 • Panel 31W, Row 31

Most people called Xavier Amado Arvizu "X," unless they called him "Javy." Xavier wasn't a big kid, but he was tough when he needed to be. Most of the time, though, he was gentle and kind. The various Vietnam memorial websites are filled with remembrances of Xavier and they all talk about his spirit and personality. "He was always singing and laughing, and was always ready and willing to listen," said Emily Mora, his younger cousin. Although Emily was 12 years younger, Xavier spent time with her and took her places. The extended Arvizu family spent lots of time together, having many gatherings and picnics and parties.

Xavier spent much of his childhood in the El Paso, Texas area, but by the time he was in high school the family had moved to Monterey Park, Calif. Xavier and his sister, Terry, lived with their parents, Amado and Mary Lou Arvizu. Xavier was very involved in activities while he was at Mark Keppel High School in Monterey Park. He played football and basketball and ran track while at Keppel, and was a yell leader. He could be found cheering on the Keppel sporting teams with a powerful yell of "Go Aztecs!" His classmates loved him and he seemed to get along with everyone. His considerate nature and easy smile won him many friends. He graduated in 1965.

Xavier's high school graduation photo. Photo courtesy of Margie Bernal and Emily Mora.

For a time after high school, Xavier attended East Los Angeles Community College. Someday he hoped to become a history teacher, but those plans would have to wait. In December 1967, Xavier was drafted into the U.S. Army. Xavier was a proud and honorable man, and for him there was no question of complying with his induction orders. He arrived at Fort Ord, Calif. for basic training just after Christmas 1967.

After completing training at Fort Ord, and then advanced individual training at Fort Sill, Okla., Xavier returned to California where he married his true love, Margie Skaron. The couple wed on May 11, 1968 and Xavier left for Vietnam shortly after. While he would have preferred to stay at home with his new wife, Xavier was proud to serve and honored to do his duty. Emily and her family were frightened for Xavier and didn't want him to go; the family had already suffered a loss in Vietnam. Emily's cousin, Lance Cpl. Alexandro Nevarez of the U.S. Marine Corps, had been killed in combat in Vietnam in 1967.

Xavier Arvizu and Margie Skaron on their wedding day. Photo courtesy of Margie Bernal and Emily Mora.

Unlike Xavier, Alex had enlisted in the military at the age of 18. He was proud to be a Marine and wanted to serve in Vietnam. His time in Vietnam had been arduous and he saw combat almost immediately upon his arrival. Alex's combat history shows that he participated in operations all over South Vietnam with the 3rd Battalion of the 9th Marines. He told his family that the situation in Vietnam was difficult, but he assured them that his Marine training had prepared him to do his job. Alex was killed by enemy gunfire on April 30, 1967 at the age of 19.

Xavier didn't talk much about the war with Margie as he didn't want to worry her. He didn't want to worry anyone. Emily Mora remembered his letters home talking about everything but the war that raged on around him. "He wrote generally about how the people had it there, the living conditions, and how much he enjoyed meeting the Vietnamese children." Emily was only 10 years old while Xavier was in Vietnam, and his letters to her were full of advice and wisdom. "He would always write to be sure to make the most of my opportunities and what I had because others had it so much worse."

While in Vietnam, Xavier was stationed with Battery A, 1st Battalion, 8th Infantry Division. He first served as a cannoneer, and then as an assistant gunner. They were stationed in Hua Ngia Province on February 24, 1969 when Xavier died after receiving multiple fragmentation wounds in combat. He was 21. ♦

Xavier with his aunt and uncle, Vera and Mike Nevarez. Photo courtesy of Margie Bernal and Emily Mora.

Alexandro Nevarez's high school graduation photo. Photo courtesy of Emily Mora.

ALEXANDRO NEVAREZ

Lance Corporal, Marine Corps • 7/13/47–4/30/67 • Panel 18E, Row 125

JAMES R WATANABE

Sergeant, Army • 9/16/44–9/26/67 • Panel 27E, Row 17

James in Army, 1967. Photo courtesy of The Watanabe family.

James Ryochiro Watanabe was born behind the high fences of the Manzanar Relocation Center. Manzanar was one of ten relocation centers built to intern persons of Japanese descent during World War II. Manzanar was located in the Owens Valley of California, an area that was swept by dust storms during 100 degree summers and buried in snow during the winters. James was born on September 16, 1944 to Goro and Hayako Watanabe, who had both been interned in the early days of the camp. The camp was not yet completed when they arrived, and they stayed in tar paper shacks. Goro and Hayako met at the camp and were both considered Kibei, or people of Japanese descent who were born in America but educated in Japan. Both had returned to the U.S. as teenagers after completing their schooling in Japan. The couple would marry behind the guard towers of the relocation camp. The family would be released from Manzanar in October 1945.

Once out of the internment camp, the family moved up and down California, leasing farmland with groups of other farmers and working the land for several years. In 1953, the family settled in the Oxnard, Calif. area, 160 miles south of Manzanar. Goro and Hayako would have seven more children, giving James four brothers and three sisters. Hayako worked primarily in agriculture and her work would inspire James' lifelong love for the outdoors. He loved to fish, either in fresh or salt water, and was active with the Future Farmers of America. James was smart, graduating as valedictorian of his eighth grade class. His grades at Hueneme High School earned him a scholarship to California Polytechnic University in 1963. He worked hard at Cal Poly, studying agriculture. He and two friends started a business called Nobel Flower Company, and James grew beautiful chrysanthemums. While James was away at college, his family's financial situation became dire. His father had returned to Japan while James was in high school and his mother was trying to raise her children on her own. Hayako had only a high school education from Japan and her English skills were limited. She could not drive, so the only jobs she could find were agricultural and did not pay well. James left school before he graduated to return and care for his family.

James seeking shelter from the sun in Vietnam. Photo courtesy of the Watanabe family.

James, his brother Gordon and sister Julia were the three oldest siblings, and all worked as much as possible to help their mother support the five siblings who were still in school. At the age of 21, James was now the head of his family. In the little spare time he had, he spent time with his fiancée, Mary Otani, often attending activities at St. Paul's Methodist Church. Shortly after returning from Cal Poly, James received his draft notice. "James was a peaceful man. He didn't want to be in a war," said his younger sister Carol. James tried to get a hardship deferment because of his place as the main wage earner for his mother and siblings, but he was denied. James was not one to shirk his responsibilities. "James seriously accepted responsibility and was always committed to using his abilities to do his best on all tasks."

James arrived at Fort Ord, Calif. for basic training just after his 22nd birthday. He was assigned the military occupational specialty of 11B10, rifleman, and was sent to Fort Polk, La. for additional training. After completing the advanced individual training, James left for Vietnam in February 1967. He was assigned to B Company, 3rd Battalion, 22nd Infantry. James would be wounded in combat in May 1967 and would receive the Purple Heart. He would be promoted through the ranks of B Company, serving as a machine gunner and eventually earning the title of squad leader.

Despite his successes in Vietnam, James missed his family. "The Vietnam hot and humid climate was very different from Southern California. He joked about going skiing when he got home just to get over the weather there," Carol said. "Rather than communicate about the war he asked for updates about home, family and friends as a diversion away from the war." The family continued to struggle financially with James overseas. Julia was working in Los Angeles and sending money home and Gordon had to drop out of school to help make ends meet. Although worried for his family back home, James continued to remain dedicated to his company and his duties as a soldier, and was rewarded with a Bronze Star for his actions in combat on September 13, 1967.

James fishing in 1964 in Oxnard, Calif. Photo courtesy of the Watanabe family.

James' baby picture, taken at Manzanar Relocation Center, Calif. 1945. Photo courtesy of the Watanabe family.

On September 26, 1967, James was acting as squad leader and was returning from a check of the company's perimeter. The company had been heavily engaged with enemy forces in the preceding days, and as James was making his way back from the perimeter, he was mistaken for an enemy soldier. He was killed by gunfire from American troops. His cause of death is listed as misadventure, the Army's code for friendly fire.

After his death, James' family struggled. His sister Carol says that "it was very hard to reconcile the facts that he was born behind barbed wire at a concentration camp in California, he served the U.S. Army so valiantly for the government that had put his family there, and he died at the hands of his own countrymen." When his family visits the memorials that bear his name, they always leave chrysanthemums, the flower that he was so talented at growing. They remember James as an optimistic young man who believed that the world could be a better place. In the valedictorian's address he gave to his eighth grade class, James expressed hope and the desire to move beyond what had been done in the past.

"With our goal, a better world, we will try to curb the threats facing it. And I am sure we will eventually succeed, because with the vast amount of knowledge at our feet, we will profit by the mistakes of the past and the wisdom of the many great men and women of the past. And if we do not succeed the next generation will take our places, profit by our mistakes and eventually our goal will be reached. A world of freedom and peace for all."

The life of this bright, intelligent young American was cut short at the age of 23. ♦

Flag left at The Wall by Julia Watanabe, James' sister.

James' graduation photo from Hueneme High School, Oxnard, Calif. in 1963. Photo courtesy of the Watanabe family.

WALTER C. WRIGHT

Airman 2nd Class, Air Force • 10/30/47–10/3/67 • Panel 27E, Row 46

Walter Clarence Wright was the only son of an only son, and his family hoped that, somehow, that would keep him out of Vietnam. Walt's parents and his three sisters held on to the hope that, even if he did have to join the military, he could be stationed stateside in a job that would allow him to serve his country but not put the Wright family name at risk. Their hopes were dashed in August 1967, and the Wright name came to an end less than three months later.

Walt was born in the Rocky Mountains, and there was no place on earth he loved more. During the school year Walt, his parents, William and Loretta, and his sisters Nancy, Claire and Marilyn, lived in Montrose, Colo. The summers were spent at the family's San Juan Ranch in Lake City, Colo. Walt was an avid outdoorsman and loved to hunt, fish and hike the areas around his home. "He knew the mountains around the Lake City area better than most and there weren't many high mountain areas he had not explored," said his sister, Marilyn. He would drive his jeep all over the Lake City area, and his faithful dog, Butch, was always with him. He was a strong young man and could take care of himself. When he camped in the mountains, he lived off of the land. Steve Carricato used to head up into the mountains with Walt. "We went by horseback. We usually fished all night and slept during the day. We carried guns and usually killed something to eat beside fish. We usually stayed seven to 10 days." Walt hoped to be a game warden or to have a career that would keep him in the mountains he so loved.

Walt's caring and giving nature could be seen not only in how he loved the land, but also in how he cared for those he loved. He was devoted to his sisters and friends and could often be found helping those in need, like the time he helped close family friend, Nancy Shorter, deal with the death of her family dog. "He was so caring, and took our dog away quickly so that my brothers were sheltered from seeing their dog lying dead. He hugged me and comforted me and knew just what to say."

Walt had a mischievous spirit and a love for fun and games. When family and friends came to visit, he would take them for rides in the mountains in his jeep. He loved to drive fast, and the passengers usually came back from the rides white as ghosts and scared out of their minds. Nancy Shorter remembered the relationship between Walt and his sisters. "He used to tease his sisters and myself until we wanted to throw him in the pond near his house. Unfortunately, it usually ended with his sister or me in the pond instead. I can still see him laughing on the bank of the pond."

In 1966, Walt realized that the time to serve his country had come. He did not want to be drafted, but would never have refused to serve. His sister Marilyn said that despite his feelings, Walt "responded for his country." Walt joined the Air Force in 1966.

Walt completed his Air Force training at Lackland Air Force Base in Texas and returned home to Colorado for additional training at Lowry Air Force Base. His training was primarily as a weapons mechanic and his first assignment was with the 331 Fighter Intercept Squadron in Texas. While there, Walt also received combat training in preparation for his next assignment–Vietnam.

When he arrived in Vietnam in August 1967, Walt was assigned to the 4th Air Control Squadron (ACS) at Nha Trang Airbase. He served on an AC-47 gunship, an aircraft that was designed to provide air support for ground troops of the Army's 7th Cavalry Regiment, and to act as a forward observer for fighter planes. It featured guns that were mounted on the pilot's side of the plane. While in Vietnam, Walt expressed fear and concern for himself and his friends, telling his family that he was doing his best in a difficult situation.

On October 3, 1967, Walter was one of seven crew members on an AC-47 gunship from the 4th ACS. The plane took off for a mission in the vicinity of Hue. It was a daylight fire mission providing suppressing fire to cover troops engaged in combat in the area. It was hit with anti-aircraft fire and the plane crashed. All seven crewmembers were killed.

"His life was so special from day one," said his sister, Nancy. "He was a true American, dedicated to the end." Walter Clarence Wright was the only resident of Lake City, Colo. to be killed in Vietnam. For his service to his country, he would be posthumously awarded the Silver Star, the Distinguished Flying Cross, an Air Medal with oak leaf cluster and a Purple Heart. ♦

Airman 2nd Class Walter C. Wright, U.S. Air Force. Photo courtesy of Marilyn Wright Plise.

Three generations of Wright men on Father's Day, 1966. Walt, William, and Clarence Wright at the family ranch in Lake City, Colo. Photo courtesy of Marilyn Wright Plise.

Walt on top of Round Mountain in Colorado, viewing the beautiful Uncompahgre Peak in the background. Photo courtesy of Marilyn Wright Plise.

ELEANOR G ALEXANDER

Captain, Army • 9/18/40–11/30/67 • Panel 31E, Row 8

Eleanor Grace Alexander wasn't content simply serving her country as a nurse in the Army Nurse Corps. She knew that her nursing skills were most needed in Vietnam, where casualties were rising and nurses and doctors were in high demand. She had trained as a nurse at D'Youville College and worked for six years at Madison Hospital, both in upstate New York. Eleanor did not join the Army to be stationed stateside; she wanted to take care of the Americans serving in combat. She volunteered to leave her job as a captain in a Fort Sam Houston training detachment to go to Vietnam. "She insisted on going over there for six months. She had to do this," remembered her sister-in-law Susanne Alexander.

Eleanor arrived in Vietnam in June 1967 and was assigned to the 85th Evacuation Hospital in Qui Nhon. She worked as one of the operating room nurses primarily treating NVA and VC in the American military hospitals. The wounded and ill enemy combatants were stabilized at the hospital before being turned over to the South Vietnamese as prisoners. The hours at the 85th Evacuation Hospital were long and the posting was a difficult one. Capt. Rhona Prescott worked with Eleanor and she remembers the conditions: "The 85th… was under Quonset huts, which were World War II equipment kind of things. There was a perimeter of concertina wire (barbed wire) with guards all around. It was a hospital for the enemy. Morale was not good." Even in this environment, Eleanor managed to maintain her composure and positive attitude. She brought a reel-to-reel tape recorder into the operating room on which she played popular music that had been sent from home and she always had a smile on her face.

Eleanor and Rhona became friends and spent time talking about their nursing experiences. Rhona had previously worked in Army field hospitals where wounded soldiers were brought directly from the field. That kind of nursing assignment was what Eleanor had come to Vietnam to do – unloading the men from the choppers and bringing them into field hospitals in an attempt to save their lives. Even though she gave her all to her assignment at the 85th, it was clear that she would rather be somewhere else. She longed to be assigned to a field hospital, even on temporary duty. She got her chance in the fall of 1967.

Her friend Rhona had the field experience that Eleanor so craved and so it was Rhona that was assigned to a temporary duty team that was heading into the field. "There was a battle gearing up called Dak To which was one of the battles that turned out to be the beginning of that infamous Tet of 1968. I was the nurse on that team, there was an anesthetist and two corpsmen. I had gone over to the officers club to get me a beer. In that five or ten minutes, the call came. I wasn't in my quarters. Eleanor was close by, my roommate went and got her and she took my gear (which included my jacket with my name on it) and since time was of an essence, she got on the helicopter with the chosen anesthetist and the correct corpsmen and she went to the duty station at another hospital in my place."

After getting to the field hospital near Pleiku, Eleanor got the orders changed to her name and stayed at the field hospital for four weeks. Her letters home from the field showed that she loved the assignment and was doing exactly what she wanted to do. The young, beautiful and charming Eleanor found her home in the field.

Eleanor was on an Air Force C-7 for her return flight to Qui Nhon on November 30, 1967. On that cloudy, rainy day, the aircraft was diverted from the runway. As it circled, it crashed into a mountainside. Due to the location of the crash, American personnel could not reach the downed plane for several days. By the time the crash site was reached, it was clear that there had been no survivors. There were bullet holes in the fuselage of the plane, but it was never verified that the plane had gone down because of enemy fire.

Eleanor is buried at St. Andrews Cemetery in Westwood, N.J. Even those who only knew her peripherally remember the joy she brought to the world around her. Harold David Parks was a truck driver at the 85th who sometimes crossed paths with Eleanor. "She was a remarkable looking young woman who was always smiling and bright-eyed." ♦

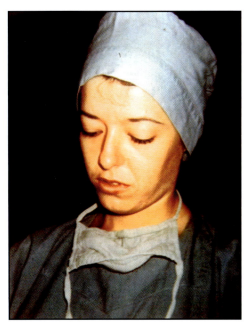

*A young Eleanor Alexander.
Photo courtesy of Walter Haan.*

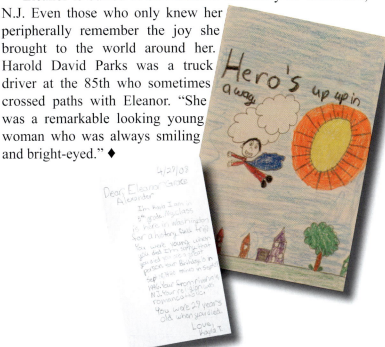

*A 5th grader named Kayla left this card for Eleanor at The Wall in 2008. From the Vietnam Veterans Memorial Collection.
Photo by Sebastián E. Encina.*

HEDWIG D ORLOWSKI

First Lieutenant, Army • 4/13/44–11/30/67 • Panel 31E, Row 15

The average age of nurses in Vietnam was 23 years and six months. These men and women may have been young, but they were faced with the challenging responsibility of caring for America's combat troops.

Hedwig Diane Orlowski had an interesting childhood, being born in Tel Aviv and living in Germany before the family settled in Detroit, Mich. Hedwig graduated from H.H. Arnold High School in Wiesbaden, Germany. The school was part of the Department of Defense Dependent school system and was primarily a school for children whose parents served in the Air Force. After returning to the U.S. and settling in Michigan, she trained to be a nurse at Mercy College in Detroit and at Hurley Hospital in Flint.

Hedwig enlisted in the Army in September 1965 and was an enlisted woman until October 1966 when she received her lieutenant's commission. She was stationed at hospitals at Fort Sam Houston in Texas and Fort Benning, Ga. before being assigned a tour of duty in Vietnam.

Hedwig arrived in Vietnam in early July 1967 and was assigned to the 67th Evacuation Hospital located at Qui Nhon. In Vietnam, nurses typically worked 12 hour shifts six days a week. Of course, nothing in Vietnam was typical. Hospitals of varying sizes were scattered all over Vietnam to treat both the wounds of combat and the diseases that came from extended tours in the sweltering jungles of Vietnam. Hospitals were often short on supplies and staff, forcing both doctors and nurses to work long hours and find sleep when and where they could. When large-scale engagements occurred, everyone in the hospital was put to work as the wounded men were brought in from the field. On some occasions, when a particular hospital received high numbers of casualties, nurses and doctors were temporarily shifted to the busier hospitals. Hedwig had been sent to Pleiku to support the hospital there in November 1967.

Hedwig was one of 22 passengers on board an Air Force C-7 that took off from Pleiku on November 30. She was returning to her post at the 67th Evacuation Hospital in Qui Nhon. The weather that day was rainy, with many clouds that reduced visibility to less than two miles. As the aircraft approached Qui Nhon, the pilot was told that he could not land and informed the airfield that he would head to Nha Trang. A few moments later, the plane crashed into the side of a mountain just three miles from the Qui Nhon airport. There were no survivors.

When Hedwig lost her life in the plane crash, she was 23 years and seven months old. ♦

Hedwig Diane Orlowski's nursing school graduation photo.

Hedwig while attending Arnold High School in Germany. She graduated in 1962. Photo courtesy of Paul C. Burton.

A memento left at The Wall in the name of 1st Lt. Orlowski. From the Vietnam Veterans Memorial Collection. Photo by Sebastián E. Encina.

Photo by Bill Shugarts

ROBERT D MASON

Seaman, Navy • 11/15/45–12/21/67 • Panel 32E, Row 37

Robert Mason wanted to be a police officer. Growing up in Maryland, he admired the police officers of Montgomery County and hoped that he could one day follow in their footsteps. Robert was an average student, and when he graduated from high school in 1965 he felt that the best way to gain the experience he needed for his future career was to join the military.

Robert was born in 1945, one of six children of Mary Louise and John Mason. Robert, his brother John and their four sisters lived in Maryland with their parents. Their father, John, was a salesman for a local meat company. Tall and thin, Robert, called Bob by his family and friends, loved Elvis Presley. While in high school, he worked for grocers in the area around his Rockville, Md. hometown.

Bob joined the Navy in November 1965 and was sent to the U.S. Naval Training Center at Great Lakes, Ill. He was proud to serve his country and to be learning skills that could help him in the future. In March 1966, he was assigned to the USS Carter Hall as a seaman apprentice and worked with the quartermaster. He served there for two months and was then given assignment at U.S. Naval Air Base at Coro, Calif. Bob would then receive his first overseas assignment in March 1966 to Camp Carter in Danang, Vietnam. He arrived there in June 1966 for a one-year tour of duty.

At Camp Carter, Bob served as a member of the Naval Support Activity. His primary duties as an investigator were looking into thefts of Navy equipment. Lt. George Maddock, an investigations officer, told John and Louise that Bob and his group "perform a very useful and deterrent function by making individuals think twice before they attempted to pilfer something from an individual or the U.S. government." He was an investigator and in letters home to his family and friends talked about working on raids looking for blackmarket items and stolen goods. Bob did his job well, and superior officers cited his inquisitive nature as a help to the team. He got along very well with other investigators and seemed to enjoy the work he was doing. Bob suffered a setback when he spent a month in a naval hospital in Yokosuka, Japan after a September incident in which he fractured his jaw.

When he enlisted, Bob had signed up for a four-year stint in the Navy. In December 1966, he extended his time in Vietnam by six months in the hopes that his next duty station would be closer to home. On his extension form, Bob said, "I like my duty in Vietnam and I feel I am doing more good here than in the United States." Bob told his parents that he just had to get through 1967, and then he would be back in the U.S. for 1968 and 1969. He would then complete his commitment to the Navy and could begin his career as a police officer.

On December 23, 1967, Louise and John received a visit from Navy casualty officers. Bob was dead, the result of a gunshot wound to the head suffered on December 21 in the room of another naval investigator. According to the Navy, Bob's gun had gone off while he was removing it from his holster to show to a friend. He was 22.

From the moment she learned of her son's death, Louise struggled to understand what had happened. Almost immediately after the funeral, she began writing letters. Bob's brother, John, was only 15 years old and helped his mother write to Bob's fellow investigators, commanding officers, and Navy officials. Bob's naval record is filled with letters to and from Louise Mason as she desperately tried to figure out how Robert had died. She quickly became bitter and believed that there was something not right about what had happened the night of December 21 in Danang. Louise believed that Bob, who had used guns since he was young, was far too careful to have his gun go off accidentally. The letters she received from naval officials were filled with Louise's notes and thoughts. On the bottom of a letter from a rear admiral in the Navy, Louise wrote, "I don't want fake sympathy, I want the honest truth." In her eyes, she never believed that she received it from anyone. Many years after his death, Louise simply wrote "finished" on another letter from the Navy.

Regardless of how Bob died or who caused his death, he was gone. Louise never recovered from her son's death. When the news came, she took the Christmas tree down and never put it up again. For the rest of her life, her only holiday decoration was a wreath with a black ribbon. Louise died in 1986 and was buried with the flag that had draped Bob's casket nearly 20 years earlier. ♦

A young Bob during his childhood in Maryland. Photo courtesy of John Mason.

Bob's senior photo from Robert Peary High School. He graduated in 1965.

Bob enjoys a moment of relaxation while stationed in Vietnam. Photo courtesy of John Mason.

BRIAN F DURR

Specialist 4th Class, Army • 1/27/47–2/8/68 • Panel 38E, Row 26

The men of A Company, 1st Battalion, 6th Infantry were close. Most of them had been drafted, and a large group of them completed their basic and advanced individual trainings together at Fort Hood, Texas. In 1967, they would go to Vietnam together. A bond of brotherhood is not uncommon in combat, but it was rare in 1967 for a company to head to Vietnam together. "Our company knew each other very well and were very close friends," remembers Don Kaiser. The men of A Company also had strong leadership, with their company commander and many of their non-commissioned officers (NCOs) having already done tours in Vietnam. The company commander nicknamed them the Gunfighters, and the name stuck.

Spc. Brian Francis Durr had been drafted into the Army in September 1966 and was among the group that trained together for a year at Fort Hood. The family had a military tradition, with one of Brian's grandfathers having fought in World War I and six uncles serving in World War II. But it was a different time, and Vietnam was a different war. Francis and Therese Durr were proud of their son's service but concerned for his safety. Brian was the oldest of eight siblings, with two brothers and five sisters. Therese Durr took solace in her Catholic faith and the family knew that serving was the right thing to do. If Brian was concerned about his future in the Army or the combat he was likely to see, he never showed any fear to his family. "He was a tough individual but you wouldn't know it by looking at him," said Kaiser.

Brian was a friendly young man whose quiet nature belied a fun-loving spirit. He loved Motown music and Western TV shows and movies. His sister Suzette remembered her big brother as leading an active, varied life. "Brian always wanted to be the first one in the spring to ski around the ice and not fall or get wet." Brian worked as a busboy at an area restaurant and spent his paychecks on gas for his Volkswagen bug and he spent hours cruising around with his girlfriend. He liked working on that car and the others he had, and he had a mind for mechanics. Brian also loved yellow roses and planted bushes all over the backyard of the family's Whitesboro, N.Y. home.

When Brian and the 1/6th first arrived in Vietnam, he was homesick. Though he had become close with the men in his company, he missed his girlfriend and his big family back home. It took him a while to adjust, but soon his letters home were filled with pride in his unit and a strong sense of brotherhood. The pride was not simply boastful. "Our company was one of the most decorated rifle companies to serve in Vietnam," said Kaiser, who served in the same company as Brian, but in a different platoon. "Our company was always sent in first because we were a well-trained and close-knit group with great leadership."

It was not until February 1968 that Brian expressed any concern at all about his life in Vietnam. In a letter dated February 7, he mentioned that they were being flown south of Danang that day to participate in an operation. The area where

Brian at sea, en route to Vietnam.
Photo courtesy of Frank and Sue Kelly.

they were headed was close to the American military base at Danang, where U.S. Marines and South Vietnamese troops had recently begun feeling the effects of what would come to be known as the Tet Offensive. The 1/6th flew by helicopter to Duong Son, an area southwest of the village of Lo Giang. They spent the night there and the next day A company moved about one–half mile northeast of Lo Giang.

On the morning of February 8, three platoons of A Company made their way across a 500-yard rice paddy toward the village. Kaiser remembered the day vividly: "Little did we know, there was a reinforced North Vietnamese Army regiment hidden in the village. We crossed the paddy to within 100 yards of the village, and the whole world opened up on us." The three platoons were soon being bombarded with automatic weapons fire, and Brian's 2nd Platoon was being hit from both the village and from trenches along the right side of the rice paddy. Brian's platoon was ordered to hold, and the 3rd Platoon, including Kaiser, was to swing to the right to try and take out the trenches. By this point, some of the men of A Company were engaged in hand-to-hand combat with the NVA. Kaiser remembered the day: "Brian and a guy named Terry Beulow were next to each other because Brian was his radio operator, they were fighting hand-to-hand and making their way to 'safety.' They were finally separated and Brian kept holding his ground, giving others cover fire as they retreated. He fought so that others could live."

Of the men from A Company that made their way toward Lo Giang that day, 19 of them were killed, including Brian. Within Brian's 2nd Platoon, only four men were not killed or wounded.

In 2010, several of the men who fought with Brian that day near Lo Giang gathered to honor his memory and the memories of all they lost that day. A memorial window from St. Anne's Catholic Church in Brian's hometown of Whitesboro was being moved to a new place of honor in front of the New Hartford American Legion Post 1376. The window, which featured Saint Anne with her arms wrapped around the Virgin Mary, was dedicated to Brian after his death. After St. Anne's merged with another area church, the building was closed to the public. The Durr family arranged for the window to be moved and the dedication of the new memorial was an occasion for the men of the 1/6th to reunite. Joe Bruggerman and Tom Charbonneau came from New York, John Martenis from New Jersey and Joe Gamache from Rhode Island. Paul Senick came in from Pennsylvania, Terry Beulow, Brian's squad leader, came from Iowa, and Don Kaiser came all the way from Texas. While A Company's time together brought them closer and served them well in battle, it made the events of February 8 that much harder. "The only problem with being so close with those guys is when people like Brian were killed, it was very hard to handle." ♦

Brian and his parents Francis and Therese Durr. Photo courtesy of Frank and Sue Kelly.

Jungle Column ♦ Samuel Alexander
Courtesy of Army Art Collection,
U.S. Army, Center of Military History.

Small Flags at Wall ♦ Dan Arant

ROBERT R BRETT

Lieutenant, Navy • 1/3/36–2/22/68 • Panel 40E, Row 58

The Rev. Robert Brett, U.S. Navy chaplain.

"Therefore take up the whole armor of God, that you may be able to withstand in the evil day, and having done all, to stand firm."
Ephesians 6:13

During his time in Vietnam, Lt. Robert Raymond Brett always stood firm — firm in his faith, firm in his duty and firm in his devotion to his men. He would be there to provide whatever care his Marines needed, whether it be physical, emotional or spiritual, regardless of what was going on around him. That was why he had joined the Navy: to be where the men in combat needed him most.

According to his family, Bob had always wanted to be a priest. Born in 1936, Bob and his four siblings, Joseph, Francis, Rosemary and Anastasia, grew up in the Philadelphia area, where he attended Catholic schools before entering the seminary at St. Mary's Manor. He professed his faith in 1956 and then went on to study at Catholic University in Washington, D.C. He graduated with a bachelor's in philosophy in 1958, and was ordained as a priest of the Society of Mary at the Basilica of the National Shrine of the Immaculate Conception in 1962. Shortly thereafter, he earned a master's degree in Latin.

Five years after his ordination, he realized that he needed to do more to support the men and women serving in Vietnam. He joined the Navy as a chaplain. After chaplain school in Newport, R.I. and Marine training at Camp Pendleton, the now Lt. Robert Brett requested overseas duty and assignment to a Marine unit in Vietnam.

It was customary for each infantry battalion to be assigned a chaplain, and Father Brett was assigned to the 26th Marines stationed at Phu Bai. He arrived in Vietnam in October 1967 and moved to Khe Sahn when the 26th moved in January 1968. He was well-liked and highly regarded by the men he served. The men respected him because they saw him out wherever they were, not simply at the masses he performed every Sunday. His base was at Hill 558, where the 26th Marines had their command post, but it was common for Father Bob, as the Marines called him, to be out at the Marine positions, regardless of weather or enemy fire. In his book *Walk With Me: A Vietnam Experience*, Lt. Col. Jerry Kurth remembered the risks that Father Bob was willing to take in order to minister to the men of the 26th Marines after they had suffered an attack that caused many casualties: "Around 7 a.m. a couple of choppers arrive at Hill 558 to pick up the replacements. Just as the last replacements board, Father Brett runs up to a chopper and tells the pilot he will be accompanying the replacements. He never bothers to ask permission or seek approval; he just feels he is needed on Hill 861A after their ordeal."

For most of Father Bob's time in Vietnam, Pfc. Alexander Chin could often be found right next to him. Chin was a 24-year old Pfc. Marine from Maryland who, because of his religious beliefs, had transferred to a non-combatant post. He was not willing to take another life, but he stood by Father Bob and together they risked their lives ministering to their Marines. The two performed every conceivable religious duty, from baptisms and communions to confessions and last rites. As the base was being attacked, Father Bob would have to perform multiple masses to make sure that all could attend. He sometimes said mass ten times a day, and each service was always packed. Kurth called him "utterly tireless as well as utterly fearless." Before his death in 2011, Kurth told Father Bob's family that Father Bob moved around to be with his troops, regardless of what any commanding officer ordered.

The Siege of Khe Sahn began in January 1968, just after Father Bob and the 26th Marines had arrived in the area. North Vietnamese Army forces attacked the Marine base on January

Father Bob. Photo courtesy of Edward Rouse.

Father Bob. Photo courtesy of Edward Rouse.

21, beginning a massive coordinated attack that would last for 77 days and take the lives of more than 200 American troops. As always, Father Bob was in the thick of the action, ministering to his Marines.

On February 22, Father Bob and Chin were at the Khe Sahn Combat Base awaiting helicopter transport back to the command post at Hill 558. Kurth had not wanted Father Bob to leave Hill 558, but relented when Father Bob accused him of "preventing him from doing his duty as a priest." As the chopper landed and Father Bob and others made their way to it, NVA rockets began hitting the base. As the rocket fire increased, Father Bob told the helicopter to take off. He headed back to the trenches, with Chin by his side. Almost immediately upon their arrival at the trench, a rocket struck directly on the trench. When the smoke of the rocket attack cleared, eight men lay dead in the trench, including Father Bob and Chin.

Father Bob was buried on the grounds of the seminary he'd attended, and Chin was laid to rest in a family plot in Princess Anne, Md. In 1998, the Brett family moved Father Bob to Chaplain's Hill in Arlington National Cemetery. As a sign of their gratitude for the faith, devotion and courage of Chin, they petitioned to have him buried right beside the chaplain. In 1999, Chin was buried with full military honors on Chaplain's Hill. Father Bob and Chin are side by side, just as they were so often in Vietnam. ♦

U.S. Marine Corps Pfc. Alexander Chin, Father Bob's assistant. The two men served their Marines together and died together during the siege of Khe Sahn.

Father Bob. Photo courtesy of Edward Rouse.

Winford McCosar

Lance Corporal, Marine Corps • 11/22/47–3/6/68 • Panel 43E, Row 28

Winford McCosar did not fear war and he did not fear death. "Native Americans usually do not fear war, it is part of being a warrior and earning honor. Most warriors do not fear death as it comes with duty," said his older brother Bunnie. Winford's willingness to serve in the military came as much from his family as it did from Native American traditions. By the time Winford joined the U.S. Marine Corps, five of his siblings had already served or were currently serving in the armed forces.

Winford, born in Oklahoma in 1947, was the eighth of 12 children born to Matthew and Nellie McCosar. From the Muscogee/Creek nation, the McCosar family had a long history in Oklahoma dating back to when Matthew's father, Bunnie, was born in 1862 in what was called Indian Territory. Matthew and Nellie worked jobs throughout Oklahoma as Winford was growing up, and the family moved often as Winford's parents and older siblings tried to find work. Matthew worked doing general home repairs and Nellie cared for the home and sewed when she could find work in factories. As Winford was growing up, the family spent time in Holdenville, Okla. and then in the areas surrounding Oklahoma City before moving to southern California.

Winford, who his friends and family called Win, liked sports and art and enjoyed working on cars with his friends. He ran track and cross country and was an average student at Bell High School in Bell, Calif. graduating in 1965. He tried to find work in the areas around Los Angeles but was not successful. Living conditions for the family were hard, and in 1966 Winford decided to follow the example of his older siblings and join the military. His siblings Shirley, Matthew Jr., and Victor had served in the Air Force, Paula was in the Navy Reserve, and Bunnie was in the Marine Corps. Winford decided to follow Bunnie's example and he enlisted in the Marines in 1966. The McCosar family was proud of Winford for making an honorable decision that would improve the family's living conditions.

Winford arrived at Marine Corps Recruit Depot San Diego in October 1966 for boot camp and then was sent to Camp Pendleton, Calif. for additional training. He was assigned the military occupational specialty of 0141, administrative man. After completing his training in March 1967, Winford was assigned to United States Naval Base at Norfolk, Va. It was while serving at Norva that Winford volunteered for duty in Vietnam. "He was proud to be a Marine and to serve beside his fellow grunts," said Bunnie, who himself would do three tours of duty in Vietnam as a helicopter mechanic.

Arriving in Vietnam in November 1967, Winford was assigned to the Headquarters and Supply Company of the 1st Battalion, 26th Marines which was stationed near Khe Sahn and had the mission of defending the combat base. When Winford was assigned, the 1st of the 26th was just beginning Operation Scotland I. The battalion was very busy during the month of December, conducting 77 night ambushes and 360 listening posts, along with more than 100 patrols of the area. In January 1968, Winford was reassigned to B Company and by the end of the month was seeing a great deal of action as North Vietnamese attacks on the Khe Sahn Combat Base (KSCB) intensified. In January and February, the battalion was forced into defensive actions, and casualties began to increase. Combat deaths and wounds requiring evacuation increased five-fold from January to February.

Winford McCosar during boot camp at Marine Corps Recruit Depot, San Diego in 1966. Photo courtesy of Bunnie McCosar.

On March 6, 1968, Winford was on an Air Force C-123 that took off from the Hue-Phu Bai airport headed back to Khe Sahn. The aircraft, flying under the call sign *Bookie 762*, was filled with parts and equipment needed by the troops at KSCB, as well as replacement Marines. The Air Force plane had five crewmen, and 44 passengers who included 42 Marines, one Navy corpsman and a civilian photographer. At approximately 3:30 p.m., *Bookie 762* made an attempt to land on the Khe Sahn runway. As they began their approach, the plane was diverted because there was a small aircraft on the runway that was not communicating with the control tower. *Bookie 762* was told to circle and make another approach. As they did so, the C-123

Lance Cpl. Winford McCosar, U.S. Marine Corps. Photo courtesy of Bunnie McCosar.

was hit with ground fire from outside the perimeter of KSCB and the plane lost three of its engines. The pilot lost control of the plane, and it crashed and exploded.

As it crashed outside the perimeter of KSCB and was in enemy territory, it was not until March 25 that American troops could reach the wreck of *Bookie 762*. By that time, the wreck had burned itself out, and between the explosion and fire, the length of time that had passed and the conditions of the jungle it was only possible to identify five of the men on board. The other 44 men, including Winford, could not be identified. The men were buried in a mass grave at Jefferson Barracks National Cemetery in St. Louis, Mo. ♦

SAMUEL R NIXON

Staff Sergeant, Army • 8/15/42–3/21/68 • Panel 45E, Row 50

In the middle of the 20th century, Mulberry, Ark. was not an easy place to find work. Located in the northwestern part of the state, the small, rural town didn't have many jobs to offer its youths. After completing Mulberry High School, William Dale Nixon tried to find a way to make a living near home but saw his best opportunity in the military. Dale, as he was called by his family, joined in the Army in 1957. His younger brother Sam followed him in 1960.

Dale and Sam were the oldest of Laura and Samuel Nixon's four sons. The family also had six girls. Their parents were day laborers, so the Nixon children knew they would have to find their own ways to make a living. For all four Nixon boys, the military gave them a way to serve their country and earn money to raise their families.

Dale, as the oldest son, led the way into the service. He liked Elvis music and loved to dance. He was tall and strong and doted on his younger sisters. Diane was much younger than Dale and remembers how happy she was when he would visit the family while home on leave. Diane left a written remberance to her brother on the website *vvmf.org*, "When you were home on leave, you'd have me to "shake out" the clothes that you'd worn the night before and put them in the dirty clothes basket. I got to keep all the change in your pockets and you always made sure there was some." Dale was married, and he and his wife Betty had a son and a daughter. He was stationed in Okinawa, Japan for a time and completed one tour of Vietnam. By the end of 1967, Dale had attained the rank of captain.

Sam, though three years younger than Dale, was almost as tall as his big brother. He was faster, too, winning trophies at track meets while at Mulberry High. He joined the Army, and after training at Fort Bragg, N.C. served at several stateside posts. Sam was compassionate and had a big heart. Although he was quiet, his big smile and giving nature earned him many friends. He and his wife, Jeffie, had a son and a daughter, and in 1967 he was a staff sergeant getting ready for his first tour in Vietnam.

Sam would leave for Vietnam just after Christmas in 1967, assigned as a field artillery crewman with B Company, 1st Battalion of the 321st Artillery. The unit was based in Thua Thien Province. Before he left for Vietnam, Sam told his mother that he would be careful while in Vietnam, telling her that he "had too much to come back to not to be careful." On March, 21, 1968, Sam died from multiple fragmentation wounds.

At the time of Sam's death, all four Nixon boys were in the Army: Sam and Dale in Vietnam, Ronald was a sergeant who had already served a tour in Vietnam, and Jerry was in training at Fort Leonard Wood, Mo. Laura Nixon was proud of her sons' service, telling a Pine Bluff newspaper that, "I felt like I tried to raise my children so when they became old enough they would know how to make decisions." When Sam died, his brother Dale was already in Vietnam, arriving in early February for his second tour, this time with C Troop, 7th Squadron of the 1st Cavalry. Dale was able to escort Sam's body back to Arkansas for burial and then return to Vietnam to finish his own tour. Once again, Laura Nixon told one of her sons to be careful in Vietnam. Her oldest son told her that he would be careful. He'd already been in Vietnam and was going back so that his younger brothers wouldn't have to.

Dale Nixon was killed in action by small arms fire on May 8, 1968, less than two months after escorting his brother's body home for burial. ♦

Staff Sgt. Samuel Nixon, U.S. Army.

Staff Sgt. Samuel Nixon, U.S. Army.

Capt. William Nixon, U.S. Army.

Capt. William Nixon, U.S. Army.

WILLIAM D NIXON

Captain, Army • 10/15/39–5/8/68 • Panel 57E, Row 7

HARVEY L. COOLEY

Specialist 4th Class, Army • 1/19/49–5/6/68 • Panel 56E, Row 4

Spc. 4th Class Harvey Lynn Cooley, U.S. Army. Photo courtesy of the Cooley family.

The name Harvey comes from a surname that came to Britain after the Norman Invasion began in 1066. It's a combination of 'haer,' which means battle, and 'vy' which means worthy. Battle worthy.

By all accounts, the young Army medic Harvey Cooley was exactly that.

Harvey Lynn Cooley was the second of eight siblings. His parents, John Carl and Annie Ruth Cooley, raised their kids in Fulton, Ky. Set on the Kentucky-Tennessee border, Fulton was a small town. John Cooley did a little bit of everything, sometimes farming, and sometimes driving a bus and working as a janitor for the local school district. Annie Ruth took care of the kids at home, which would eventually include two foster sons as well as her own brood. Harvey was the second oldest and second son, and his siblings remember him having a great sense of humor. "He liked to kid around a lot," said his sister Pat, who at 19 months younger was the closest in age to Harvey. Harvey attended Carroll High School in Fulton, and though he was a good student, he hated school. He dropped out when he was in the 11th grade. Shortly thereafter, the family headed south and moved to Tennessee, eventually settling outside Memphis.

After quitting school, Harvey was looking for work. By 1966, both of his parents were working at Methodist Hospital in downtown Memphis. Soon, Harvey found work there as well, as a physical therapy assistant. He fell in love with the job and felt proud to be able to help people. He was tall and thin and was energized by the work he was doing. In November 1966, Harvey was working at the hospital when he met Mildred Roane, who was known as Millie. He was instantly smitten with her, and the feeling was mutual. She lived in the Memphis area with her mother, who was a patient at the hospital when Millie and Harvey met. The young pair were married just a few weeks later on December 10, 1966.

Harvey and Millie moved down to Houston, Texas where her father lived. Harvey was very much in love with his new wife. They enjoyed going to drive-ins and movies at the local theater, and Harvey began looking for full-time work to support he and Millie. The Cooley family would soon grow, as Millie discovered she was pregnant and due at the end of the year. Harvey's young family needed stability; the Houston job market didn't seem to have anything for Harvey and he knew the military would catch up to him eventually. He enlisted in the U.S. Army in April 1967. Harvey had just turned 18.

Harvey arrived at Fort Polk, La. on April 14, 1967. It was there that he met David Lawson, another young soldier from Helena, Ark. The two became fast friends, and the intense eight weeks of basic training bonded them together like brothers. They had learned to be soldiers together and that was a difficult bond to break. Based on his experience at the hospital in Memphis, Harvey was sent to Fort Sam Houston in Texas, while David was sent to Fort Sill, Okla. training in field artillery. Despite their close bond, they feared they'd never see each other again.

In June 1967, Harvey arrived at Fort Sam Houston for his 10-week combat medic training. During this training, he learned the skills required of a medic serving alongside combat troops. Instructed in basic medical skills such as injections, hygiene and splinting, Harvey would also learn how to treat injuries specific to combat, such as shock, amputations and severe burns. There was also an emphasis on survival, with a one-week lesson that culminated in a four-man team of medics working together to carry a patient a quarter mile through a simulated jungle environment. Harvey completed his training in September 1967 and was given orders for a one-year tour of duty in Vietnam. At Fort Sill, Lawson had received a similar set of orders.

During the first week of September, Harvey found himself at Fort Ord, Calif. waiting to depart for Vietnam. As he was

Harvey with his siblings prior to leaving for Vietnam. Photo courtesy of the Cooley family.

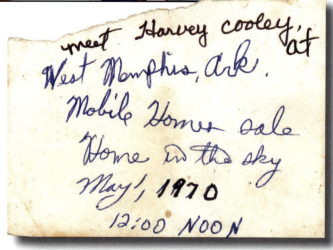

The note that Harvey wrote to his friend David Lawson just before leaving for Vietnam in 1969. David kept this note for 40 years before he could share it with Harvey's family. Courtesy of David Lawson.

walking, Harvey ran into his old friend. Both soldiers were headed to Vietnam and the two friends had only a few minutes to catch up before heading overseas. They didn't want to lose touch with each other again, so they made plans to meet after their tours in Vietnam were over. They selected May 1, 1970 for the date of their reunion. They'd meet at noon in West Memphis, Ark. and catch up after their long year in Vietnam. Harvey wrote his information down on the note and Lawson stuck the note in his wallet before they parted ways.

Spc. Cooley arrived in Vietnam and was assigned to the headquarters company of the 4th Battalion, 12th Infantry, 199th Infantry Brigade. The 119th Light Infantry Brigade, nicknamed the Redcatchers, had arrived in Vietnam in December 1966 and quickly established itself as a reliable and formidable group. Harvey was assigned as a combat medic. Being a medic requires skill and courage and demands grace and intellect under pressure. When a soldier is wounded, it is the medic's job to tend to that soldier, even as the war rages on around them. The medic would go out on patrols with his platoon and treat them for everything from heat stroke and dehydration to bullet and shrapnel wounds. The medic was a critically important member of the platoon, and his soldiers relied on him for the treatment of headaches and the dispensation of morphine to calm the pain of a critical wound. As a medic, the men in Harvey's platoon called him "Doc."

Doc Cooley was only in Vietnam a short while when he became very ill. Diagnosed with parasites, he was sent back to the states for treatment and was given temporary assignment to Fort Campbell, Ky. while he was receiving treatment for his illness. His illness proved to be somewhat good news, as it allowed him to be home for the birth of his son. On November 12, 1967, his wife Millie gave birth to a baby boy: Harvey Lynn Cooley Jr.

While back in Memphis, Harvey reluctantly shared some of his experiences in Vietnam. He told of water everywhere, and how they would often have to walk through rice paddies, rivers and streams with water up to his neck. While he liked the men he was serving with, he hated Vietnam. He had seen terrible things in his short time in Vietnam, things that he felt no one should have to see and that no one should have to go through. He even hoped that his illness would be severe enough that he wouldn't have to go back. Now that he had a son, the last thing he wanted to do was go back to Vietnam. At only 19 years old, Harvey was still very much a boy and he had seen many things in Vietnam that he couldn't get out of his head. He wanted to stay in Memphis. His illness improved and by April 1968 it was clear that Doc Cooley was going back to Vietnam. When he found out he was headed back, he punched a hole in the wall at his parents' house.

Doc Cooley left Memphis on Easter Sunday, 1968 and arrived back in Vietnam shortly thereafter. He was assigned to D Company, 4th Battalion, 12th Infantry of the 199th Infantry Bridgade. He was back with the Redcatchers. He replaced Doc Ramiro Chavez, who had been serving as D Company's medic since January, 1968. The Redcatchers had seen a great deal of action during the Tet Offensive of January, 1968, and by the time Doc Cooley arrived back in Vietnam they were still in the field nearly all of the time. The group was proud, but tired when Doc Cooley returned.

Vietnam in May is extremely hot, with the moisture Doc Cooley hated hanging in the air. D Company was patrolling the area around Fire Support Base Stephanie on the morning of May 6, 1968 in support of ongoing operations in the area. While out in the rice paddies, D Company encountered Viet Cong forces that seemed to be well-established in the area. In the quick bursts of enemy fire, three members of D Company were wounded. Doc Cooley rushed into action. He treated two of the wounded, and while he was doing so, D Company managed to push the enemy back and the firing slowed down. At this point, the third wounded man began to make his way toward Doc Cooley. Robert Tonsetic was there, and he described the action in his 2007 book *Days of Valor*: "Pfc. Raymond Witzig began to crawl toward Specialist Cooley's location. When Cooley saw that the man's wounds were too severe for him to move further, he ran forward and picked up the wounded soldier. As he carried Witzig back toward the cover of a rice paddy dike, the NVA opened fire." Witzig and Harvey were killed.

Gently, Ever So Gently. ♦ Frank Thomas

Despite his misgivings about going back to Vietnam, Harvey gave everything for his men. He never hesitated to rush to their aid and gave his life to save the men in his company. Although he had not wanted to be back in Vietnam, an outside observer would never have known that. He put his fears and apprehension behind him and focused on the battle that faced him. His training had prepared him to tend to his men, and that is exactly what he would do. His utmost concern was that the men of his company be taken care of, even if that meant sacrificing his own life. For his actions on May 6, Harvey was awarded the Silver Star. His citation states, "By his

War Dogs Sacrifice ♦ Carolyn Marshall

Right: Pfc. Raymond Witzig, the soldier that Harvey was aiding on May 6, 1968, when they were hit by small arms fire. Both were killed. Photo courtesy of Ram Chavez.

heroic actions, the lives of two wounded soldiers were saved." As his name revealed, he was indeed battle ready. Harvey was only 19 when he was killed.

Back home in Memphis, Millie Cooley was now a widow and her young Harvey Jr. was only six months old. Harvey's parents would help her raise Harvey's son, who they called Lynn. John and Annie Cooley would never fix the hole that Harvey had punched in the wall before he went back to Vietnam.

Lawson would serve his tour in Vietnam and make it safely back to Arkansas. The May 1, 1970 meeting date with Harvey came and went. Lawson wasn't up for the meeting and wrote Harvey a letter asking if they could postpone the meeting. Harvey never responded. Lawson assumed that his friend Harvey didn't make it back from Vietnam, as he truly believed that Harvey would have responded if he was able. Lawson never forgot his friend Harvey, and though they were never able to meet after Vietnam, Lawson always kept the note that Harvey had written at Fort Ord in 1967.

Thanks to the advent of the Internet, Lawson was able to locate information about Harvey. He learned how Harvey had died and was able to reconnect with members of Harvey's family. Lawson had many phone conversations with Harvey's sister Nancy and his youngest brother Bob. He learned that Harvey's son had also joined the military, serving in the Army just as his father had. Lawson was also able to travel to Oak Grove Cemetery with Harvey's brother Bob and finally have the meeting that he and Harvey were supposed to have in May 1970.

When Lawson first began searching to learn what had happened to his friend Harvey, he came across a poem that Harvey's younger sister Nancy had written for him in 1998. She had posted the poem on several Vietnam memorial websites. It is called "Dear Brother." ♦

*Dear Brother,
It's been thirty long years
since you've been gone
When you left to fight
that war so far from home.
It was such an awful war
And you were just a boy,
But you fought the fight so bravely,
And I'm so proud of my brother.

Dear Brother,
I know you can hear me
I know you can see me
From up there in heaven
Cause you're my guardian angel.

Your baby boy has grown
And has a family of his own.
Though they never met you
They know every thing about you
And in their eyes you stand so tall
And they sure love their grandpa.

Dear Brother,
I know you can hear me
I know you can see me
From up there in heaven
Cause you're my guardian angel.

I still have all your letters
I still carry your pictures
with me everyday.
I remember all the good times
that we shared.
And just wanted you to know
I still care.

Dear Brother,
I know you can hear me
I know you can see me
From up there in heaven
Cause you're my guardian angel.

I placed some flowers on your grave today
And got down on my knees to pray
To the Father up above
To always hold you in his love.
I think about you everyday.
I love you still and miss you so
And Dear Brother,
you'll always be my hero.*

PAMELA D DONOVAN

Second Lieutenant, Army • 3/25/42–7/8/68 • Panel 53W, Row 43

Born in England to Irish parents, Pamela Donovan lived many places before her family settled in Massachusetts in 1956. Her parents, Edward (Ted) and Joyce Donovan, raised their children in Ireland, England and Canada before coming to the United States. Ted and Joyce managed Our Lady of Sorrows Library at St. Gabriel's Monastery in Brighton. The library loaned religious and inspirational books recorded on cassettes to the blind.

The Donovans were a faithful family and Pamela expressed an interest in religious service before settling on nursing as a career. After her graduation from Newton Country Day School, she attended St. Elizabeth's Hospital School of Nursing. She became a registered nurse in 1965. Pamela was a kind and compassionate young woman and was very concerned for the needs of others. It was not surprising that she was moved by news coverage coming out of Vietnam. She knew that she had skills that could help the men serving in combat, so she began researching what it would take to serve as a nurse in Vietnam. Although she was not American by birth, she felt that she had to do something for her adopted country. In late 1967, she applied for U.S. citizenship and enlisted in the Army.

Pamela joined the Army Nurse Corps in October of 1967 and was sent to Fort Sam Houston for training, and once that was completed in January of 1968 she was assigned to Brooke General Hospital. She left for Vietnam on March 8, 1968, with assignment to the 85th Evacuation Hospital, located in South Vietnam. The 85th Evacuation Hospital was primitive by modern standards, with both exam and operating rooms in Quonset huts, but the doctors and nurses assigned there provided lifesaving care to the American troops who they treated. She wrote home often to her parents and heaped praise on the courage and morale of the men she was treating.

About a month after Pamela had arrived in Vietnam, her mother received notification that Pamela had suffered severe sunburn while on a beach in Vietnam and was hospitalized for treatment. Joyce and Ted Donovan were not overly concerned about Pamela's health as they received letters and cassettes from her, and she always seemed to be in good spirits and on the way to recovery. In June, Pamela managed to send letters of encouragement to her mother, who was hospitalized at the time. Pamela wrote her mother every day. She seemed to be healing well and looking forward to a chance to travel after finishing her tour in Vietnam, specifically mentioning how she would like to see Japan and Australia.

Joyce and Ted Donovan were stunned when, on July 4, they received a telegram from the Army telling them that Pamela had been hospitalized in serious condition after being found unconscious in her room. Even more shocking was the cause: an overdose of barbiturates. Reeling from the news, the Donovans attempted to find out more about their daughter's condition, but within days a car pulled up at the house bearing Army officers: Pamela had died on July 8 at the 3rd Field Hospital in Saigon, where she had been moved for more advanced treatment. The cause of death was listed as pneumonia caused by a barbiturate overdose.

In her book *Grasping the Nettle*, Joyce Donovan tells of a letter she and her husband received from Pamela after she died. Dated July 3, Pamela told of attending mass and communion, and of giving her confession to the chaplain. She told her parents that she felt like a new person. The Donovans made many phone calls to Army and Red Cross personnel in the U.S. and Vietnam, but never received much information about how their daughter had died. They buried Pamela in her adopted country and returned to England. ♦

2nd Lt. Pamela Donovan, U.S. Army.

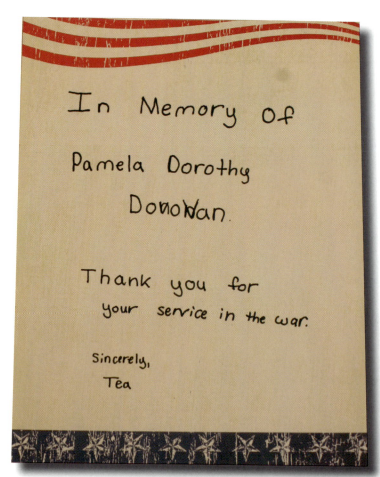

This note was left in memory of Pamela as part of a class field trip to The Wall. From the Vietnam Veterans Memorial Collection. Photo by Sebastián E. Encina.

ANNIE RUTH GRAHAM

Lieutenant Colonel, Army ♦ 11/7/16–8/14/68 ♦ Panel 48W, Row 12

When Annie Ruth Graham first joined the Army, many of the men she would eventually care for in Vietnam had not even been born. When she arrived in Vietnam in 1968, most of the men she treated were young enough to be her sons.

Annie joined the Army in February 1942 when she was 23. Her first posting was as a general duty nurse at Fort Jackson, S.C., but by March 1943 she was serving overseas during the height of World War II. She served as nurse at both 57th Station Hospital in Algeria and Tunisia from 1943 to 1945 and then at the 171st Evacuation Hospital in Italy from February through November 1945. By the time she returned from World War II and was taken off of active duty, she held the rank of First Lieutenant. She was awarded the World War II Victory Medal and the European-African-Mid East Campaign Medal with two bronze service stars.

Annie returned to active duty in January 1951, several months after the U.S. entered the Korean War. She served for one year at Fort Rucker, Ala. before being sent to Osaka Army Hospital in Japan, where she would serve as a staff nurse in the general surgery and orthopedic surgery wards before being promoted to head nurse of the dependent section. Annie stayed at Osaka from October 1952 until August 1954. She had been promoted to the rank of major when she was sent to her next posting at Fort Leonard Wood, Mo. Annie would go back overseas from 1958 through 1960 before returning home to a three-year position as the head nurse in the department of surgery at Walter Reed Hospital in Washington, D.C.

In 1966, Annie was promoted to the rank of lieutenant colonel. She had served as head nurse at a U.S. Army hospital in Ethiopia, and then as assistant chief nurse at Womack Army Hospital in North Carolina. After her promotion, she was given orders to Vietnam. She arrived in Saigon on November 18, 1967 before heading to her position as chief nurse of the 91st Evacuation Hospital in Tuy Hoa, Vietnam. The 91st Evac was a 400-bed facility that provided both inpatient and outpatient services and also treated Vietnamese civilians. Annie was responsible for all nursing services at the hospital. On Christmas of 1967, Annie wrote a letter home to her family, "Our hospital is located directly on the beach of the South China Sea which is perfectly beautiful but quite treacherous. It is monsoon season now so we have torrential rains at times. The climate is quite humid but the nights are really rather pleasant. Getting used to my new outfit (tropical fatigues, jungle boots, and "baseball cap") is not as "exciting" as in World War II but I'm quite sure I'll manage to survive it all!"

Annie led and coordinated the hospital's nursing staff during the Tet Offensive in early 1968, and the hospital ran smoothly despite the chaos of the increased casualties. For her service at the 91st Evac, Annie would be awarded the Legion of Merit medal. The citation specifically mentions her efficiency, organization and leadership, but also calls attention to her caring and giving nature. "Displaying a sincere interest in the welfare of the Vietnamese civilians, she often spent her off duty hours visiting the nationals, who, as innocent victims, suffered the consequences of war."

On August 8, 1968, Annie suffered what appeared to be a fainting spell. But, her condition was much more severe. She was transported to an Army Hospital in Tachikawa, Japan where she was diagnosed with a subarchnoid hemorrhage. She was in a coma for six days before passing away on August 14, 1968 at the age of 51. ♦

Annie Ruth Graham in the early years of her Army career.

Lt. Col. Annie Ruth Graham, U.S. Army.

Annie in a lighter moment. Photo courtesy of Christine Kirby.

A hand-painted American flag left in Annie's honor at The Wall. From the Vietnam Veterans Memorial Collection. Photo by Sebastián E. Encina.

ROGER J BARTHOLOMEW

Lieutenant Colonel, Army • 11/2/32–11/27/68 • Panel 38W, Row 70

They called him "Black Bart." His skills as a pilot were well-known, and he was considered one of the toughest pilots in the Army. He'd flown at both Landing Zone (LZ) X-Ray and LZ Albany during the heavy fighting in the Ia Drang Valley in 1965, and was mentioned by Col. Harold Moore and Joseph Galloway in the book *We Were Soldiers Once…And Young*. A dedicated, career soldier, Roger Jay Bartholomew would serve his country in Korea and Vietnam and earn the Distinguished Flying Cross, three Army Commendation Medals and two Purple Hearts.

Back home with his wife, Shirley, and three children, he was simply Bart. He was born in Oregon in 1935, the youngest child of Jay and Lela Bartholomew. Bart grew up on a ranch at the base of Mount Hood, where his parents raised cattle. He was a Boy Scout and participated in 4-H events when he was growing up. After high school, he put himself through Oregon State University, where he earned a degree in agriculture. After finishing at Oregon State, he joined the Army as a commissioned officer.

Bart wanted to fly, and completed training at Fort Benning, Ga.; Fort Sill, Okla. and Fort Leavenworth, Kan. He was very patriotic and wanted to serve his country as an aviator. He would fly both helicopters and fixed wing aircraft during his career with the Army. In the late 1950s, he met Shirley Andrews while he was stationed in Omaha, Neb. When Shirley and Bart were married in 1959, Bart was serving as a pilot for the commander of the 16th Army Corps. Bart and Shirley would have three children: Laura, Lisa and Jay. The family moved around a lot as Bart's assignments changed, and the three Bartholomew kids lived on Army bases all over the country. Lisa Bartholomew Hanson remembers her father's "brilliant blue eyes," and how he "took us to the pool a lot when he was home. He loved being a dad and letting us rough house with him."

Bart first went to Vietnam in 1965, where he served as an aerial rocket artillery commander. Before leaving, he told his wife that it was better to fight the enemy on their own ground rather than on ours, and that the U.S. should do everything in its power to win the war in Vietnam. Bart would certainly do everything in his power. In November 1965 he was part of the battles in the Ia Drang Valley. The helicopters of C Battery, 2nd Battalion, 20th Artillery were under Bart's command in November as aerial rocket artillery (ARA) support for the men of the 1st Cavalry Division as they fought for four arduous days in Vietnam's Central Highlands. Bart and his pilots flew constantly, firing rockets at the NVA elements on the ground. It was a difficult task, as the NVA had infiltrated American positions and the NVA and American troops were all mixed together. The artillery helicopters could not support the ground troops, because they simply could not tell who was who. Bart is quoted in *We Were Soldiers Once…And Young* describing the conditions at LZ Albany: "We had tactical air, ARA, and artillery and still we couldn't do a damned thing. It was the most helpless, hopeless thing I ever witnessed." Hundreds of Americans died during those days in the Ia Drang Valley, but Bart completed his tour and made it home to his family.

Photo courtesy of the Bartholomew Family.

Bart's second tour began in October 1968. He was a lieutenant colonel at this time, assigned to command the newly-formed 4th Battalion, 77th Artillery of the 101st Airborne Division. By that point, he was a 15-year veteran of the Army and had seen combat many times. He was not afraid to fly in dangerous situations, and his family would find out years later that he had volunteered for many difficult missions. On November 27, he was the pilot of a UH-1C (Huey) helicopter flying near Da Nang. He was flying an ARA mission near Firebase Tomahawk. During an engagement with enemy forces, another battalion was ambushed. Bart went to the aid of the ambushed battalion and was attempting to clear their escape route. Shirley Bartholomew received an account of what happened next: "Disregarding his own safety, Colonel Bartholomew flew his lone aircraft back into the area and located a large enemy unit moving in to block the withdrawal. Colonel Bartholomew engaged that force with rockets and machine gun fire. Although wounded in his second pass, he delivered more rockets and machine gun fire in the

The pilot they called "Black Bart" in front of one of the many types of aircraft he flew for the Army. Photo courtesy of The Bartholomew Family.

enemy positions, thereby saving the friendly element." On one of the passes over the enemy troops, Bart's aircraft was struck by ground fire and crashed. Bart, the helicopter's three other crew members and one passenger were killed.

Bart's family was preparing to celebrate a holiday when Shirley Bartholomew was notified about her husband's crash. Bart's daughter Lisa said, "It was Thanksgiving morning and my sister and brother and I were watching the parades." Bart was first reported missing and the next day Shirley received a telegram stating that Bart's remains had been found.

After his death, Shirley Bartholomew and her three children kept Bart's memory alive. Shirley often talked to her children about their father, and his young son, Jay, would often tell people that his father was "the best flier in the Army." Shirley always told her children that Bart died doing something he loved, and he believed in what he was fighting for. "To us he's a great hero." ♦

Lt. Col. Roger Bartholomew, U.S. Army. Photo courtesy of the Bartholomew family.

Gunner ♦ Richard Yaco
National Museum of Marine Corps, Art Collection
Triangle, Va.

MORTON H SINGER

Captain, Army • 10/25/36–12/17/68 • Panel 36W, Row 37

Capt. Morton Singer, U.S. Army.

There is a Jewish proverb that states, "I ask not for a lighter burden, but for broader shoulders." Chaplain Morton Singer, a Rabbi from New York had those broad shoulders, both literally and figuratively. Born in 1936, Morton was the younger of two boys, both of whom would go on to become rabbis. Morton was a strong man, and he believed in the health of the mind, body and spirit. Although he had a gentle soul and was supremely kind, he was a very physically powerful man. He had a brown belt in karate and was an Olympic-caliber weightlifter. Morton also had a beautiful voice and loved the popular rock 'n' roll music of the day.

Rabbi Singer had married his wife, Eva, in her native Guatemala, and the couple had two daughters, Vera and Karina. The family lived in New York, where Morton taught youngsters both the Torah and how to be healthy. His students at both the Yeshiva and Shul of Great Neck, Long Island remembered his confidence, and that he seemed comfortable in whatever he was doing. They remembered him strolling the gymnasium in a track suit and arriving in his black Chevy Impala. He demanded the best from his students, because he wanted them to believe that they could do anything they dreamed. He had a powerful personality to go along with his physical strength, and he left an indelible mark on everyone he met. He was proud of who he was – a husband, a father, a weightlifter, a Jew, a soldier.

Rabbi Singer was a captain in the U.S. Army and a trained paratrooper who had been stationed at Fort Benning, Fort Bragg and Fort Sill during his Army career. In 1967, Singer volunteered to serve in Israel's Six Day War and then one year later volunteered to go to Vietnam. He felt a strong calling to go and would not be dissuaded. Although his brother, Rabbi Norman Singer, had supported Morton's service in Israel, he did not approve of Morton going to Vietnam. But, Morton had a sense of duty and responsibility to both his country and his religion. He was dedicated to serving the men fighting in the jungles of Vietnam. He arrived to begin his Vietnam service in November 1968 and was assigned to Headquarters Company of XXIV Corps. To the men he served, he brought his joyful spirit and his knowledge of the Torah. He believed in the importance of worship during wartime.

On December 18, 1968, Singer was one of 40 passengers on an Air Force C-123 airplane. The plane, also bearing four Air Force crew members, took off from Phan Rang. It was a ferry flight, taking troops from one part of Vietnam to the other. Morton was on his way to conduct Hanukkah services for men in the field. Somehow, the wrong type of fuel was loaded into the plane, and it crashed southwest of Chu Lai Air Base. Three of the crew members and 11 passengers were killed in the crash, including Morton. He was 32.

On October 24, 2011, Morton was one of 14 Jewish chaplains honored on the Jewish Chaplains Memorial at Arlington National Cemetery. ♦

Army Chaplain, Rabbi Morton Singer, is on the right, photo taken at Fort Sill in 1968.

Waiting to Lift Off ♦ James Pollock, 1967

DAVID A LAND

Seaman, Navy • 4/5/49–1/14/69 • Panel 34W, Row 2

"Then made answer John Alden: 'The name of friendship is sacred. What you demand in that name, I have not the power to deny you!'"
– The Courtship of Miles Standish,
by Henry Wadsworth Longfellow

When his son David was born in 1949, Elvert Land didn't have much difficulty selecting a middle name for his third child: "John Alden was my hero. He was youthful, courageous, and good looking. That's what I wanted my son to be like." Elvert, who was called E.H. by business associates and Ed by friends, had high hopes for his son, so he named him after the 16th century Mayflower passenger.

David Alden Land was born to Ed and his wife, Peggy, on April 5, 1949. He was the younger brother to Michael and Diane Land, and five years later would be joined by his younger brother Joe. David was a fun, smiling, athletic young man who idolized the cowboys he saw in movies and on television. As a young boy, David's heroes were Roy Rogers and Gene Autry. When he wasn't wearing his cowboy hat, David could be found wearing a coonskin cap like Davy Crockett's. The Land family had a ranch in Butler County, Kan. but kept their main home in Wichita. Ed bought the ranch so that he and the boys would have a place to raise horses and cattle. The Land family was close and religious when David was growing up. It was a peaceful, faithful life for the Land family.

Most of the time, David could be found with his best friend Ralph Bickford. The two had met while in the seventh grade at Robinson Junior High School and had remained close while at Southeast High School. Ralph's sister, Judy, commented that, "They never left each other's side and were considered sons at the other's home." Ralph's shy and intellectual persona was a complement to David's gregarious and outgoing nature. Ralph, like David, enjoyed sports and the outdoors. The two would often take hunting trips with David's family and other Wichita friends. In the summers, they worked on the Land family ranch, building barns and corrals. There was a tack room in a small barn that David claimed as his own. The hideaway had an old, overstuffed chair and a potbellied stove. David and Ralph would spend hours out there talking. David dreamed of owning a horse, and his father told him that if he worked hard on the farm, he would buy him one. David could not wait for that day. In the meantime, the boys could often be found driving around Wichita and talking about everything under the sun. "As the younger brother, I was usually in the backseat," said Joe Land. "They might not have known it, but I was always listening to their conversations. Sometimes they had really deep, philosophical talks, but often times they were just talking about music or singing along to the radio."

Ralph was slightly older than David, and was the son of Christy Bickford Jr. and his wife Mary. Christy Bickford worked at the Boeing Aircraft plant in Wichita and Mary was a harpist who played with the Wichita Symphony Orchestra and taught at Wichita State University. Christy was called "Bic," so Ralph was sometimes called "Little Bic." Ralph lived about three miles from the Land family in Wichita with his parents and sister Judy. Mary would sometimes entertain Ralph and his friends by playing Beatles' songs on her harp. Ralph was very mechanically-inclined and had hoped to pursue an engineering degree after his graduation from high school and become a gunsmith when he was older. He worked for Ed Land at Land Manufacturing as a tool and die operator, and he took his interests home with him. Ralph had a lathe in his parents' basement that he used to make rifles.

As Ralph and David approached their high school graduation, many of their conversations centered around the situation in Southeast Asia. Like many young men, they were concerned about how Vietnam would change their lives and whether the draft would send them overseas. Joe Land remembers those conversations well: "In Wichita at that time, you were either a patriot or a hippie, there was very little in between. But no matter how scared they were, they were going to do their duty. There was no way that they would shirk their responsibilities. To them, that was worse than death." Ralph and David knew that enlisting in the military would give them some control over their destinies, so in 1967 they both took steps to serve their country on their own terms. In July, David enlisted in the U.S. Navy Reserve. David had chosen the Navy in part because of his father's service during World War II. David trained at Naval Station Great Lakes, Ill. and then started his freshman year at Friends University in Wichita.

Much like David, Ralph followed in his father's footsteps. Christy Bickford had been in the Army during World War II and he came from a long line of military service. An ancestor on his father's side had received the Medal of Honor at Vicksburg in 1863. Rather than taking his chances with the draft, Ralph joined the National Guard while in his first semester at Friends University. Ralph's sister, Judy said that he was very patriotic and had a very strong sense of duty. He was sent to Fort Ord in Monterey, Calif. for basic training. He hoped to complete his training and then return to Friends University to continue his

RALPH N BICKFORD

Corporal, Army • 1/21/49–3/22/69 • Panel 28W, Row 8

Ralph Bickford's senior photo, Southeast High School. Photo courtesy of Judy Eby.

David Land's senior photo, Southeast High School. Photo courtesy of Joe Land.

David on a river bank in Vietnam on December 26, 1968. Photo courtesy of Joe Land.

his education in engineering. He arrived at basic training in February 1968, but was stricken with spinal meningitis during training. Ralph became critically ill and was in a California military hospital. Initially, the Bickford family was told that Ralph would not live through the night. His parents flew to California the next morning and stayed with him for a week.

David was still back in Wichita, participating in Navy Reserve activities and finishing up his first year of college. He was thrilled to discover that his father was going to buy him a horse as a thank you gesture for all of his work on the ranch. David chose Rega, a beautiful chestnut-brown yearling from a group that Ed had bought on a buying trip to Oklahoma. Shortly after Rega arrived at the Land ranch, David learned of Ralph's illness. He was devastated and worried for his friend. After surviving the most dangerous part of the illness, Army doctors agreed to send Ralph back home to Kansas to recover. Ed gave David his choice: he could have Rega, or Ed would buy a plane ticket to California so that David bring Ralph home. David didn't hesitate and told his father he wanted to go get his best friend. Ed was so moved by David's loyalty that he purchased Rega anyway. David flew to California, picked up Ralph at the military hospital, and the pair flew back to Wichita the next day. "David was a nervous wreck until Ralph got better," said Judy. "He mothered Ralph, much to Ralph's irritation."

Ralph's illness set his training back a few weeks, and by the time he finished, his unit, the 69th Brigade of the Kansas National Guard, had been called to active duty, and Ralph was sent to Fort Carson, Colo. in August 1968. At the same time Ralph was arriving in Colorado, David was making the decision to volunteer for active duty in the Navy. On July 27, he signed a form saying that he was willing to serve "24 months of active duty for general assignment afloat or ashore." He was promoted to the rank of seaman and assigned to the mobile riverine force (MRF). The MRF addressed the large amount of rivers, canals and other waterways throughout South Vietnam. David was sent to Mare Island Naval Shipyard in Vallejo, Calif. There he underwent an 11-week training course designed to prepare him for service in what was commonly referred to as the "Brownwater Navy." While at Mare Island, David met many of the men he would serve alongside in Vietnam. One of these men was Bill Peterson. During the training, Bill was a boat captain and David was a crew member serving under him. Even though he was eight years older, Bill remembers growing extremely close to the young seaman. "David was fun-loving, but was very kind and tender-hearted." After completion of the course, the group received their orders. They were heading to Vietnam.

David came back to Wichita on leave before heading to Vietnam and was able to visit all of his friends and family. He was a very sentimental young man, even heading to his elementary school to visit with his former teachers before leaving. On the day that he was heading to the airport, David's brother Mike took the day off of work and Joe was kept home from school so the whole family could be together. David's grandparents traveled from Oklahoma and Ralph Bickford went with them to see David off at the airport. His younger brother Joe remembers the November day vividly. "Dave lingered as long as he could, gave his mother a big hug and a kiss and ran up the stairs. He was the last one on the plane." Ed, overcome with emotion, collapsed into his own father's arms as he watched David head off to war.

Once in Vietnam, David was assigned to an armored transport craft (ATC), or Tango boat. The Tango was a converted landing craft, mechanized. It featured a bow ramp that could be raised and lowered in order to load gear and troops. It was fitted with gun positions that typically held 20mm guns. A flat deck had been added to allow for helicopters to land. Victor Unruh served on another Tango boat in David's unit. He described conditions onboard these boats as difficult at best: "I was on a Tango boat, which had a crew of seven and only had beds for four. Each of us had one locker for our personal effects, and it was the size of a gym locker. Our nourishment was derived from C-rations which we would heat up using chunks of C-4 plastic explosives." There were no showers on board, and David told his parents that while on operations, they would be so dirty and sweaty that "it all turned into a rank mud that the mosquitoes love." Not only were the conditions difficult, missions were dangerous and casualty rates were high. The MRF worked in conjunction with the U.S. Army's 9th Infantry Division, along with South Vietnamese troops. Joe Land has had many conversations with men who served with his brother, and learned the challenges David faced every day. "The MRF boats were often like sitting ducks. They would patrol the river, and were being shot at on a regular basis. It was very easy for the enemy to spot the boats and fire before the MRF knew what hit them."

On December 28, David was on his boat, T-151-5, just after noon. The boat was on a patrol on Can Gao a Song Cai Lon, a canal 35 kilometers southeast of Rach Soi base. The boat was attacked with B-40 rockets and automatic weapons fire as it made its way along the canal.

David and another crewman were wounded. In a letter home, David told his grandfather about the incident and about how he felt during the attack: "I was wounded while under heavy enemy fire. I'm fine now though and I'll be back at it again soon. I took a small piece of shrapnel just left of chin that lodged in the side of neck. It was close, but God was watching over me. There's no sense pretending I'm not scared. I've never been so scared in all my life, but I was so close to death that day and He didn't call me away, so maybe He'll see me through till I return home." David's letter was sent to his paternal grandfather, E. Homer Land, an evangelist in the Nazarene Church and a very religious man. In that letter, and one to his parents from just after the incident, David reveals how his faith was getting him through his time in Vietnam. He told his grandfather and his parents that he knew God was with him in battle: "When the shooting's all over I always seem to be singing church hymns. The other day just before we entered battle, I read a prayer from my serviceman's prayer book over the phonetical phone hook up to all battle stations on my boat. God did show mercy upon us." After his injury, David was sent to the USS Nueces to recover. His injury was not severe, and he was in good spirits. After spending a few days in the hospital, David felt that he needed to get back to T-151-5. Victor Unruh said that David felt an obligation to get back to his boat. "David had checked himself out of sickbay to come out with us. When he heard we were going out again he wanted to be with his crewmates," said Unruh. It was January 13.

David and the crew of T-151-5 were traveling on the Rach Cai Nhut Canal in a formation. It was about 2 p.m. in Vietnam and 1 a.m. back in Wichita. The boats were sweeping for mines, using grappling hooks deployed from the bottom of the tango boats to snap the cables of the mines. Suddenly, there was an explosion. The boat "sustained severe damage, including the loss of the helicopter platform and the bending up of the hull. When the boat reentered the water it immediately sank," said Unruh, whose Tango boat was just ahead of David's. A search and rescue operation began immediately, but neither David nor Jose Campos could be found. The rescue was called on account of darkness.

As far as the Lands knew, David was still in sickbay on the USS Nueces. The last letter they received from him contained the news of his injury and had been dated December 29. They knew he was in good condition and his wound was healing well. On January 14, it was around 9 p.m. in Wichita when the Land family heard a knock on the door. They had been at church and a man from Ed's office had told them a Navy officer was looking for them. When the Navy officer entered the home, he informed them that David was missing in action.

When she heard the news about her son, Peggy Land collapsed to the floor. Two days later, they learned that David's body had been found. David was dead at 19. Just before signing himself out of the sickbay, he had written one last letter to his parents: "I know enough has been said about how we're going to take everything, but let me say this and then we won't mention it any more. What happens we have no say over. God is in complete control. No matter what happens, we will accept it and keep on going. Worry will only make you old before your time. So — your concern is very, very deeply appreciated, but please don't worry. Life goes on."

Ralph Bickford received the news of David's death while he was training at Fort Carson, Colo. He was able to return home to Wichita to serve as a pallbearer at David's funeral, and as she had so many times before, Mary Bickford played her harp for David. Ralph was not the only of David's best friends to attend the funeral. Ed Land made arrangements for Rega to attend David's graveside service. It is said that when the hearse bearing David's body pulled into Lakeview Gardens Cemetery, Rega became very difficult to handle and seemed as though she was trying to get to the casket. Rega would live for nearly 20 more years, dying in 1988.

*Ralph and David, best friends since junior high.
Photo courtesy of Joe Land.*

*David in his father's office at Land Manufacturing.
Photo courtesy of Joe Land.*

*Bud Sankey prepares David's beloved horse Rega at David's grave-side service.
Photo courtesy of Joe Land.*

*David and his beloved horse Rega, just before David left for Vietnam.
Photo courtesy of Joe Land.*

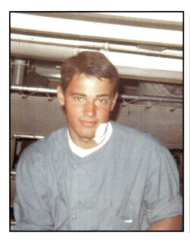  

David on the USS Nueces after being wounded on December 28, 1968. Photo courtesy of Joe Land.

David Land on a pier overlooking Oakland Bay. Ed Land remembered this pier from his own time in the military during WWII. Photo courtesy of Joe Land.

David Land and Ralph Bickford at the airport in 1968. David would leave for Vietnam that day. Photo courtesy of Joe Land.

Ralph spent a lot of time with David's parents on that leave in Wichita, before he too would have to head off to Vietnam. His parents had asked for Ralph to undergo a medical examination after David's death to make sure he was physically able to handle Vietnam. He was less than a year removed from his bout with spinal meningitis and had suffered a car accident in Colorado that left him with severe head injuries. When the results of the Army physical indicated he was fit for duty, Ralph told his parents he knew it was his time to serve and refused to let his parents or area politicians intervene to keep him home. "He didn't see why he should stay in the States while others were going," said his father, Christy. "I think he felt it was necessary for him to go." David's death had also had a profound impact on Ralph and he commented to David's pastor that he hoped to finish what David started in Vietnam. Before he left, Ralph spent every evening with David's sister Diane. The two relied on each other for comfort during the ordeal and before he left Ralph told Diane that he had been in love with her for many years. The two promised each other that they would marry when Ralph returned from war.

When he arrived in Vietnam in March 1969, Ralph was assigned to B Company of 1st Battalion, 502nd Infantry. He was a rifleman in an infantry company, the very job he was afraid he would get if he took his chances with the draft. He had ended up in Vietnam anyway. Before he left, he told his mother that he could not allow himself to get upset about where he was headed or how his life had ended up. He didn't know what faced him, so he tried not to worry. The 1/502nd was stationed in Thua Thien Province. He joined a battalion that was seeing a lot of enemy action in the area of Fire Support Base (FSB) Veghel. On March 20, A and B Companies had established a landing zone and a control base at Dong A Tay. The next two days consisted of heavy contact, and on March 22, B Company was conducting a reconnaissance in force when they were engaged by a North Vietnamese Army company. The engagement lasted two and a half hours, resulting in five wounded Americans and three members of B Company killed in action. Ralph was one of the three KIAs. He was 20.

On March 23, Ed and Peggy Land had attended a ceremony to receive David's medals. After they received his Purple Heart with Gold Star and his other Vietnam campaign medals, they went to the home of Christy and Mary Bickford to have lunch. In a near repeat of January 16, the Lands heard a knock on the door. Where before it had been a Navy officer bringing them the news of David's death, it was now an Army officer bringing the Bickfords the horrible news of Ralph's passing.

As Ralph and David were so often together in life, the families thought it only fitting that they be together in death. "There was never a thought that David and Ralph wouldn't be buried together," said David's brother Joe. Their close friendship was one that inspired both families and is remembered by those that knew them. They lie side by side at Lakeview Gardens Cemetery in Wichita. ♦

"All save the dear old friendship, and that shall grow older and dearer!"

Quote from The Courtship of Miles Standish, by Henry Wadsworth Longfellow.

The graves of Ralph Bickford and David Land, side by side at Lakeview Gardens Cemetery, Wichita, Kan. Photo courtesy of Joe Land.

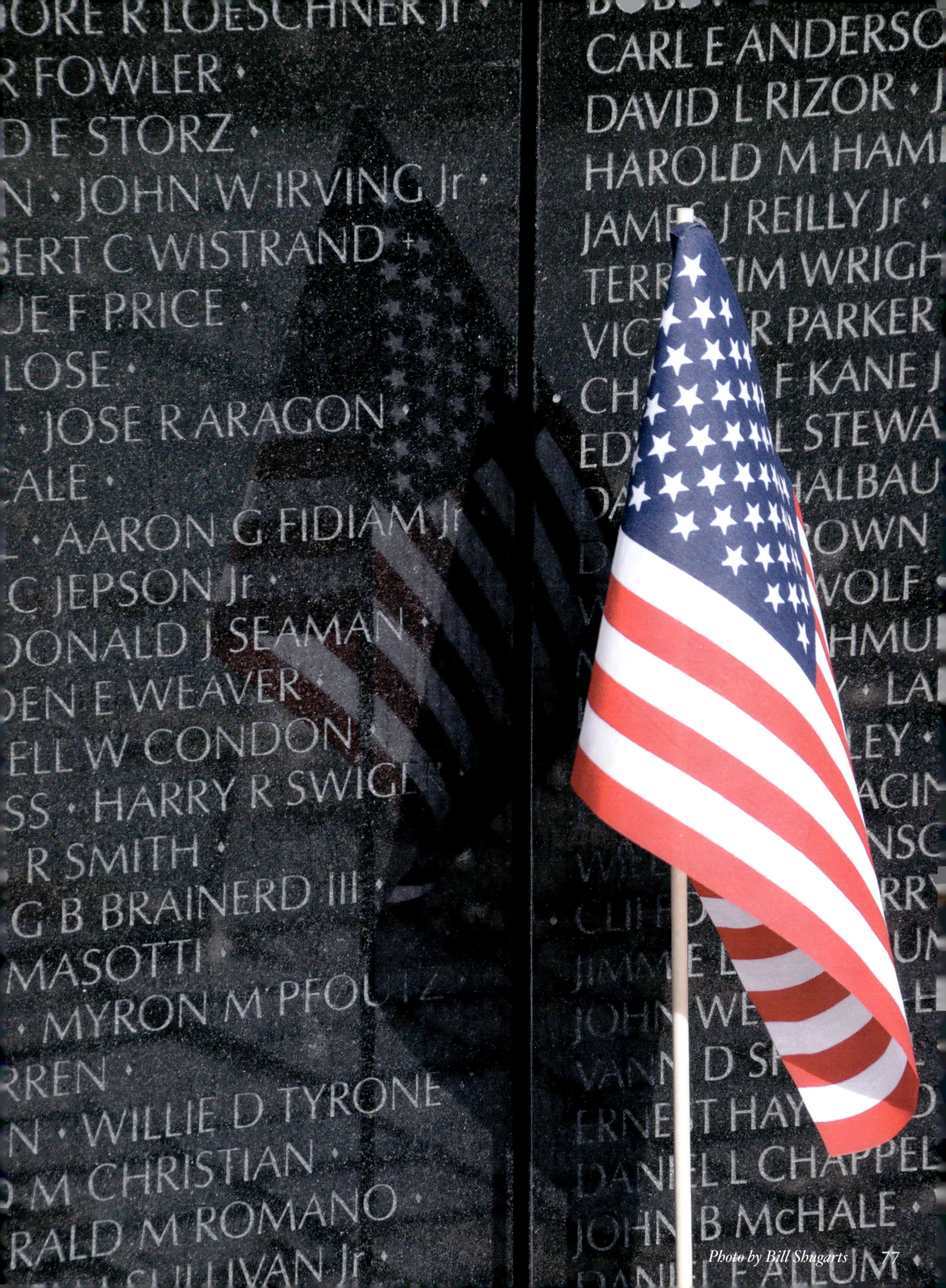

Photo by Bill Shugarts

Price Tags-Vietnam ♦ Bernie Duff, 2011

HOWARD LEARY

Sergeant First Class, Army • 8/11/32–2/19/69 • Panel 32W, Row 58

In order to become president of the Gold Star Wives of America (GSW), a woman must be efficient, personable and committed to advancing the mission of the organization. She also must meet the requirement that binds all GSW members together—she has lost her spouse to military service. Jeannette Blackman Early easily met all of the former criteria, and unfortunately met the latter requirement as well. Her husband, Sgt. 1st Class Howard Lee Early, died in Vietnam in 1969.

Howard Lee was a career Army soldier, dedicating his life to the service of his country. From the small town of Jonesville, La., Howard left his family in 1951 to enlist. His parents, Gable and Georgia Early, were farmers. Family legend is that Howard left the farm and walked the 45 miles to Alexandria so that he could sign up. He lied about his age too, telling the Army he was born in 1932 rather than 1935. However he got there and however old he was, Howard Lee would prove to be a dedicated and talented Army soldier during his 18-year career.

After training, Howard's Army career would take him all over the globe. He was first posted to the 5th Armored Division at Fort Chaffee, Ark. before serving a one-year tour during the Korean War with the service battery of the 48th Field Artillery Battalion. After returning from Korea, Howard was posted at the Aberdeen Proving Ground, Md. and at Fort Knox, Ky. before heading back overseas for a three-year post in Germany. He served there in 1954 through 1957 and returned from 1959 to 1961. In the interim, he was stationed at Fort Knox.

When Howard was on leave from Germany in 1961, he was back home in Jonesville when he met Jeannette Blackman, a teacher at an area school. The pair quickly courted and were married on Christmas Eve, 1961. Their son Fabian was born in 1963 while the family was stationed at Fort Campbell, Ky., and their twins Alphonso and Alonzo were born in 1964. The war in southeast Asia was just beginning in March 1965 when Howard was sent to join the 2nd Battalion of the 5th Cavalry and then the 1st Battalion of the 23rd Infantry. He served a one-year tour in Vietnam before returning home to his family.

Howard's career took a new direction when he attended the Drill Sergeant School at Fort Polk, La. Once the training was completed, Howard and his family moved to Fort Sam Houston, Texas where he would serve as a drill sergeant from 1966 to 1968. He enjoyed the relationships he formed with both his students and his colleagues there and engaged in a competition with the other drill instructors to see who could come away with the most top class honors. Howard always enjoyed the responsibility that the Army gave him and regardless of where he was or what he was assigned to do, he always wanted to be the best.

Most career non-commissioned officers did more than one tour of duty in Vietnam and Howard was no different. He arrived in Vietnam for his second tour in July 1968 and was first assigned to the 503rd Infantry Division as platoon sergeant. After about six months, he was transferred to a position as a light weapons infantry advisor with a mobile advisory team within the Military Assistance Command, Vietnam (MACV). He was serving in that role when he and a team of two other MACV members and a group of South Vietnamese troops were sent on a patrol to engage a Viet Cong patrol in the area. Howard and his team were soon ambushed and were pinned down by enemy forces in a hard to reach area. By nightfall, the team did not respond to radio communications. The next morning, Howard's body and the bodies of two other MACV team members were recovered. On the night of February 19, 1969, Jeannette Early answered her door to the two Army officers bearing the news of her husband's death.

In 2011, Jeannette Blackman Early was elected national president of the Gold Star Wives of America. ♦

This formal portrait of Howard still graces the home of his widow Jeannette.

Sgt. 1st Class Howard Lee Early, U.S. Army. Photo courtesy of Jeannette Early.

RONALD V HACKER

Sergeant, Army • 4/8/48–4/3/69 • Panel 27W, Row 5

Ronald Hacker was born in Weston, W. Va. on April 8, 1948. He was the son of Fred and Virginia Hacker. The Hacker family lived on a small farm in West Virginia, and Ronnie was close to his siblings. The kids would spend summer evenings chasing fireflies and Ronnie taught his younger sister Nancy to surf on a creek near their home. Ronnie was always smiling and having fun, and Nancy remembers that things were always more fun when he was around. "I only knew Ronnie as a young child but he was my best friend and I adored my big brother." Nancy also remembers the time when Ronnie got into it with a skunk and their mother made him hang his clothes on the barbed wire fence along the field. The family separated in 1957 when Ronnie and his father moved to Massillon, Ohio.

After a short time at Massillon's Washington High School, Ronnie dropped out in April 1964 at age 15 to work in the oil fields of East Canton. He usually worked 12 hour days, seven days a week. Sometimes he would pull double shifts if the person on the next shift failed to show up. Ronnie was a hard worker, putting in long hours and never complaining. He soon rose to the job of roughneck. In that position, he was responsible for the majority of the drilling, and for transporting, repairing and assembling the drilling equipment. It was a difficult job, but Ronnie excelled at it. He talked about someday owning his own rig so that he could retire with a good income by the time he was 40.

Ronnie in his basic training photograph, 1968. Photo courtesy of Darelynn Hacker Clay.

In 1966, Ronnie met Darelynn Shook. Their first date was on Christmas Eve; they went to the drive-in movies on a double date. He was 18, and she was 16. He fell for her almost immediately and the two were soon inseparable. They spent time playing billiards at one of Ronnie's friend's houses and going to drive-in movies. They also listened to a lot of Willie Nelson and Johnny Cash because Ronnie loved country music. They had many friends, and although Ronnie worked nearly every day, they made time to be together. Ronnie and Darelynn were married on August 12, 1967.

Unfortunately, Ronnie and Darelynn married as the war in Vietnam was reaching its peak and troop levels were nearing 500,000. Ronnie first received a notice from a draft board in West Virginia, but was able to notify them that he was currently living in Ohio. On Valentine's Day, 1968, the Ohio induction notice came. Though his father, Fred, had served in World War II, Ronnie didn't have any desire to join the military. He would rather stay in the oil fields, continuing to make a living so that he and Darelynn could start a family.

Ronnie in Vietnam. Photo courtesy of Darelynn Hacker Clay.

By March 1968, Ronnie was at Fort Knox, Ky. completing his basic training. His young wife Darelynn was staying with Ronnie's grandmother in Massillon. Looking forward to coming home on leave after he completed, he told his wife about how he didn't want to be in the Army and that he often woke up wishing his new life as a soldier was a bad dream. But, Ronnie was not one to back down or give up, so he would stay and do his job for the next two years. Initially, he had been thinking about trying to qualify for an airborne unit, but feared that would guarantee him a trip to Vietnam and he was doing his best to make sure that he made it home to Darelynn safely. He talked about how much his wife meant to him and how much he missed her. Ronnie was clearly very much in love with Darelynn, and signed his letters home from Fort Knox "R.H. + D.H. Forever and Ever."

5 March 1968

"Hi Honey, I love you a whole big bunch. I'm still waiting on my German chocolate cake you were making for me. We're going on a hike tomorrow to the rifle range for target practice. I'm going to get me an expert medal for my dress uniform, then you can have it. I'll get it just for you 'cause I love you so much. Remember when we were at the drive in when I told you I loved you for the first time? You didn't believe me, did you? Now that I have time to think once in a while, I see all the fun we missed by me working all the time. As soon as I get out of the service I'm going to work five days a week only. So we can make up for all the fun we missed. With all my love, Ronnie"

Ronnie at LZ Green in November of 1968. Photo courtesy of Darelynn Hacker Clay.

A newlywed Ronald Hacker, before his time in Vietnam. Photo courtesy of Darelynn Hacker Clay.

Ronnie & Darelynn on their wedding day, August 12, 1967. Photo courtesy of Darelynn Hacker Clay.

Ronnie arrived in Vietnam in early September 1968, just seven months after receiving his induction letter. The number of troops in Vietnam had steadily risen during the summer of 1968, and would reach its highest number of 537,000 troops right around the same time that Ronnie arrived in Vietnam. He was assigned to C Company, 1st Battalion, 22nd Infantry Regiment of the 4th Infantry Division. He was assigned a post as an assistant gunner on an M60 machine gun. He drew Snoopy on his helmet cover, alongside "R.H. + D.H." and the countdown of the days he had left in Vietnam.

16 September 1968
"Hi honey, What's you doin? Right now we're about 12 miles from Saigon or so they say. Anyway, we're clear out of the human race. This place we're at now was a firebase for the 173 Airborne until about 10 days ago. I'm on guard duty right now about 100 meters out in jungle from the firebase. You wouldn't believe what it's like here it's all swamp and grass about 7 feet tall and all kinds of crazy animals. Right now it's about 100 degrees but it seems hotter but the sky is getting dark so I know it's going to rain. You wouldn't believe how different everyone is over here. When I first came they all acted like they had known me for 10 years. They're a really a good bunch of guys."

25 October 1968
"Hi honey, Here's what has happened in the past two days. There has been a cease fire on both sides, we do not bomb North Vietnam but some North Vietnamese Army (NVA) don't know because they stay out for months without hearing from the top people. But the word is that there were 6,000-8,000 NVA with tanks about 2 miles from us coming our way when we decided to hit them. So they stopped and turned around and went back across the border. Our higher intelligence tells us that all NVA forces that were in South Vietnam are gone! I don't believe it but that's what they said. I hope so! I haven't heard a blast from a gun in two whole days. I don't know, but something big is up. Hope so. This war may soon be over. I love you and don't forget it. Love, Ronnie"

By early October, Ronnie's hard work and dedication were noticed by superiors. Just as in the oil fields, he was beginning to rise through the ranks and be given more responsibility within his company. He was appointed team leader of the B team within his squad, and was given the task of communicating orders to the other members of the team. The B team was a rifle team and Ronnie would take his team out on patrols. They would go out into the field with weapons, a radio and enough food and water for a few days, reporting any movement that they saw. Ronnie was especially pleased because the team leader position was a promotion to the rank of specialist. Three months after that, if he was still a team leader, he'd be promoted to the rank of sergeant.

11 December 1968
"Dearest Darelynn,
We are now at Dak-To on top of a mountain and I mean a mountain! The elevation is 1575 and that's almost straight up from any side. When we came in today we had to walk about 4 miles through real thick jungle and over all of these mountains. It wouldn't have been so bad if I'd had a little less to carry but I had to carry my pack which had my bedroll, 9 quarts of water, 9 meals of C-rations and everything else that belongs to me. All of that weighed about 70 pounds plus my weapon, a M60 machine gun that weighs 28 pounds and 500 rounds of ammo that weighs about 15 pounds. It was over 100 pounds that I was carrying. Honey, I am gonna take some pictures of this place tomorrow so you can see what it looks like. It's beautiful. Why people want to destroy such a place I'll never understand. Well honey, I'm gonna close for now, my candle is about to burn out so I'm gonna say good night. Love ya a whole big bunch! Your hubby, Ronnie"

While in Vietnam, Ronnie often found himself deep in thought. He spent a lot of time thinking about his future and what his life with Darelynn would be like. He wanted a big family with at least four kids, and hoped to make enough money so that he could spend more time with his family. He knew for sure that he would keep his promise to only work five days a week, so that he wouldn't miss out on anything like he had before he left for the Army. He didn't like being in Vietnam, and expressed his frustration at those protesting the war back in the U.S. He believed that he was there so that his children wouldn't have to fight a war when they were older. The thought was enough to get him through the long days and the very cold nights in the mountains near Dak To.

17 March 1969

"Hi honey. We're at Poly-Cliane now (Author's note: probably referring to Poli Klang, a firebase) I guess we're gonna be here for quite some time. There's quite a lot of contact with the VC and NVA in this area around here. The only thing we do now is look for "Charlie." I don't want to find him. <u>I'm getting too short!</u> 159 days I think! We walk from 6:30 in the morning to 5 p.m. then we have 1 ½ hours before dark to cut 25-30 meters of brush down in front of our position, build a bunker, eat, and then go to sleep and pull about 2 hours guard at night. I never thought in my life I'd ever be doing some of the things I'm doing now. I haven't had a hot meal in so long I forget what hot food tastes like. I haven't had a bath in a month, except for going swimming in a river for a few minutes. Well, I'm gonna go for now. Be good and remember I love you. Love, Ronnie"

In February 1969, Ronnie was up for a promotion to sergeant and had been taken off of his M60 machine gun. His recent elevation to team leader had meant additional patrols into the surrounding jungles in February and March that included encounters with both monkeys and bears. He was counting down to R & R leave in May and to the end of his tour in the fall. His letters to Darelynn were still filled with his love and thoughts for the future, but more and more were imploring her not to worry about him. In a letter dated March 30, he marveled that he would be 21 in just 10 days and he thanked Darelynn for helping him get to where he was. He knew that he was a hard man to understand and he thanked his young wife for standing by him. He promised Darelynn that he would be okay.

Ronnie was serving as a squad leader on April 3, 1969. His company was involved in an operation in the Cu Don Valley complex west of Kontum, South Vietnam. They immediately began receiving heavy enemy fire and the point squad suffered four wounded men. Ronnie volunteered to lead soldiers to the wounded squad's area to assist and had the foresight to bring enough ammunition for both his men and the wounded soldiers. Ronnie's actions would earn him the Silver Star for heroism:

"Exhibiting exceptional ability and coolness while under heavy fire he then maneuvered his men to positions from which they engaged the enemy with accurate and effective cover fire, allowing the wounded to be evacuated from the area. Seeing one of his men wounded by the intense hostile fire, Sergeant Hacker rushed to his side."

Under intense enemy fire, Ronnie saw a man from his team wounded and he could not stand idly by. He ran to that the soldier and picked him up to carry him to safety. As he was trying to rescue that wounded man, Ronnie was killed. He was 20. ♦

Ronnie on a hill in Vietnam. He found the country beautiful and described the breathtaking vistas to Darelynn in letters. Photo courtesy of Darelynn Hacker Clay.

SAMUEL W. BELL

Staff Sergeant, Marine Corps • 6/18/35–5/10/69 • Panel 25W, Row 35

Samuel Wayne Bell was a lifer. He wanted to dedicate his life to the military and to the service of his country. He joined the Air Force in 1952, spent eight years in blue, including two years in the Korean War. He had tried civilian life for a year after being discharged from the Air Force, but, as his wife Susan said, "the motto of the Corps, '*Semper Fidelis*' drew him in, for he believed in that motto, 'Always faithful' – to God and country and family." Samuel believed he had a calling to serve his country and was willing to give his life in that service. He joined the Marine Corps in 1961.

Born in California's Napa Valley in 1935, Samuel was one of five children. He came from a military tradition, with one of his brothers serving in World War II and two others serving in the Army between World War II and Korea. His mother's first husband had died of mustard gas poisoning sustained in World War I. "It was the expectation to give service to your country," Susan said. Samuel, called Wayne by family and friends, was not an overly motivated student and left Napa Valley High School to join the Air Force.

After serving in Korea, Japan and at several stateside Air Force bases, Wayne was discharged. His love for service continued when he joined the Marine Corps. He married the former Susan Deck in 1964 and by the time of their wedding he had already served one tour in Vietnam. He would return twice more. Susan was pregnant with their daughter, Marquessa, in 1966 when Wayne went back to Vietnam. "He hated leaving his family, since I was pregnant with his first child, he didn't see the entire pregnancy and arrived home from his first tour when his daughter was five months old," remembered Susan. "He loved the job—the Corps, his men, his country as well as his family."

Like many soldiers, his complaints from Vietnam were the weather and the living conditions: the mud, the humidity, the rain. As a combat veteran, he also grieved for the men he had lost. Wayne also realized that his Marines, as well as the people of Vietnam, would be forever changed by the war around them. His wife said that Wayne "was very aware of the results and grieved over them in his letters and in his conversations later." Nevertheless, Wayne fervently believed that the American cause in Vietnam was a just one, and that it was the United States' responsibility to bring freedom to those oppressed or living under tyranny.

Wayne returned to his wife and daughter in California after his second tour of duty in Vietnam. He was stationed at Camp Pendleton for most of 1967 and 1968. Wayne was an accomplished, talented man. He loved being in the military but also was a gourmet chef and a gifted dancer. He even taught dance at Arthur Murray studios for a time. "He sang all the time," said Susan, "and he loved old, black and white movies." He liked driving fast cars and was known on the Marine bases as one of the most charitable men around, giving to orphans, widows and children. He was a compassionate man who loved kids. He particularly doted on his daughter, who he considered a gift from God.

At Camp Pendleton, Wayne was a driver for the base's chief of staff. He and Susan bought a home in Barstow and were enjoying life surrounded by people they knew. Wayne left for his third tour of duty in Vietnam in April 1969. This time, he was serving with D Company, 1st Battalion, 3rd Marines of the 3rd Marine Division. He was a platoon sergeant, and his men called him "Scotty" for his Scottish heritage. He was well-liked by his men, and they respected him. Gary Stanley served under Wayne and remembered that he "gave us confidence in our ability to do what we needed to accomplish. You were someone we knew we could count on to teach us and lead us right."

Wayne had been in Vietnam for about a month on May 10, 1969. His platoon had been among a group of Marines that had been moved to areas near the Demilitarized Zone (DMZ) between North and South Vietnam. By May 10, their company had seen heavy fighting for much of May, including a day long fire fight on May 1 that saw eight Marines and a Navy corpsman killed. Near the DMZ was a hill called Mutter's Ridge, named for the colonel who had first captured the ridge in 1966. Wayne was the platoon sergeant for 3rd Platoon, and he was stationed on a small hill with his men. The platoon was hit by NVA forces at around 3:30 a.m. and the engagement lasted for three hours. The Marines fought the NVA, who attacked with the strength of at least two platoons, but the Marines got the NVA off the hill twice. The fighting was intense, in some cases coming down to hand-to-hand combat. At least 25 men of the platoon were wounded, and six Marines lost their lives, including Wayne.

At their new home in Barstow, Susan was notified of her husband's death. "The base chaplain and the detail from headquarters came in a Marine Corps green vehicle that day. It was the second time the car had been on our street in a month with death notifications for Marines deployed in combat in Vietnam." But she knew that her husband believed in what he was doing in Vietnam. "He truly believed we lived in the greatest country on earth." ♦

SHARON A LANE

First Lieutenant, Army • 7/7/43–6/8/69 • Panel 23W, Row 112

Sharon Lane at the beginning of her nursing career.

One of the often overlooked parts of the Vietnam War was the number of civilian casualties. It is estimated that 50,000 to 2 million Vietnamese civilians lost their lives during the years 1960-1975, and hundreds of thousands more were wounded. In 1967, the U.S. Army founded the Civilian War Casualty Hospitalization Program to provide treatment for Vietnamese people suffering from war-related injuries. These patients could be treated at military hospitals that had available beds and would be cared for by American personnel. For many American doctors and nurses, treating Vietnamese patients was a difficult task. It was emotionally draining, and many medical personnel struggled with the job of treating patients that may have been supporting enemy forces. Sharon Lane wasn't one of them.

Sharon Ann Lane was born in Ohio in 1943 and grew up in the Canton area. She lived in the town of North Industry for most of her life and graduated from Canton South High School in 1961. In the fall of that year, she enrolled in Aultman School of Nursing in Canton and graduated from there in 1965. Her mother, Kay, said that "She never wanted to stop learning." She worked at the Aultman hospital for two years and decided to join the Army Nurse Corps in 1968. "She just wanted to better herself and felt she could help in the service," her father John remembered in a newspaper interview.

Sharon was trained in military nursing at Fort Sam Houston in Texas in 1968, and was then stationed at Fitzsimmons General Hospital in Denver, Colo. from June 1968 through April 1969. While at Fitzsimmons, she worked in the tuberculosis ward and then was commissioned as a first lieutenant, and was transferred to the cardiac intensive care unit. She left for Vietnam in early April.

When she arrived in Vietnam, Sharon was assigned to the 312th Evacuation Hospital at Chu Lai. She first worked in the intensive care unit but was then transferred to Ward 4, sometimes referred to as the Vietnamese Ward. She was a good nurse and possessed the personality traits necessary to keep sane in a combat hospital environment. Those who served with her remember that her patients loved her, and that she was particularly admired by her Vietnamese patients because of the kindness she showed them. "They appreciated her tenderness and concern for them," remembered her immediate supervisor in Vietnam, Capt. Lorraine Montz. Sharon liked working with the Vietnamese and wanted to stay in the ward. She had turned down at least one transfer to leave the unit. She also enjoyed the people she was working with and in her letters home really only complained about the heat of Vietnam.

Ward 4 was made up of two Quonset huts called 4A and 4B with a hallway running between them. Sharon had switched to the night shift in early June and was looking forward to not having to wake up early. In the early morning hours of June 6, 1969, Sharon and another nurse were enjoying a few quiet moments before waking the patients for the day. Just before 6 am, incoming fire rained down on the area and a 122mm rocket hit the hallway between Wards 4A and 4B, sending pieces of shrapnel flying in every direction. One piece flew through the wall of the Quonset hut and struck Sharon as she sat on a bed. It punctured her aorta, killing her in seconds. More than two dozen Americans and Vietnamese were wounded in the attack. A young Vietnamese boy who was a patient in the hospital also lost his life.

Sharon was killed just weeks before her 26th birthday. She is the only American military woman to have died as a result of direct combat action during the Vietnam War. "I have lost a wonderful daughter," said her mother. The family would never be the same after Sharon's death. The many memorials in her name, including a women's center and a bronze statue at Aultman hospital, and roads in Colorado and Virginia, do not bring her daughter back. Kay kept Sharon's room unchanged for decades after she buried her daughter. ♦

1st Lt. Sharon Lane, killed by a rocket attack on the 312th Evacuation Hospital in 1969.

MICHAEL H PAINTER

Engineman 1st Class, Coast Guard • 2/28/43–8/8/69 • Panel 20W, Row 115

During the Vietnam War, more than 8,000 Coast Guardsmen served on vessels in Southeast Asia. Vietnam's 1,200 mile coastline and myriad rivers made the Coast Guard a critical element of the U.S. plan in Vietnam.

Michael Harris Painter was 25 when he arrived in Vietnam in November 1968. He had joined the Coast Guard in 1964 and trained at the Coast Guard base in Alameda, Calif. From January 1965 to April 1968, Michael would be stationed with the Yaquina Bay Group in Newport, Ore. In April 1968, he re-enlisted in the Coast Guard for six more years. Michael's last posting before Vietnam was on the Coast Guard Light Vessel (WLV) Columbia along the Columbia River. He was onboard WLV Columbia from July 1968 until his assignment to Division 12 in February 1969. When he left for Vietnam, he left his wife, Faye, and son, Brian.

He was assigned to Coastal Squadron One, Division 12 based out of Da Nang. He would serve as loader and gunner on United States Coast Guard Cutters (USCGC) and would also work with the Vector program that trained Vietnamese Navy personnel. His first assignment in Vietnam was on the USCGC Point Dume, and he served aboard her for most of his tour. While he was on board, he was part of the mortar crew and participated in more than 60 missions. According to Coast Guard records, during this time the Point Dume was responsible for more than 30 enemy killed in action, the destruction of more than 150 structures and the sinking of 62 boats.

After completing his time on the Point Dume, Michael volunteered to serve on the USCGC Point Arden. Like the Point Dume, the Point Arden was an 82-foot cutter that carried a crew of two officers and eight enlisted men. On August 9, 1969, Michael was onboard the Point Arden on what the Coast Guard called a "harassment and interdiction mission." Michael was on the bow working with Lt. j.g Michael Kirkpatrick at firing the mortars. They were firing at suspected enemy positions. The gun, an 80mm mortar, had to be loaded by hand before firing. A shell exploded inside the firing tube, and the ensuing blast shattered both metal weapons and flung them into the air. Both Painter and Kirkpatrick were killed in the explosion.

Engineman 1st Class Michael Harris Painter, U.S. Coast Guard

Michael's son, Brian, spent his career in the Coast Guard, rising to the rank of senior chief. In 2007, he represented the Coast Guard at the 25th Anniversary of The Wall. He, like many other "Coasties," attempts to make sure that all Americans are aware of the Coast Guard's role in Vietnam. "People are surprised that our beloved Coast Guard played a part in that war. The public should know," said David Nelson, who served in Vietnam at the same time as Michael Painter. Seven Coasties lost their lives in Vietnam and those who served with them strive to keep their memories alive.

Monsoon Initiative ♦ Frank Thomas

DOUGLAS S KEMPF

Specialist 4th Class, Army • 7/12/47–9/5/69 • Panel 18W, Row 40

Multi-faceted. Looking back on her high school sweetheart and first love, that's the word that Cathy Parrish Kempf Heck kept repeating: Doug was multi-faceted. Capable of being macho and arrogant, but at the same time gentle and loving, Doug Kempf was many things to many people. He was strong-willed and outgoing, but had a soft spot for children and doted on Cathy's grandmother. One of the things that Cathy loved most about Doug was that he had so many sides to him. Doug was a person who loved life and participated in all aspects of it.

The youngest of Ortha and Gilbert (Gib) Kempf's three boys, Doug grew up in a close-knit Ohio family. Ortha and her sister Beatrice were extremely close, so close that they married their husbands in a double wedding on June 16, 1939. Though Beatrice, her husband Max June and their children lived in Bowling Green, Ohio, the Kempf and June families visited each other often. Because Doug was the youngest of three boys, he often took on his cousin Ron June as de facto younger brother, passing on all of the teasing and torment that Doug had received from his older brothers, Terry and Denny. He loved practical jokes and seemed to be always smiling and laughing. Ortha had her hands full with the three boys, the cousins, and all of the neighborhood kids that often found themselves at the Kempf's unique Coshocton home.

Gib was the sheriff of Coshocton, Ohio from 1948 to 1956, and while serving in that position he and his family lived in a large house attached to the jail. Neighborhood kids would play in the alley behind the jail, and Ron June remembers playing kickball and football in the long hallway that separated the house from the jail. When cells were empty, Ron would find himself locked in by Doug. "He'd tell me that it was a real shame, but they didn't know where the keys were for the cell I was in," said Ron. "And he'd leave me in there for a bit. He thought that was real funny." Along with Gib's job as sheriff came a job for his wife Ortha. She ran the jail and that included preparing all of the meals for prisoners in the jail. The prisoners ate well. Ortha fed them the same meals she fed her own family. Family legend has it that arrests would increase around the holidays because men struggling to make ends meet would cause trouble so that they could be in jail for Ortha's Christmas or Easter meals.

After Gib was no longer sheriff, the family decided to stay in Coshocton. Doug went to Coshocton High School and quickly established a reputation as quite the ladies' man. "He was a man's man," remembers Cathy. "He sometimes stashed his unfiltered Camels in a rolled-up T-shirt sleeve or shirt collar." He enjoyed going out and having fun, and his larger than life personality often made him the center of attention. Doug was a senior and Cathy a sophomore when they had a sociology class together.

At first, Cathy was overwhelmed by Doug's outgoing personality. Doug's personable nature was the polar opposite of Cathy's shy, soft-spoken demeanor. One of their first dates was to a Sadie Hawkins dance. It was a themed dance and the students were dressed in overalls and pigtails reminiscent of the *Li'l Abner* comic strip. Cathy remembers Doug dragging her out to the center of the dance floor where all of a sudden he just dropped down into the splits and popped right back up. In time, Doug's personality would win Cathy over.

Once they were together, Cathy began to see the very soft, gentle side of Doug that he didn't reveal to many people. Cathy's grandmother was a wonderful cook, and Doug would sit with her in the kitchen, talking as he watched her bake. He was a big fan of her cookies and would often eat them right off the tray, fresh from the oven. He was fiercely protective of Cathy, defending her honor with force when he felt it necessary. While they were dating, Cathy worked as a lifeguard at a neighborhood pool. A classmate asked her out, and when she politely declined, the classmate called her a derogatory name. When Doug heard about the insult, "He gave the classmate quite a black eye," said Cathy. "That evening at a dance, Doug held him by his shirt collar and marched him over to where I was and forced the boy to apologize to me."

Behind all of Doug's machismo and arrogance was a highly intelligent young man. He earned good grades, was a member of the National Honor Society and understood that he needed to do well in high school to succeed in life. After graduation, Doug went on to Ohio State University. After vacillating between medicine and dentistry, he decided to register himself as pre-med. After working long summers at Stone Container while in high school, Doug had saved up the money to pay for his own education. He kept working at the factory during the summer so that he wouldn't be in debt to anyone when he started his life as a doctor. He would marry Cathy and the two would start a family together.

Specialist 4th Class Douglas Kempf, U.S. Army Medic. Photo courtesy of CJ Heck.

Doug in Vietnam. Photo courtesy of CJ Heck.

The Heck and Kempf families on the night of Doug & Cathy's engagement. Christmas Eve, 1968. Photo courtesy of CJ Heck.

Doug & Cathy at the altar of Custer Memorial Chapel on their wedding day in 1969. Photo courtesy of CJ Heck.

Cathy remembers that they wanted two boys and a girl. Cathy knew that Doug would be a great father and wanted their boys to take after Doug's strength of character. His dreams were simple and he believed that his hard work would lead him to a happy life. Doug proposed to Cathy on Christmas Eve 1968 in front of both of their families. Cathy said yes and the dreams of the young couple took another step towards becoming reality.

In the U.S. in the 1960s, the dreams and plans of tens of thousands of young men and women were put on hold. After the 1968 fall semester, Doug was forced to take a semester off. Within a month of failing to enroll in classes in Columbus, Doug was drafted into the Army. His dream of becoming a doctor would be postponed. He would get his medical training not in the classrooms of Ohio State, but in the jungles of Vietnam.

Although his Army service would keep him from returning to Ohio State, it would not keep him from marrying Cathy. Doug and Cathy were married on January 11, 1969 at the Custer Memorial Chapel in Coshocton. After the wedding, Doug and Cathy moved to Fayetteville, N.C. where Doug was completing his basic training. Cathy remembers those early days with Doug fondly. "Doug and I shared a good life from January to May. We were military-poor and living in a trailer on base at Fort Bragg in Fayetteville, N.C. but we didn't care. We were together and we were happy. There, we loved and laughed and planned our future for when he returned." After Fort Bragg, Doug went on to Fort Sam Houston in Texas for his medical training, and after completing his medic training was assigned to the 199th Light Infantry Brigade. He arrived in Vietnam on June 1, 1969.

Assigned to D Company, 4th Battalion, 12th Infantry, Doug soon became "Doc" to those he served with. His personality served him well in Vietnam and he was everyone's friend. His comrades not only saw him as a doctor and a friend, but as someone they could rely on for reassurance and support. Although Doug was only 21 when he arrived in Vietnam, his confidence and good nature led those he served with to see him as an older brother. He took care of everyone's wounds and helped make new members of the unit feel comfortable. While stationed with D Company, Doug would often head into the surrounding villages to care for the Vietnamese children living there. He was never scared; he just believed that the kids needed his help and that he was going to give it. To him, that was part of what being a medic meant—helping everyone that you were able to help. He didn't care that he may have been putting himself in danger by going out into the villages; he had such a soft spot for children that he simply had to take care of them. He would take care of cuts and scrapes, insect bites and fevers. He often brought other soldiers with him, and they consistently marveled at how good he was with young Vietnamese who lived around him.

As good as he was to the kids, his job in Vietnam was to care for his men. By all accounts he did that admirably. He could often be found taking care of the wounds caused by life in the jungles of Vietnam: trench foot, dehydration, blisters and sunburns, and the leeches that would periodically show up on his soldiers. Of course, not all of the injuries sustained by his soldiers were as simple as those, and injuries caused by the bullets and bombs of the enemy were Doug's job as well.

It was a September afternoon in what was then the Long Khanh province, South Vietnam. D Company was in an area 12 kilometers west/southwest of Xuan Loc. The mission was to be two weeks long, but almost immediately the company walked into an ambush and began taking heavy fire. Doug was in the back with Lt. James McCraney, and they soon heard the cries of "medic!" coming from the front of the line. Doug jumped up to run to his men, but was held back by his commanding officer when it became clear that the wounded men were being tended to. Time passed and the cries of "medic!" grew louder. The area had been cleared of enemy activity and Doug never hesitated to make his way to the wounded men. As he was tending to one of his wounded soldiers, Doug was hit by a sniper's bullet. An enemy soldier had been hiding in the trees and Doug was mortally wounded. According to those who were there, he never knew what hit him. He was 22, and would earn a Bronze Star with a V device for valor for his actions that day.

It was not until five days later that Cathy Parrish Kempf found out that Doug had been killed. She recalled the day that she learned of Doug's death in a story she wrote entitled "From Bride to Widow." The story is posted in its entirety on her blog "Memoirs from Nam," a writing community designed to aid Vietnam veterans and their families with healing the wounds of their time in Vietnam. Cathy recalls, "My mother called me at work, 'Honey, you'd better come home. There are some people here who need to talk to you. It's about Doug.'" The blog continued, "I didn't say anything. I dropped the phone and, with my heart in my throat, I ran in my dress and high heels out of the building and up the street. I didn't stop running until nearly four blocks later, when I got to the house I grew up in, where I had always felt so safe and loved. Parked in front of the house and looking out of place, was a large black car. I raced up the front steps and in the door. Just inside stood two uniformed men locked to attention, their hands behind their backs, and hats tucked under their arms. Their faces were somber. Daddy and mama stood nearby. He had his arm around Mama's waist and she was crying. *"Mrs. Kempf, we regret to inform you that your husband, Specialist Douglas S. Kempf, was killed in action in Vietnam on September 5 ..."*

"I didn't hear the rest of what he had to say. Daddy said I fainted where I stood, just inside the front door in the foyer. When I came around, I was on the couch in my parents' living room, and then I remembered. Oh my God, I remembered and I wanted to die, too. I was devoid of all feeling, except grief."

That horrible day was followed by days and weeks that Cathy doesn't remember. The time following Doug's death was a terrible one for the entire Kempf family. Doug's time in Vietnam had been tense for the whole family and now their worst fears had been realized. Doug, so joyful and with such a loving, giving heart, was gone. Doug was buried on September 18 in Coshocton County's Memory Gardens. Almost immediately after his death, the family established a memorial fund in Doug's name at Coshocton High School. In the weeks after his death, the fund grew rapidly. Doug had been loved in Coshocton and the town would not soon forget him. The fund raised enough money to be self-perpetuating, and as of 2012, the Douglas S. Kempf Memorial Scholarship is still being given out at Coshocton High School to a worthy student looking to pursue higher education.

Cathy never forgot her first love, Doug. An author, Cathy, who now goes by CJ, writes often of her husband and the pain she felt after his death. "Back then, nobody wanted to talk about it. I often felt I should just let Doug go and move on, and was told that more than once." Allowing herself to write about her grief has given CJ the opportunity to speak with others who experienced the Vietnam War. It also enabled her to connect with one of the men who was with Doug on the day that he died, Lt. James McCraney. They were able to speak on the phone about Doug's last days in Vietnam, and although it was a difficult conversation for both of them, it was immensely helpful. "Each time someone writes in and shares their experiences, dealing with Doug's death gets a little bit easier," CJ said. She believes that the wives, parents, siblings and children of those killed in Vietnam experienced a severe trauma when their loved ones were killed and that many have never dealt with that loss. For her, writing about Doug and what it was like to lose him allows her to move forward with her life and to understand his place in a world that he left so many years ago. ♦

Doug & Cathy on their wedding day, January 11, 1969. Photo courtesy of CJ Heck.

"Job Well Done, Brother" ♦ © Roland Castanie

Photo by Bill Shugarts

FRANCIS E CORTOR Jr

Sergeant, Army • 5/23/47–10/21/69 • Panel 17W, Row 100

Frances Cortor Turley lost her son Duke to mortar fire in Vietnam in October 1969. The last time she had seen Duke had been in June of that year when he boarded a TWA flight bound for Washington as he made his way to Vietnam for his second tour of duty. He waved to her from the window and then he was gone.

Duke was her oldest, the first of four boys born to Frances and her husband Francis Cortor Sr. Three people in one house with the same name got confusing, so Frances took to calling her son Duke and the name stuck. Duke was an active young man and loved playing sports and music. While at Esther High School in Esther, Mo., he was on the basketball team until pneumatic fever sidelined him. Many young men would be devastated when told they couldn't play the sport they loved, but after Duke's illness he returned to the team as a manager. His mother said that, "He was willing to help anyone do anything, and although he may not have won any awards, he was always there to help the boys that did." His contributions were long remembered, sticking with his high school coach for more than 40 years. "I saw his coach recently at church," said his mother in a 2012 interview. "He told me that Duke was one of the finest gentlemen he ever knew."

Duke got along with everyone and was active in many groups. He was a Boy Scout and was involved in the Royal Ambassadors, a Baptist group for young men. He often went on mission trips with his youth groups, and he made an impression wherever he went for his kindness, courtesy and respect for all.

After graduation, Duke went to college for one year before entering the Army in 1966. He was first sent to Fort Leonard Wood, Mo. for his basic training, and then went to Fort Ord and Fort Benning for training in his military occupational specialty of infantry fire crewman. Duke was stationed stateside for 1967 and early 1968 and was assigned to companies at Fort Benning, Ga. and Fort Carson, Colo. His first assignment to Vietnam came in July 1968 when he arrived with E Company, 1st Battalion of the 11th Infantry.

In Vietnam, his duties on an indirect fire crew involved leading a mortar squad and then being a forward observer. Duke's Baptist faith brought him some measure of peace during the war and he once told his mother that "God is my point man." He served admirably in his roles, again gaining the respect of those who knew him. He finished his tour in Vietnam and returned home to Missouri on leave in April 1969. While home, he informed his mother that he had re-upped for another enlistment and that

Sergeant Francis Edwin Cortor, Jr., U.S. Army. Photo courtesy of Frances Cortor Turley.

Duke, upper left, with his three younger brothers. Photo courtesy of Frances Cortor Turley.

This photograph of Duke still hangs in a place of honor in his mother's home, 43 years after his death. Photo courtesy of Frances Cortor Turley.

he would be returning to Vietnam when his leave was up. He returned to Vietnam in June 1969 after waving to his mother from that TWA jet. That was the last time Frances Cortor Turley would see her son alive.

For his second tour, Duke was again assigned to the 1st Battalion of the 11th Infantry, this time with B Company. The battalion was stationed in Quang Tri province near Hill 174, an area that was referred to as Rocket Ridge. Duke was a sergeant by this time and was serving as a team leader within B Company. The battalion had received some casualties on the morning of October 21, 1969. Thomas Combs of Bravo Company was there that day and remembered the action. "Sergeant Cortor was not in my platoon, but he volunteered to go with me and a few other men in my unit on repeated attempts to recover the bodies of two men in my platoon who had been killed earlier during a mortar attack. Each time we crested the hill in the recovery attempt, we were driven back by additional mortar fire." Duke kept charging and was not dissuaded by the mortars falling all around him and sending shrapnel into the air. According to his Silver Star citation, Duke just kept going. "Although the company was ordered to withdraw from the hilltop, Sergeant Cortor, with complete disregard for his own safety, returned to his position, braving heavy enemy fire to recover the bodies of two of his fallen comrades." Duke had died as he lived, helping others.

After Duke's death, his mother struggled to keep going. "His brothers and others did not grow up knowing his love and concern for them–our family was no longer whole." She found solace helping returning veterans and the families of those that had lost sons to war. She became involved in the Gold Star Mothers of America and found comfort with women who had been through the same type of devastating loss that she had. She was elected national president of the group in 1996 and traveled with the group to Vietnam, where she stood near the place where Duke died and said a prayer. To this day, she remains active in Veterans causes, volunteering her time weekly operating a coffee cart at Jefferson National Barracks in St. Louis. While at the barracks, Frances Cortor Turley drives past the cemetery where her Duke is buried. Someday, she hopes to be buried beside him. ◆

People Reflected in Wall ◆ Leroy Lawson

Hot LZ ♦ Bernie Duff

MICHAEL D CASEY

Captain, Army • 6/18/46–1/23/70 • Panel 14W, Row 59

Capt. Michael Casey grew up without a father. John Wesley Casey died at the age of 47 in October of 1947, leaving behind his wife, Bertha, and seven children. The youngest of those was Michael Dale, born just 15 months before his father died. Bertha raised their children in the Brushy Mountain area on the western edge of the Ozark Mountains. The Casey children covered a wide age range, with the oldest, Doris, being 20 years older than Michael, who they called their "little squirrel." By the time Michael was born, his older brother John had already served in the Navy in World War II.

The Brushy Mountain area was rural and the Caseys' nearest neighbor was a quarter mile away. Their life was simple, and their house did not have electricity until 1950. The Casey children relied on themselves for entertainment. They spent countless hours roaming the foothills of the Ozarks, swimming at local swimming holes, and playing games such as red rover, kick the can and tag. The Caseys lived among some of the most beautiful sights nature had to offer. Their yard was not fenced in, and instead they were surrounded by trees, streams and the rolling hills of the western Ozarks. The family was Baptist and had a strong faith. There was a great deal of patriotism in the area, and many young men from the Brushy Mountain region went into the military to serve their country. Along with his brother John's service during World War II, Michael also had his father's Navy service in World War I and his brother Donald's Air Force service to look up to.

After her husband's death, Bertha was on her own. In addition to her husband's small pension from his Navy service, she took work wherever she could find it. "My mother made a living by the sweat of her brow," said her daughter Bonnie. Bertha did everything she could to put food on the table for her children: growing a garden, repairing and making clothes, and washing clothes in water heated in a kettle outside. Bertha also relied on her older children to make ends meet and help raise the younger ones. "We didn't have a lot of money, but we had a whole lot of love," said Bonnie.

In 1962, Michael told his older sister Bivra that he wanted to attend the Oklahoma Military Academy (OMA). Bivra was 17 years older than Michael and had been a key force in his life. She adored her younger siblings but took special interest in her youngest brother. According to their sister Bonnie, Bivra took Michael's request seriously. "She did some research about the academy and learned that it was rated as an outstanding military school. She came to the conclusion that since Michael had no father figure at home that this could be a God send for him. She decided he would benefit from the classes, the on campus organizations, and the expectations for the cadets. Bivra made sure that Michael understood the strict requirements for the OMA cadets, and after a series of discussions the decision was made: Michael would enter OMA for his junior year in 1962. "She was convinced that under the influence of those military men that Michael would become a great American. Bivra helped him enroll and paid all fees for him. Her love for her siblings and mother were never ending," said Bonnie.

The Oklahoma Military Academy was founded in 1919. The school, located in Claremore, Okla., was designed as a state-sponsored military school that would include academic courses, military training and vocational skill instruction. Cadets at OMA had to be 14 years of age, and while it started as a four-year secondary school, it would eventually grow to include a two-year junior college program. Known for its academic and military rigor, OMA grew in reputation as its graduates rose through the ranks of the U.S. military.

Michael started at OMA in the fall of 1962 and was immediately immersed in the campus life at the academy. He became involved in the chapel counsel, the drill team, the Saber Society and the marching band. Michael was a dedicated student who took his education seriously and was often rewarded for high marks while at OMA. He was also a member of both the outstanding company and best drill platoon. He graduated from OMA on May 4, 1964.

Maj. Gen. Teddy Sanford of the U.S. Army had accepted an invitation from the

Capt. Michael Dale Casey, U.S. Army. Photo courtesy of the Casey family.

Holding a rifle that was found in a cache of enemy weapons in 1970. Photo courtesy of the Casey family.

OMA Board of Regents to address the Class of 1964. Sanford had joined the Oklahoma National Guard in 1922 at the age of 15 and had gone on to distinguished service in World War II and Korea before being named commanding general of the Army's XIX Corps out of Fort Chafee, Ark. The words that Sanford spoke that day would change the lives of the Casey family forever.

Sanford began his speech with a topic that must have struck Michael immediately: growing up without a father. "My early life as a youth and in early manhood was not an easy one. I lost my father at the early age of 12. The thing that my friends had that I didn't have was a father. This, I never forgot, and I never mentioned. If I had any envy, this was it," Sanford began. A hero of two wars, Sanford had combat ribbons from all over the world and had been awarded virtually every military honor that the Army could bestow on a soldier. Yet Sanford had not grown up in a life of privilege, but in a rural area of Oklahoma, just as Michael had. He had also grown up without a father, just as Michael had.

Michael Casey and Maj. Gen. Teddy Sanford, Fort Chaffee, Ark., 1964. This meeting with General Sanford helped Michael decide to make the military a career. Photo courtesy of the Casey family.

When Michael Casey and the rest of the OMA Class of 1964 were listening to Sanford speak that day in May, the United States was less than three months away from becoming involved in Vietnam. Sanford touched on the fact that many of these young men would go on to a military life, and that they, like generations before them, were likely to see combat. As he spoke that day, many of the young men in the audience must have been seriously considering his words and wondering where their futures would take them. As high school graduates, they were now faced with many choices for their future. Sanford encouraged them to take those choices seriously and to consider what it meant to be a man in the world. "You must be a man and face up to the reality of the world," Sanford said. "You and I were born males, but it takes a lot of work, and thought, and will, and determination to be a man. Face life bravely, accept its responsibility."

Michael was so moved by Sanford's words that he wrote a letter of appreciation to the general expressing the newfound desire to embark on a military career. The general in turn invited Michael to visit Fort Chaffee as his special guest for a day. Michael was able to spend part of the day with the general and enjoyed the visit of Fort Chaffee. Michael also saw some of the activities of the 45th Division that day and his experience solidified his desire to enter the military.

Michael Casey looks back at his family as he prepares to board the plane for his first tour of duty in Vietnam, 1968. Photo courtesy of the Casey family.

Michael Casey receiving a Bronze Star Medal for valor from Gen. William Westmoreland in 1968. Photo courtesy of the Casey family.

Michael went back to OMA in the fall to continue his education at the junior college level. He completed a two-year degree in 1966 and headed to Oklahoma State University to study military science. Oklahoma State had previously been Oklahoma A&M University and was where Sanford received his degree in 1936. Michael spent one year there and was involved with the ROTC. He entered the Army Reserve in July 1967 and was commissioned as a second lieutenant. His service would begin in October. As he was not on active duty until the fall, Michael spent the summer of 1967 in Venezuela working with his brother-in-law Rufus Mock. Rufus, married to Michael's sister, Bivra, worked as a wire-line engineer on oil platforms. Michael's work that summer allowed him to learn a trade, and when he returned from Venezuela, he had a new plan. He would serve his country, and when his career with the military was over he would return to Venezuela and work on the rigs.

Michael Casey in the jungles of Vietnam.

Michael, his mother Bertha, and his nephew Joe Wes Long. This photo was taken the day that Michael left for his first tour in Vietnam in 1968. Photo courtesy of the Casey family.

While in Vietnam in 1969, Michael rested on a Cobra gunship waiting for a flight back to the operation base. Photo courtesy of the Casey family.

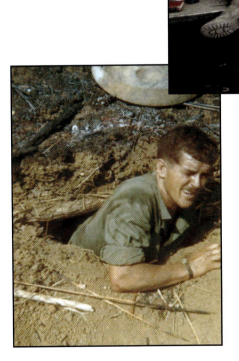

Michael exiting a Viet Cong spider hole after a search. Vietnam, 1969. Photo courtesy of the Casey family.

During the latter part of 1967 through September 1968, Michael received basic training at Fort Benning, Ga. followed by training in his military occupational specialty at Fort Hood, Texas. Michael's MOS was 1542, or infantry unit commander. In addition to the combat training that all soldiers received at Fort Hood, Michael would have the added responsibility of learning the skills necessary to lead a platoon into combat. Like most lieutenants, Michael was quite young. He was only 21 years old when he was training to take as many as 60 men into combat. While training, Michael was well aware that his leadership would take him to Vietnam. His sister Bonnie recalls that Michael had no hesitation about joining the military during a time of war. "He felt good about being in the Army and was ready to serve where needed. He was a soldier who was ready to accomplish, to his best God given ability, all the orders that were given to him by his commanders. He had no questions about it."

In October 1968, Michael arrived in Vietnam where he was promoted to first lieutenant and assigned to the Army's 7th Squadron of the 17th Cavalry. He was a platoon commander for A Troop, "The Ruthless Riders." Troop A had arrived in Vietnam in 1967. Casey was assigned to lead the aero rifle platoon. In Vietnam, an air cavalry troop was divided into three critically important platoons: the scout platoon, the weapons platoon and the rifle platoon. Each of the platoons had a different role to play in the operation of the unit. In an October 1968 letter, he reported that he had 31 men under his command; "The light observations and the Cobras go out and find Viet Cong, and if they can't take care of them from the air they load me and my men in the lift ships and insert us on the ground in the general vicinity and they guide us to them and we attempt to take care of them. Also, if one of our ships is shot down they insert us immediately so we can secure the ship." During the latter part of 1968, A Troop operated in the area of Ban Me Thout, and then moved near Pleiku and then southeast of Kontum. Action was heavy in the area at the time. Casey described the nights as "like the 4th of July. We just sleep through it."

By all accounts, Michael was well-respected by the men with whom he served. A former commanding officer of A Troop, Maj. H. Marshall once told his family how much Michael meant to his men. "The aero rifle platoon showed more respect for him than any other officer I ever met because he is one more among them." In photos taken by the men who served with Michael in Vietnam, it is evident that Michael truly was one of the guys. He can be seen playing cards, sharing a toast with both his commanding officer and a private, and guiding a helicopter to a safe landing. His soldiers called him "Blue," which in air cavalry squadron signified that he was the leader of the aero rifle, or blue, platoon. "By calling him 'Blue,' they mean more than just saying 'Sir,'" said Marshall. His actions on the battlefield gave his men even more reason to respect him; he would not send them anywhere that he would not go himself. In the photos that the men of A Troop shared, Michael can always be found right in the middle of things. By the end of his tour, he was wounded twice. The first wound occurred when he was checking out a Vietnamese 'spider hole' and an explosion ruptured his eardrum. The second was the result of a helicopter crash.

After serving a full year in Vietnam, Michael decided that his work there was not done, and he told his family that he had volunteered for another six months in-country. He was able to return to Oklahoma and visit his family before extending his stay. While he was home, he often talked about the men he served with. "Michael had a heartfelt and deep brotherly love for his warrior comrades on and off the battlefield," recalled his sister Bonnie. "When he returned home before going back for a second tour, at times he would stand and stare out the kitchen window then turn around and say, 'they are the best' and 'they are the greatest.'" However, he also realized the danger he was facing by going back. He spoke frankly with his sister Doris on that trip home, telling her that he understood that the odds weren't on his side. "Everyone is going to die," Michael told her. "I'm not afraid to die. I've lived with death for nearly a year. We are all going to die. It's not that we die, it's how we die."

When Michael returned to Vietnam in late September 1969, he was promoted to captain and given a relatively safe post within the 7/17th, that of a club officer. But, he was not comfortable with the idea of staying behind while his men went into combat. He again volunteered, this time to move back to a forward area where he could lead his troops. That was where he felt he belonged. Michael continued to serve as an aero rifle platoon leader with A Troop and was in that capacity on January 23, 1970. They were near Binh Dinh that day when they were called to attempt a rescue of a long range reconnaissance patrol that had been ambushed and suffered casualties. There were two members of the patrol trying to get a wounded soldier to the helicopter that Michael had just exited. He assisted these soldiers and then headed back to pick up another wounded patrol member. As he approached the soldier, he was struck with a barrage of gunfire from an enemy soldier. Michael immediately placed himself between the wounded man and the enemy and fired accurately enough to wound the enemy. Michael's wounds were fatal, but the soldier he was protecting survived and returned home.

Michael's death was felt throughout his hometown and the surrounding area. In one of the many thank you notes that she wrote after her son's funeral, Bertha Casey said, "Mike, being the youngest of my seven children, was the pride and joy of my entire family; therefore his death came as a great shock and loss." There were so many people that wanted to attend his funeral service at the First Baptist Church of Sallisaw, that it was broadcast over radio station KRBB. A news station from Tulsa reported news of his death, as did a newspaper in Maracaibo, Venezuela, where he had worked before his Army service.

In addition to the Silver Star he earned in the incident in which he lost his life, he was awarded the Bronze Star, two Purple Hearts, the Air Medal, the Army Commendation Medal and the Vietnamese Cross with Palm, the highest award the Vietnamese government could give to an American soldier. In a letter to Mike's mother after his death, Maj. Ronald Maxson said, "Mike had the greatest love. He lay down his life for his brother. We all are better men for having experienced the touch of Mike's life." ♦

Heading Home ♦ John Stuart

MIGUEL KEITH

Lance Corporal, Marine Corps • 6/2/51–5/8/70 • Panel 11W, Row 132

While he was in high school, Miguel Keith never kept a job for more than a month or two. He'd always find another, but his inability to stay in one place was frustrating for his parents. The Marine Corps, Miguel said, would be different. He was right.

Miguel Keith left North High School in Omaha, Neb. when he was 17 years old. He began his boot camp at Marine Corps Recruit Depot in San Diego in January 1969, and it became clear to both his parents and his fellow recruits that Miguel would find success. "A lot of boys had quit during boot camp," his mother said. "He told us he was going to finish this job and make us proud of him." His fellow recruits saw a young man with the ability to lead, a trait that his first grade teacher had seen almost a lifetime before. Sidney Foy, who taught Miguel at The Baird School in Texas, remembered that Miguel always took the lead.

His personality certainly helped. Miguel had a wonderful smile and a bright, caring nature that people seemed to respond to. He had many friends and would do anything for them. He could often be found helping people and was respectful of everyone, whether they were a friend or a complete stranger. Those who knew him remembered Miguel as dedicated, and when something or someone mattered to him he would never give up on them. He would carry that dedication into his Marine Corps service. Robert R. Gallegos was in Platoon 1081 with Miguel at Marine Corps Recruit Depot in San Diego in 1969. The two, both small in stature, often stood together in formation. "Even then, you could tell there was something special about Miguel." Robert remembered a young man whose passion for the Marine Corps was displayed at all times. "Miguel was driven to be the best at everything he did. He had a sense of duty far and above anyone else around us."

Lance Cpl. Miguel Keith, U.S. Marine Corps.

After he completed boot camp in San Diego, Miguel went to Camp Pendleton where he was trained in his military occupational specialty as a machine gunner. Almost immediately after his training at Camp Pendleton, he was told that he could go to Vietnam or request another assignment. He told his parents that he had made a commitment to his fellow Marines and would head overseas. Before leaving the United States, Miguel made a late-night phone call to his mother expressing nerves about what he was getting into. "I tried to make him believe he was ready to go and do a good job," said his mother. Miguel arrived in Vietnam in November 1969, less than a year after joining the Marine Corps.

Once in Vietnam, Miguel was assigned to the 1st Combined Action Group based in Quang Ngai province. While in Vietnam, he was promoted to the rank of lance corporal. Miguel wrote many letters home to his family, and most were directed toward his stepfather, who had raised him and had also been a Marine. "Dad, take care of Mom" was a common note in Miguel's letters. The longer he was in Vietnam, however, the more fear began to come through in his letters. The fighting was heavy, and in April, Miguel began to think, for the first time, that he might not make it home from Vietnam. He was right.

Lance Cpl. Miguel Keith, U.S. Marine Corps.

On May 8, 1970, Miguel was acting as a machine gunner when his platoon was attacked by enemy forces. He was wounded in the initial enemy attack but continued fighting against a force that outnumbered his platoon. Despite his wounds, he raced to check on the platoon's positions and noticed a group of five enemy soldiers approaching the command post. He fired his machine gun as he rushed toward them and took out three of the five before a hand grenade detonated beside him. He still did not fall. Bleeding heavily from his wounds, Miguel moved toward a group of more than 20 enemy soldiers. He charged the group, spraying machine gun fire among them as he attacked. He struck four of them and the others fled. His wounds finally became too much for him and Miguel died. He would have turned 19 years old in 25 days.

For his courageous actions on May 8, 1970, Miguel was awarded the Congressional Medal of Honor, the highest military honor bestowed by the United States. What Miguel did that day didn't surprise those who knew him. His mother said that Miguel was kindhearted and had always helped those he cared about. "He was always thinking of the other man…he would do anything for a friend." ♦

BARTON S CREED

Lieutenant Commander, Navy 4/3/45–3/13/71 • Panel 4W, Row 43

Bart's picture in the 1967 United States Naval Academy yearbook.

Bart and Susan at the U.S. Naval Academy's Ring Dance. Photo courtesy of Susan Creed Percy.

Bart and Susan goof around at the home of a family friend. Photo courtesy of Susan Creed Percy.

Barton Sheldon Creed was born on April 3, 1945 to Verna Creed and her husband, George Creed Jr. Bart was the youngest, being born two years after his brother, George III. Bart went to Peekskill Military Academy (PMA), where he breezed through the academics and was an all-state football player. The Creed brothers were often boys being boys, and they could be found playing football and baseball in the streets and parks of Peekskill, N.Y. with other neighborhood kids. At PMA, Bart was respected by the other students and younger students often looked up to him. Bart graduated from PMA in 1963, and earned an appointment to the United States Naval Academy in Annapolis, Md.

Although he wasn't sure he wanted to attend the Naval Academy, once he got there Bart soon began thoroughly enjoying the Annapolis experience. He enjoyed it so much that his academics struggled. He was on his battalion's lacrosse team all four of his years at Annapolis and was in the Gun Club. He kept himself busy, collecting stamps and coins, as well as adding to a collection of guns that his father had started for him. Bart liked to have fun and had a strong sense of adventure. Classmate Robert Treis called Bart "wild as a hatter, crazy as a bedbug, but nothing too dangerous." The USNA 1967 yearbook, *The Lucky Bag,* said that, "Putting his magnetic personality to use on the weekends made the weekdays rough, and Plebe Calculus became a battle but Bart won. His personality and desire will contribute to his success in his chosen career."

In 1965, Bart was a midshipman in his junior year at the Naval Academy. He had been on a summer cruise, and the ship had docked at Myrtle Beach, S.C. By coincidence, Susan Page was also in Myrtle Beach that summer. Susan, a junior at Greensboro College, was visiting her brother John, who was stationed at Myrtle Beach with the Air Force. One summer evening, Susan and a friend had joined her brother at the Officer's Club for a meal. That same night, Bart walked into the club and into Susan's life. "Right away, Bart stood out, and not just because he was wearing a Navy uniform in an Air Force club," said Susan. She remembers how tall and handsome Bart was, and soon she and the 20-year-old sailor with dark blonde hair were talking. Bart and Susan began dating nearly immediately, and Bart's days of chasing women were over. The pair were engaged to be married in the fall of 1966.

Bart graduated from the Naval Academy on June 7, 1967. That day, he heard of an opening at the Naval Academy chapel. A wedding had been cancelled, and the hard to secure Chapel was now available for him and Susan to be married. It seemed like fate, as though he and Susan were meant to be married there. Susan and Bart's parents only had one problem with the idea: the chapel's availability was for the next day. Bart's sense of adventure won out over Susan's hesitations, and the wedding was held the next day, June 8, 1967.

After Bart's commissioning, the graduation and the wedding, the new Mr. and Mrs. Barton Creed began their lives and Bart's military career. Bart was going to fly planes for the Navy and the first stop for pilot training was Pensacola, Fla. The six-week program at Pensacola led to additional training at Naval Air Station (NAS) Meridian, Miss. and NAS Jacksonville, Fla. Eventually, Bart and Susan would be stationed at NAS Lemoore in central California. By 1970, they had two children, a son, Scott, born in 1969 and a daughter, Judith Page, born in 1970. Bart adored his children, and though his aviation training was rigorous, Bart was able to spend time with the kids. Despite the fun he loved to have, Bart was highly respected by his fellow aviators.

Bart and Susan both knew his aviation training would take him to Southeast Asia at some point, but it wasn't in him to worry. "Bart's motto was 'don't worry 'til you have to,'" said Susan. "He felt it was his duty to take part; he wanted to go to Vietnam. He believed in liberty and thought helping the people of Vietnam was a noble thing." Bart had been training on the A7 Corsair II at Jacksonville and it was this single-seat plane that he would fly in Vietnam. The Navy's A7E Corsair II was a derivative of the F-8 fighter jet, but it had been streamlined and redesigned so that it was more cost-effective and efficient. It was accurate, fast and highly maneuverable, perfect for the types of flights it would need to take in the skies over Vietnam, Laos and Cambodia.

In October 1970, Bart and Susan made the trip from NAS Lemoore to Oakland, where Bart would board the USS Ranger and head to

Vietnam. Susan remembers the Ranger being "imposing and foreboding." Susan noticed that her husband seemed energized by the reality that he was on his way to do what he had been trained to do. Susan was nervous as she saw her husband off, but tried not to let Bart know of her fears. She sent Bart off to Vietnam and went home to care for their children, both under the age of two.

The USS Ranger arrived in the Gulf of Tonkin in November 1970. Bart was serving with Attack Squadron 113, "The Stingers." While on the Ranger, Bart made many friends. He was friendly with men from all walks of life and made no distinction between officers and enlisted men. Between March and November, Bart had flown more than 100 missions off the Ranger. Combat was heavy in the areas he was flying, and Bart was cautious and realistic about the combat he was seeing.

On the morning of March 13, 1971, Bart took off from the USS Ranger in his A7E Corsair II. His mission that morning was to bomb a section of the Ho Chi Minh Trail in northern Laos. The trail, once barely noticeable and difficult to travel, had become 12,000 miles of well-maintained trails and paved roads that stretched throughout Cambodia, Laos and Vietnam. The Ho Chi Minh Trail was the key to North Vietnamese strategy and operations, as it was necessary to move troops, supplies and weapons throughout the region. Bart launched from the USS Ranger that morning and headed toward the Laotian portion of the Ho Chi Minh Trail. He was the leader of a two-plane team that was headed to attack entrenched enemy positions. He had completed the bombing run and volunteered to go after some enemy trucks that had been spotted in the area. He was in the area of Ban Sung, an area covered by heavy jungle that had been the seat of North Vietnamese activity, when his aircraft started receiving heavy fire from anti-aircraft artillery. At about 11:15 a.m., his plane was hit by fire from enemy ground forces, and Bart was forced to eject as his A7E Corsair II went hurtling to the ground.

Bart survived the ejection and landed in the jungle-covered valley alive but injured. Once on the ground, he reported to the Ranger that he had probably broken an arm and a leg from the ejection, but he was able to give his position on the ground and stay in contact. The crew of the Ranger scrambled to find and rescue Bart. A forward air controller was able to establish and maintain contact with Bart very quickly, and search and rescue helicopters were sent to the area. The first attempt to rescue Bart was made shortly after he went down. On that attempt, the rescue helicopter was able to hover over Bart's position despite noticing movement in the immediate area. A rescue man was able to get close to the ground over Bart, but the enemy began heavy fire and the helicopter had to retreat because of damage to the machine and injuries to the crew. Shortly after this attempt, Bart sent a transmission, "Pick me up, pick me up now! They are here!" This would be the last transmission received from Bart.

Despite no longer hearing from Bart, the rescue attempt continued. Search and rescue planes and two helicopters attempted to clear the area where Bart made his last transmission, but the ground fire became significantly more intense and both helicopters were hit. Both of the helicopters on this rescue attempt failed to make it back to the base and there were injuries. Rescue efforts continued. By this point, it was determined that Bart had been moved as he could no longer be seen by the search and rescue plane, and his parachute was also in a new location. About 15 minutes after the second attempt, a third attempt failed, again because of heavy ground fire. After dark, they tried again, and a helicopter crew member finally made it to the ground. There was no sign of Bart.

The morning of March 14, a FAC was given permission to fly over the area where Bart had gone down. There was still no sign of him, but his parachute had been spread out on the ground about 500 meters from his last known position. This was believed by many to be a plot by the North Vietnamese Army to draw American troops to the area. Naval aviators, who had been through survival training as Bart had in Pensacola, would never draw attention to themselves in this way. Pilots continued to search for Bart in the area, but no further trace of him was seen.

Susan was at her college reunion when she learned over the phone that Bart had been shot down. Bart's parents were at home in Peekskill. They only knew that he had been shot down; details of the incident were initially scarce. Once they heard that Bart's plane had been hit and he was missing, all they could do was wait. In North Carolina with her mother and children, Susan wanted so badly to believe her husband had lived. After the initial notification of the incident, the Creeds had been told that Bart had been alive on the ground and had communicated with rescuers. As time passed, they all began to struggle with the questions about what had happened to their husband and son. There didn't seem to be anyone that Susan could

Bart in the cockpit of an F4E. Photo courtesy of Susan Creed Percy.

Bart with his son, Scott Sheldon Creed. Photo courtesy of Susan Creed Percy.

Lt. Cmdr. Barton Sheldon Creed, U.S. Navy. Photo courtesy of Susan Creed Percy.

talk to about Bart, and after a bit longer in North Carolina, her mother suggested she go back to NAS Lemoore where she would be surrounded by those who had known and loved Bart. This proved to be the right move, as Susan would find comfort with the families of Bart's fellow aviators and with the men of Bart's squadron when they returned from Vietnam.

As more time passed however, Bart's missing in action status became hard on the Creed family. Initially, Verna Creed believed her son was alive. The Navy had told her that rescuers had seen Bart alive and they believed he had been captured. "For two years, we presumed he would come out of Laos alive. We were shocked when the list of prisoners was released and his name wasn't on it." By the end of the war and the last American deaths in 1975, Bart had been officially declared presumed killed in action. He was posthumously promoted to lieutenant commander. He was 25.

Although she had remarried, Susan never forgot Bart. She spoke often of Bart and her children knew who their father was. "Scott and Page learned about their father through those who knew him best. They knew the good parts of him and the bad parts of him. We never spared them the details." Susan also made sure that George Jr. and Verna Creed were involved in her children's lives. It was important that they knew Bart was being remembered, and that he was a part of his children's lives. Both of Bart's children enjoyed military life, and both would choose to attend the U.S. Naval Academy, just as their father had done. Scott would go on to be a Marine aviator, and Page would serve on an aircraft carrier, caring for planes similar to those her father flew.

As years passed, the Creed family was realistic about Bart's fate. "At first, I went back and forth between believing he had been captured and that he was gone. I just wanted him to be alive," said Susan. "His parents were very realistic as time passed, and they became very involved in the National League of Families." The National League of POW/MIA Families was founded in 1970 and was an organization designed to facilitate the release of all prisoners of war and discover what had happened to those who had not come home. Knowing that there were others out there waiting for word on their husbands, sons and brothers was a relief to the Creed family.

Also in the early 1970s, an organization called Voices in Vital America (VIVA) had been founded to bring attention to the issue of prisoners of war and those missing in action in Vietnam. VIVA's largest publicity tool was a simple silver or copper bracelet bearing the name of a POW or MIA in Vietnam. The bracelets became were popular in the 1970s, with VIVA eventually distributing nearly five million bracelets during its seven year existence. Verna Creed received a bracelet with Bart's name on it and wore it for the rest of her life. In 1996, she had worn it for 25 years when she told a North Carolina newspaper, "I don't know why I still wear it, I guess it's just sentiment. I'll never take it off. I know he's not alive. I have not thought of such a thing, but the bracelet is just a part of him." According to her daughter-in-law Susan, she wore it until her death in 2007. She had waited 36 years for her Bart to come home, but there was still no sign of him.

In May of 2011, the U.S. government's Joint Prisoners of War, Missing in Action Accounting Command (JPAC) informed the Creed family that they had strong evidence of Bart's fate. A group of North Vietnamese soldiers serving in the area where Bart was last seen reported that he had indeed survived the crash, but that he had been killed shortly thereafter. Bart had never been a prisoner, and had most likely died the same day his plane went down. For the first time, Susan felt sure that her husband Bart had died in the jungles of Laos. "JPAC believes that they have strong evidence of where Bart is buried, and that they are getting closer to finding him. The tree line has moved and the jungle has grown over, but I am hopeful they will find him." ♦

Bart Creed's MIA bracelet rests among others in the Vietnam Veterans Memorial Collection. Photo by Kimberly Dyer.

ALVIN ADIKAI Jr.

Private First Class, Army • 1/21/49–3/14/71 • Panel 4W, Row 45

During the Vietnam War, more than 42,000 Native Americans served in Vietnam, and 90 percent of them enlisted to serve their country. Native Americans had defended their homeland for centuries, and 226 men who identified themselves as Native American gave their lives in Vietnam. Alvin Adikai Jr. was one of those 226.

Born on January 21, 1949 to Alvin Adikai Sr. and Ann Keedah in Gallup, N.M., Alvin was the oldest of the couple's two sons. His younger brother, Leon, was born five years later. Eventually, Alvin's parents divorced and his mother married Ralph Bennett. In 1960, Alvin's sister, Ralphina Bennett, was born. The family lived in Window Rock, Ariz., 27 miles northwest of Gallup and just over the Arizona/New Mexico border. Named for the 200 foot tall rock that overlooked the town, Window Rock was comprised primarily of Navajo, and was the administrative capitol for the Navajo tribe. Ann Bennett worked as a secretary for the Navajo Tribal Council.

Alvin was a quiet young man who loved sports, music and reading. He was unfailingly polite and respectful and could often be found with a book in his hand. Although he was small in stature, Alvin's athletic skills were known throughout Window Rock. While growing up, he played little league baseball and basketball, and the love for those sports continued when Alvin attended Window Rock High School. He played second base for the baseball team and received three varsity letters in the sport. He was also the point guard on the basketball team, lettering twice in that sport. Chucko, as his friends called him, loved the music of the day, including Led Zeppelin, The Doors, Jimi Hendrix and Janis Joplin. Alvin's grades were excellent and he graduated with high marks in the class of 1967.

After graduation, Alvin headed to the Western State College of Engineering in Inglewood, Calif. While he was there, his sister and mother took the train out to visit him. "He took us to Disneyland and rode every ride with me. We also went to the movies, where he and I watched a "Hells Angels" movie marathon," remembered Ralphina. "My best memories of him include having him as a protector. As the baby in the family, my older brother Leon always teased and tormented me, and Alvin would always come to my rescue." Alvin graduated from Western State with an associate's degree in electronic technology.

Like so many Native Americans before him, Alvin enlisted in the U.S. Army in September 1969. After signing up for a three-year tour of duty, he attended basic training at Fort Lewis, Wash., and then was sent to Fort Sill, Okla. for advanced individual training. His military occupational specialty was in line with his education and skills. He would serve as a 31B20, or field radio mechanic. After completion of his training, he was assigned to the 4th Battalion of the 18th Infantry in what was then West Berlin, Germany. He arrived in Germany in February 1970, and stayed there until August of that year when tragedy called him home.

On August 9, 1970, Alvin's younger brother, Leon, drowned at the age of 16. The Adikai/Bennett family was devastated by Leon's untimely death, and Alvin felt guilty leaving the family so soon after his brother's death. But he had made a commitment and just two months after Leon died, Alvin was in Vietnam. Assigned to the headquarters company of 2nd Battalion, 502nd Infantry, Alvin was a good soldier who kept to himself. He served ably in Vietnam, quietly doing his job. He never expressed any fear to his family while he was in Vietnam, and never commented on the war or what he was doing. Five months after arriving in Vietnam, Alvin was assigned to a mine sweeping team. Norm Friedman was also assigned to this detail. "We were told the morning of March 14, 1971 that we were on detail for a mine sweep along a dirt road from Mai Loc Village to Highway One. This detail was done every morning. About halfway to the end, our sergeant told us that since we hadn't found any mines previously that the guys with the mine sweeping devices should get on the truck with the rest of us and drive to Highway One. There were seven of us on detail, and we picked up four ARVN soldiers on the way. Eleven altogether with some guys hanging off the front bumper and some dangling off the rear tailgate. A few minutes later, as we rounded a curve, the enemy were waiting for us with what's called a command detonated type mine." The enemy saw the truck approaching the explosive device, waited until it was directly over it, and detonated the mine. Four of the men on the truck were killed, including Alvin. He was 22. ♦

Pfc. Alvin Adikai, Jr. U.S. Army.

Alvin at basic training at Fort Lewis, Wash. in November 1969. Photo courtesy of Ralphina Hernandez.

Alvin's senior portrait from Window Rock High School. He graduated with the class of 1967. Photo courtesy of Ralphina Hernandez.

JOHNNY ARTHUR

Specialist 5th Class, Army • 9/6/49–6/10/71 • Panel 3W, Row 71

John Arthur Sr. and his wife, Evangeline, had a big and close-knit family. The family's farm in Fruitland, N.M. was home to their nine children, along with a niece and nephew that they raised as their own. The farm had a two-acre garden where Evangeline grew tomatoes, carrots, beets, green beans, peppers and onions. Beyond that were acres of corn, watermelon, potatoes and alfalfa, and orchards filled with fruit. The crops were more than enough to feed the large family after Evangeline canned them in the fall.

The family lived on the Navajo Reservation, and John Sr. worked as an irrigation ditch rider for the tribe when he wasn't working on the farm. Evangeline was busy raising the children, but still managed to be involved in church and community activities. Their son Johnny was one of the younger members of the large Arthur brood, with five siblings and his two cousins older than him. Like most of the family, he worked on the farm in the summer time. Johnny attended Navajo Methodist Mission in Farmington, N.M. This was a private boarding school in a nearby town that bordered the reservation. All of the Arthur children went there after John Sr. and Evangeline decided that their children wouldn't attend Bureau of Indian Affairs Schools as they had.

Spc. 5th Class Johnny Arthur, U.S. Army. Photo courtesy of Ryndall Arthur.

Johnny was a very intelligent student at the Navajo Methodist Mission, but after 10th grade he decided to transfer to Kirtland Central High School. He preferred to be closer to home, and by attending Kirtland he could live at home, but Kirtland was 15 miles from the Arthur farm, and there was no bus service. Johnny was dedicated to his studies. He hitched rides to school. He loved horses and was a jockey for a time. Johnny also played football while in high school.

After high school, Johnny worked for the Department of Economic Opportunity doing home improvement and repairs for the Navajo community. It was through his job that he met Judith Bekise. The two would marry in 1969. Together they had one son, Ryndall, and Johnny would adopt Judith's son, Dion.

As the war in Vietnam wore on, Johnny decided that he needed to serve. The military could provide him an opportunity to help his country while at the same time allowing him to care for his family. He enlisted in the Army in September 1969. He was not the first member of his family to join the military, with four uncles having served before him. Johnny joined with several of his friends. His cousin, Ernest, who had been raised as Johnny's brother, joined the Marines at the same time. Johnny's family was proud of his patriotism but was afraid as they had seen so many losses on the evening news.

In Vietnam, Johnny sits inside a UH-1C helicopter. Photo courtesy of Bruce Whitney.

Johnny did his basic training at Fort Ord, Calif. and then went to Fort Bragg, N.C. for aviation brigade training. He knew he would have to go to Vietnam, and he was not afraid. In fact, he was proud, and he wanted to be a part of what was happening and do his share. Johnny's tour of Vietnam started in September 1970, and he was assigned to the 192nd Company of the 1st Aviation Brigade. He worked as a mechanic on helicopters and enjoyed flying. He hoped to use the skills he was learning in the Army to be an airline mechanic after he returned from the war.

On June 10, 1971, Johnny was serving as a crew chief on an Army Uh-1C helicopter. The helicopter, called a Huey, was to provide supporting fire for another helicopter that was extracting some Vietnamese troops from an area near Pleiku. Johnny, the door gunner Louie Gooch Montoya and the two pilots were doing their job when they were hit with enemy fire. The pilot put in a mayday call, but the helicopter crashed into the jungle. The two pilots were pulled from the fire by a crew chief from another helicopter in the area, but Johnny and Montoya were killed in the crash. Johnny was 21. ♦

Johnny in a UH-1C helicopter. The soldier on the right is Louie Gooch Montoya, who was also killed in the crash on June 10, 1971. Photo courtesy of CPT Robert E. Goolsby.

ROBERT A BRETT Jr

Captain, Air Force • 4/16/48–9/29/72 • Panel 1W, Row 75

Melissa Brett Coven describes her older brother, Robert Arthur Brett Jr. as "an amazing, funny, typically frustrating older brother." He never met anyone he couldn't get along with, and Melissa said she was 10 years old before she realized that her big brother's given name wasn't "Lefty." He "excelled in every endeavor but most especially if it was in pursuit of his goal to fly."

Lefty was born in 1948 to Robert Brett Sr. and his wife, Florence. Lefty had two brothers and two sisters. Robert Brett Sr. was an Air Force officer, and his postings took his family all over the U.S. and Japan. The Brett children grew up on air bases, which Melissa described as "like small towns…we always had lots of kids to play with." From his earliest days, Lefty wanted to be an Air Force pilot.

Lefty loved playing baseball, and Sandy Koufax was his favorite player. Growing up, he liked watching the television show "Combat," and named his dog after the character Kirby, primarily so when they were hunting he could repeat the show's signature line, "Take the point, Kirby." The family settled in Oregon in 1962 when Robert Sr. was stationed at Adair Air Station, and Lefty graduated from Corvallis High School in 1966. He went to Oregon State University, where he joined AFROTC. While at Oregon State, he went to Williams Air Force Base in Arizona for undergraduate pilot training. His goal was to become a pilot with the Thunderbirds, the Air Force demonstration team that flew F-4s in precision formations. Lefty earned a degree in political science as a distinguished military graduate and was commissioned into the Air Force in 1970.

Two years before his graduation, Lefty had married Patrice Costello. The young couple's first few years of marriage were filled with Lefty's training, but by 1972 things had settled down a bit and they welcomed a daughter, Camille, born in January. Lefty believed in what the United States was doing in Vietnam and wanted to be there doing his part. His father had been in Vietnam in 1966-1967 and Lefty believed it was now his turn. He left for Vietnam in the fall of 1972, when his daughter was only nine months old.

"Lefty" Brett during his pilot training at Williams Air Force Base in Arizona. Photo courtesy of Melissa Brett Coven.

Lefty was stationed in Thailand at Takhli Airbase with 429th Tactical Fighter Squadron of the 474th Tactical Fighter Wing. He flew F-111s, an Air Force tactical fighter plane. Shortly after he arrived in Vietnam, he was in command of an F-111 flown by Maj. William Coltman. They were flying through a thunderstorm over Laos on September 28, on the way to North Vietnam, when they went out of radio contact. When they failed to return to Takhli Airbase by the early morning hours of September 29, they were declared missing in action.

Robert Brett Sr. had retired from the Air Force as a lieutenant colonel the year before Lefty went to Vietnam. After Lefty's disappearance, Robert Brett was persistent in his efforts to find his son. He served on the board of the National League of POW/MIA Families. He wanted to make sure that his son and others like him were not forgotten. "If the American public allows the administration to write off these men, then I feel it is a national tragedy, a national shame that each citizen will have to bear the responsibility for."

The Brett family's long search for Lefty ended in 2002. On August 28, 2000, his remains and those of Coltman were recovered and identified in 2002. Nearly 30 years after the F-111 went down, Lefty was finally home. "The crash site in Laos was excavated in 2000 and some small bone fragments (too small and degraded for DNA testing) and a tooth were found along with identifiable pieces of the aircraft," said Lefty's sister Melissa. "The tooth was identified as belonging to Col. Coltman. The bone fragments are in a co-mingled grave at Arlington with both their names on the headstone." ♦

Henry L. Aderholt

Sergeant, Army • 5/20/47–12/12/72 • Panel 12W, Row 83

Sgt. Henry Lester Aderholt, U.S. Army. Photo courtesy of Karen Hopkins.

Photo courtesy of Karen Hopkins.

Margaret Aderholt holding her five week old son Henry Lester at Turkey Creek Falls, Pinson, Ala., June 1947. Photo courtesy of Karen Hopkins.

In 1962, Judy Woodall and Henry Aderholt had a lunch study hall together at Hewitt-Trussville High School in Alabama. Judy was from Center Point, and Henry from Pinson, but both of those small towns sent their students to Hewitt-Trussville as they were without high schools of their own. Judy had home economics right before the lunch study, and she sometimes brought Henry whatever they had made in class that day. The first thing she brought him was blueberry muffins. Judy fell in love with the handsome, tall, broad-shouldered Henry almost immediately. The two grew closer, occasionally getting in trouble for holding hands and cuddling in their English class. The next year, as 11th graders, they no longer had classes together. But they did have the same history teacher. One day, Henry borrowed Judy's history book and wrote "H.A. + J.W." in it. The next day, she did the same. In his auto mechanics class, Henry made Judy a heart out of metal scraps and put "H.A. + J.W." in it. She gladly accepted, and he gave her a ring that had two hearts joined with a small diamond in the center. "By then we knew we would always be together," said Judy, looking back on those early years. "He knew that I loved him, and I knew that he loved me."

Henry Lester Aderholt was born on May 20, 1947, the only child of Margaret and Lester Aderholt. Lester Aderholt, called Red by those who knew him, was an auto mechanic and his wife, Margaret, stayed at home. The family called him Henry Lester to distinguish him from his grandfather Henry Shepard Sr. and his uncle Henry Shepard Jr. In 1955, Red passed away from tuberculosis at the Memphis VA Hospital. His mother eventually married Emmett Hopkins, and Henry soon had a sister, Karen. Henry was 11 years old when Karen was born, and he doted on his younger sister. As a little girl, Karen had trouble saying Henry's name, so she began calling him "Hingie." The name stuck.

Eventually, Henry's mother and stepfather began moving around as part of Emmett's job on construction pipelines, and Henry moved to live with his maternal grandmother, Daisy, and his uncle Clyde Shepard on their 280-acre dairy farm in Pinson. A small, rural town about 12 miles north of Birmingham, Pinson was the kind of town where everyone knew everyone. Henry grew up in this environment, spending time with the large extended family that frequented his grandmother Daisy's farm. He and his cousins trained the horses and were often out riding. He had picked up a love for fixing things from his father and enjoyed working on cars and rebuilding engines. Intelligent, Henry did well in school, but after transferring to a high school in nearby Tarrant, he dropped out. He wanted to earn money, so he went out to work for his step-father, Emmett, who at the time was living in South Dakota. When he'd earned enough money to buy a car, he came back home to Pinson and his love, Judy.

Once back in Pinson, Henry got a job working in the parts department of Ed Mollison's Chevrolet. Just as on his family's dairy farm and at his previous job at a Pinson service station, Henry was a hard worker. By this time, Judy had taken community college courses and was working as an operator at South Central Bell. Henry worked during the day at the Chevy dealer and Judy worked many weekends and nights. They were together whenever possible and Henry often went to church with Judy's family on Sundays. Judy's family thought highly of Henry, and Henry often spent time with Judy's father, Leslie, in the small workshop in the back of the Woodall's Center Point home.

The couple married on October 29, 1966 in the church that Henry often attended with the Woodalls. After their marriage, they first lived in a small trailer on his grandmother's land in Pinson and then in an apartment in Birmingham. They were both working but didn't have much money. "We had a car and a bed," said Judy. "We didn't have a whole lot, but we knew we belonged together and that's all there was."

During the summer of 1967, a letter came in the mail telling Henry to report to Montgomery for his Army physical. Henry went and passed the tests with flying colors. He told Judy he knew he would be leaving soon. A visit to an Army recruiter verified that and the news that his induction letter was in the mail led Henry to enlist. The recruiter promised him a four-month up-front leave if he enlisted for an extra year and Henry decided that was the best plan. Those months would give him the time to get his beloved Judy settled in closer to Center Point, as he hated the idea of her living in Birmingham by herself.

Henry left for basic training at Fort Benning, Ga. in January 1968. Both his mother and his maternal grandmother were scared to death for him. They understood that Henry felt it was his duty to serve his country, but they were still worried. Judy understood Henry's need to serve but didn't really understand military life. Still, she made the four-hour drive from Center Point to Fort Benning as often as she could, driving up in the early morning and returning late at night. After completing basic training, Henry was sent to Fort Leonard Wood, Mo. for advanced individual training in heavy truck equipment and operations. He finished first in his class.

By June 1968, Henry was in Vietnam. Stationed at Cam Ranh Bay, Henry was part of 539th Supply Company and was working in the motor pool. In a letter to Leslie and Frances Woodall (who he called Maw and Paw), he described his duties and responsibilities. Henry worked as a mechanic, repairing anything that needed fixing on the vehicles. He worked 13-15 hour days, seven days a week. He was supposed to have two half days off per week, but had only had one in the month he'd been at Cam Ranh Bay. The hard-working Henry didn't seemed to mind, telling Paw Woodall, "When I'm working the time passes faster. I've only got 339 days left."

In March 1969, Henry and Judy met in Hawaii for Henry's R&R leave from Vietnam. It was on this trip to Hawaii that Henry told Judy he wanted to do another tour in Vietnam. "Henry always wanted to help someone," Judy said. "He was very dedicated and very helpful. He just had that sort of spirit." Henry told Judy that if he went back to Vietnam, the Army would cut a year from the service he owed them. After he came back from Vietnam, he would be out of the Army. After finishing up his first tour, Henry returned to the U.S. in December 1969.

For his second tour of Vietnam, Henry's MOS had changed. This time, he served with the 119th Assault Helicopter Company stationed at Camp Holloway near Pleiku in South Vietnam. This time, he was a door gunner on a UH-1H Huey helicopter. The door gunner on a Huey was responsible for firing at ground targets during the helicopter's flight. Henry loved being on the helicopters and often told Judy and Karen how he wanted to learn to fly them one day. He told Karen that he was thinking of making his living as a helicopter pilot after he got out of the Army.

On February 14, 1970, Henry was the door gunner on Gator 586, a Huey with tail number 66-16586. Gator 586 was on a resupply mission heading to LZ Challenge. They came under heavy fire, and during the firefight, Henry was hit in the abdomen with a single bullet. He fell off of the helicopter and landed on his back. As the chopper took off from LZ Challenge, it was still receiving enemy fire. Henry told ground troops near him to tell the choppers to wait for an air strike before returning to pick him up. Even gravely wounded, Henry was thinking about the men of his unit and didn't want them risking all of their lives for his. The bullet from the enemy AK-47 had destroyed many of his internal organs and partially severed his spine. As he lay on the ground, Henry was injured so badly that the morphine was not helping. He was eventually evacuated to a field hospital, where he underwent a surgical procedure that circumvented the injured parts of his stomach and connected his esophagus directly to his intestines.

While Henry was being treated in Vietnam, his young wife went on with her life, unaware of her husband's injuries. She knew nothing of what had happened to Henry until one week later, when she received a telegram telling her that her husband had been "slightly wounded" in combat in Vietnam. The following day, Judy received another telegram telling her that Henry's condition was "severe," and that there was "cause for concern." Apparently Henry's injury was serious enough that the Army wanted his mother's current address so that she could be notified. Desperate to know more about what had happened to Henry, Judy began calling the Department of the Army. Initially, she was told that she would hear more in two weeks. "I told them that there was no way I would wait two weeks to learn more about my husband. I called a friend who worked for a congressman and he was able to expedite the process. I got a call from the Army, but all they would tell me was that Henry was paralyzed from the waist down."

Judy finally saw her husband when he arrived at Martin Army Hospital at Fort Benning. Her husband, who had been 6 feet, 1 inch, 210 pounds of muscle when she had last seen him in January, was now skin and bones. Henry was very weak and underwent another surgery while at Martin. During this procedure, Henry's heart stopped, but doctors were able to revive him. The 23-year-old Henry got well enough to be sent home to Alabama. In October of 1970, an Army physical

Judy Woodall and Henry Aderholt on their wedding day, 1966. Photo courtesy of Karen Hopkins.

Henry and Judy in front of their Camaro in 1969. Photo courtesy of Karen Hopkins.

Henry and his mother Margaret. Photo courtesy of Karen Hopkins.

Henry and his little sister, Karen, at Shepherd's Dairy in Pinson, Ala. in 1961. Photo courtesy of Karen Hopkins.

evaluation board declared Henry's injuries to be a result of armed conflict in Vietnam and granted him an honorable discharge because of his disability.

After his discharge from the hospital and the Army, Henry and Judy moved in with her parents in Center Point. Henry was lucky that the wound hadn't killed him, and that he wasn't totally paralyzed. His spinal cord had been 60 percent severed, with the other 40 percent only having been damaged. This allowed Henry, who had to be in a wheelchair the majority of the time, some movement of his right leg. He had enough movement that he could work the pedals of a car, and one of the first things Henry did when he was back in Alabama was buy a Volkswagen Beetle. He and Judy drove it down to Fort Rucker in southeast Alabama to visit Danny Stewart, who had been a helicopter pilot during Henry's second tour, and the two had become friends. Danny and Henry cut the little Beetle in half to make a dune buggy that Henry could drive. Back in Center Point, Paw Woodall crafted a wooden stick with a notch to help Henry work the clutch.

A year or so after Henry's discharge, he and Judy built a house 25 miles from Pinson. The VA helped them build the house so that it accommodated Henry's wheelchair. Henry was still very gaunt and quite weak. Judy began to notice that he was not gaining weight and while he didn't get much worse, he never really got better, either. "I didn't realize what was happening to him, and I don't know that he did, either," Judy said. He began to do less and less, and soon was spending most of his time in bed or sitting in the wheelchair. By this point, his condition was worsening. One day Judy found him in bed, staring off into space. She tried to get her husband to talk to her and to tell her what his name was. When Henry couldn't, she knew something was terribly wrong. She and his uncle got Henry to the hospital, but they were told that Henry would never be well enough to go home.

In the hospital, Henry's condition worsened. He was suffering from malabsorption syndrome, a condition that limits the intestine's ability to absorb nutrients from food. Although he had been eating, Henry's body simply could not turn the food into what it needed to survive and he was slowly wasting away. After a call from Judy, Henry's mother and sister drove through the night to be with him. His wife, sister and mother were by his side when Henry succumbed to his injuries on December 12, 1972, two years and 10 months after his injury in Vietnam.

Because Henry had been shot in Vietnam and died of his wounds, Judy assumed Henry's name would be on the Vietnam Veterans Memorial when it was dedicated in 1982. In time, however, she learned that Henry's name had not been included among those who died in Vietnam. As Judy wasn't aware of how the military worked, she simply went on with her life and didn't think much about The Wall. But she never stopped thinking of Henry. Even though she had remarried and was raising two children on her own after a divorce, she often thought of her first love.

In 2006, Judy received an invitation in the mail to join the Gold Star Wives. The organization was founded in 1945 by World War II widows and is designed to provide support and friendship to the spouses of those who lose their lives while serving in the U.S. military. When she became involved in the Birmingham, Ala. chapter of the group, Judy began to realize that Henry's name should be on The Wall. With Henry's records in hand, Judy contacted the Vietnam Veterans Memorial Fund about having Henry's name added. In April of 2011, Judy was notified that her request had been approved and that Henry's name would at last appear in the place of honor it so deserved.

On May 30, 2011 Judy was in Washington D.C. to see her late husband's name officially added to The Wall along with the names of four other soldiers. The VVMF had also honored Judy that day by asking her to lead the crowd in the Pledge of Allegiance. As she placed her hand over her heart and recited those words, Judy stood in front of the black granite wall that now bore her Henry's name. His name brought the total number of names on The Wall to 58,272. ◆

Henry and Judy.
Photo courtesy of Karen Hopkins.

Judy leading the Pledge of Allegiance at the VVMF Memorial Day ceremony on May 30, 2011 in Washington, D.C. Photo by Dave Scavone.

EMMET R GALBRETH II

Captain, Air Force • 9/28/43–5/28/73 • Panel 1W, Row 118

Reid during flight training at Sheppard Air Force Base. Photo courtesy of Sandi Galbreth.

Located in Xieng Khouang Province in northern Laos, the Plain of Jars is filled with massive sandstone urns and unexploded bombs. The urns most likely date to a civilization more than 1,500 years old, and the bombs were dropped between 1965 and 1973. The urns were most likely used as part of a burial ritual, and the bombs were used to quell the Pathet Lao resistance. It was over this unique location that the life of Capt. Emmet Reid Galbreth II came to an end.

Emmet Galbreth Sr. and his wife, Bonnie, raised their only child, whom they called Reid, in Sherman, Texas. Reid was a smiling and energetic young man who loved sports and cars. He played football at Sherman High School, enjoyed sailing and skiing and was well-liked and well-regarded by his friends. His father sold cars, so Reid could often be seen driving the newest, most interesting cars. The family also had some land south of Sherman, and his friend Bob Goodman remembered heading there with Reid where they would ride cows.

Born in 1943, Reid finished high school and headed to the University of Texas at Austin where he majored in engineering. He took a job at Collins Radio, but soon realized that military service was heading his way. In 1969, Reid joined the Air Force with the hopes of getting a stateside assignment, or at the very least, having less time overseas. Although he did not want to leave his family, Reid felt that his contributions would help keep the country safe. He trained at Sheppard Air Force Base in Wichita Falls, Texas. He got his wings on December 13, 1969, and then drove his 1969 Porsche to Dallas to marry Sandi.

Reid was stationed in Florida for two six-month training sessions, and then at Loring Air Force Base in Limestone, Maine. These postings gave Reid time with his young family, which by 1971 included a daughter, Brittany. Soon Reid was given his overseas assignment, the 56th Air Commando Wing based out of Udorn, Thailand. The Galbreth family was concerned for Reid's safety, having lost a cousin in the Korean War, and Reid's father to illness while Reid was in college.

Reid's assignment with the 56th, which soon was renamed the 56th Special Operations Wing, was the training of Laotian pilots. It was in this assignment that Reid's true nature came forth. The pilots he trained were young Laotian boys, usually only 16 or 17 years old. His wife, Sandi, said that Reid was very concerned about the fate of these young men, to whom he became quite close. "He said the boys couldn't speak much English and didn't understand what he was telling them when he instructed them during flight time. He feared for their lives… and hated that the boys he came to care about might end up a statistic." In order to give his young trainees the best chance for survival, in his off hours Reid had them to his room where he taught them English. "Reid worked extra hard to keep the boys alive and in good health," said Sandi. In return, the young men showed him respect and gratitude, giving him gifts of musical instruments and hand-carved Buddhist pendants as tokens of their appreciation.

The United States, North Vietnam and South Vietnam in January 1973 signed the Paris Peace Accords calling for a cease-fire. American troops and bases were still located throughout the region, including Udorn in Thailand. Reid was flying training missions, and occasionally, bombing missions into Laos. On May 28, 1973, Reid and a Laotian pilot took off on a mission over the Plain of Jars. During the flight, the plane malfunctioned. According to the Air Force, Reid's canopy would not open and he could not eject. Reid went down with his plane. He was 29 years old.

After his death, Sandi received letters and phone calls from the Laotian men that he trained. "They all expressed sincere appreciation for his caring, happy attitude and that he had them at his bungalow in an attempt to teach them English. They expressed their own loss at his death." Amazingly, the Laotian student flying with Reid that day managed to survive the crash and Sandi was able to talk to him, as well. ♦

Sandi Galbreth pins wings on Reid. Photo courtesy of Sandi Galbreth.

MARY T KLINKER

Captain, Air Force • 10/3/47–4/4/75 • Panel 1W, Row 122

Capt. Mary Therese Klinker, U.S. Air Force.

As Saigon was falling in April 1975, President Gerald Ford instructed the U.S. Air Force to assist with the evacuation of thousands of Vietnamese orphans from the war-torn country. The evacuation, called "Operation Babylift," began on April 4. Air Force C-5A cargo planes would be used to evacuate the orphans from hospitals and orphanages.

Mary Therese Klinker was an Air Force captain stationed at Clark Air Force Base in the Philippines when "Operation Babylift" began. Mary grew up in Lafayette, Ind. with her parents, four brothers and a sister. She attended Central High School in Lafayette and joined the Air Force in 1969 after graduating from St. Elizabeth School of nursing. During her six years in the Air Force, she had served as a flight nurse and then as an instructor and evaluator. She loved helping people, and the humanitarian mission of "Operation Babylift" appealed to her, so she volunteered to assist on the flights.

The C-5As would pick up orphans, their caretakers and medical staff at Tan Son Nhut Air Base in Saigon. Hundreds of orphans would be loaded onto each plane for the flight back to Clark Air Force Base and then on to the United States. It was a tenuous and stressful situation, as the C-5As were not designed for medical evacuations. C-5As were some of the world's largest aircraft at that time and were used to transport tanks and helicopters, not critically-ill children. Additionally, many of the flight nurses were not accustomed to serving on that type of plane. Still, all were committed to getting the orphans safely out of Vietnam. Sister Susan Carol McDonald, a Sister of Loretto who worked with many orphanages in the area, described the size and limitations of the C-5A. "The cargo hold of the C-5A was the size of a large gymnasium (it could hold more than 16 city buses parked side by side), had netting on the floor, and a few seats along the side of the plane. It was not configured for passengers, there were no seat belts and no possibility for oxygen, should that be needed." The staff at the orphanages knew it was a risky mission, but keeping the children in the orphanages would result in many deaths. Orphanages and hospitals were having trouble getting supplies, and it was believed the C-5As would be the last way out of Vietnam for many of the Vietnamese orphans.

McDonald and her team loaded their children onto the cargo plane. The upper deck, which included troop seats, would carry some 22 infants, all of whom were very ill and required oxygen. Children aged three and up were put into the cargo area with a team of medical staff, including Mary. Also on board the plane were civilian personnel, such as embassy staff and the wives and children of Department of Defense officials.

Approximately 15 minutes after take-off on April 4, just as the plane reached cruising altitude, an explosion ripped off the lower cargo doors. Several passengers, including some children, were thrown from the cargo hold. The entire cargo compartment decompressed immediately. Rather than getting herself to safety, Mary began caring for those in need. As the plane lost power and altitude, the pilot made a skillful turn and was able to turn the plane around in an attempt to get back to Tan Son Nhut. A few miles from the air base, the C-5A crashed into a rice paddy. The plane broke into four pieces and skidded for a half mile before coming to a stop in mud and water.

Amazingly, more than 100 people survived the horrific crash, with most of them being on the upper deck of the plane. At least 180 children, civilians, orphanage staff and American military personnel were killed in the crash, including Mary. She was 27. For her actions that day she was awarded the Airman's Medal and the Meritorious Service Medal. ♦

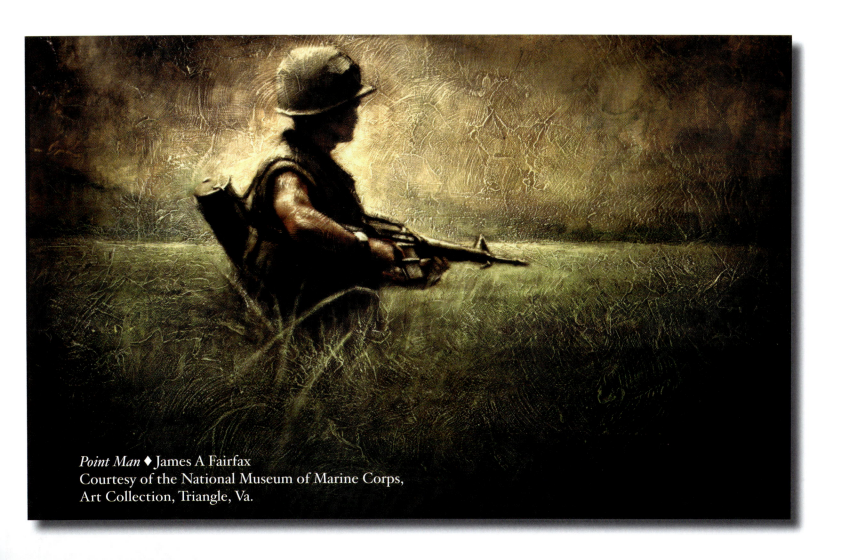
Point Man ♦ James A Fairfax
Courtesy of the National Museum of Marine Corps,
Art Collection, Triangle, Va.

Photo by Jim Lee

Bibliography

1997 Khe Sahn Reunion Transcript. (n.d.). Retrieved May 9, 2012, from http://www.geocities.com/pentagon/4867/reuniontext.html

43 Killed in Navy Carrier Blaze; Loss Navy's Worst of Viet War. (1966, October 26). *The Detroit News*, pp. 1A, 6A.

A brother's love. (1970, September 24). *Navajo Times*, p. 2.

Abrams, V. (2003, February 21). War Hero's widow faces Eviction. *The Birmingham News*. Retrieved April 23, 2012, from http://www.homeofheroes.com/news/archives/2003/0213_leonard.html

Air America. (2004, June 1). *About Air America*. Retrieved May 21, 2012, from http://www.air-america.org/About/About.shtml

Ala. soldier added to Vietnam Memorial. (2011, June 2). Retrieved from Fox10Tv.com: http://www.fox10tv.com/dpp/news/military/ala-soldier-added-to-vietnam-memorial

Alvin Adikai Jr. (1971, March 30). *Arizona Republic*, p. 43.

Alvin Adikai Jr. Killed in Vietnam. (1971, March 25). *Navajo Times*, pp. 1,3.

Annual Historic Supplement-1969. (2008, November 2). Retrieved from First Strike 1/502: http://firststrike1st502nd.multiply.com/journal/item/1195

Arkansan, with One Brother Dead, Took Fatal 2d Tour. (1968, May). *The Pine Bluff Commercial*.

Austin, L. (1984, November 11). 15 Years and Counting: Time Refuses to Heal Vietnam Wounds. *The Wichita Eagle-Beacon*, pp. 1A, 6A, 7A.

Award Medals Posthumously. (1975, August 11). *Valparaiso Vidette Messenger*, p. 8.

Berger, S. (2004, December 9). History haunts the Plain of Jars. *The Telegraph*. Retrieved May 13, 2012, from http://www.telegraph.co.uk/news/worldnews/asia/laos/1478626/History-haunts-the-Plain-of-Jars.html

Boat Specifications. (2012, May 7). Retrieved May 9, 2012, from Coastal Squadron One: Swift Boat Crew Directory: http://www.swiftboats.net/extras/boat_specifications.htm

Bogdan, J. (2009, October 21). Remembering a fallen soldier. *Utica Observer-Dispatch*. Retrieved May 14, 2012, from http://www.uticaod.com/news/x927262495/Remembering-a-fallen-soldier

Boniface, R. (2008). *Migs Over North Vietnam: The Vietnam People's Air Force in Combat, 1965-75*. Mechanicsburg: Stackpole Books.

Boyett, J. (1971, September 11). Hero Termed 'Friendly'. *Abilene Reporter News*, p. 15. Retrieved May 24, 2012, from http://newspaperarchive.com/

Busch, M. (2011, May 30). Pinson, Alabama-born Vietnam veteran added to Vietnam Veterans Memorial Wall. *The Birmingham News*. Retrieved February 3, 2012, from http://blog.al.com/spotnews/2011/05/pinson_alabama-born_vietnam_ve.html

C-123 Down! (n.d.). Retrieved May 9, 2012, from The Virtual Wall: http://www.virtualwall.org/units/c123down.htm

CAPTAIN ROBERT "LEFTY" BRETT MEMORIAL SCHOLARSHIP. (n.d.). Retrieved May 23, 2012, from The Benton County Foundation: http://www.bentoncountyfoundation.org/scholarships/captain-robert-lefty-brett

Carrier Takes Dead Back to Philippines. (1966, October 27). *The Detroit News*, p. 10C.

Cauley, J. R. (1972, May 24). Gold Star Mothers Act. *The Kansas City Times*, p. 14.

Congressional Medal of Honor Society. (2012). *Archive Statistics*. Retrieved May 14, 2012, from Congressional Medal of Honor Society: http://www.cmohs.org/medal-statistics.php

Criser, T. (2003). *The Ghost in the Orange Closet*. : TLC Advertising.

Crotty, R. (1970, August 28). Memorial Honors Inseperable Pals. *The Wichita Beacon*.

Davies, P. (2009). *USN F-4 Phantom II Vs VPAF MiG-17/19*: Vietnam 1965-73. Oxford: Osprey.

DeWitt, R. (2011, May 29). Greene County to recognize Vietnam hero after 44 years. *Tuscaloosa News*. Retrieved April 23, 2012, from http://www.tuscaloosanews.com/article/20110529/news/110529614

Donald S. Metz, D. P. (1991). MidAmerica Nazarene College: The Pioneer Years 1966-1991. Kansas City: Nazarene Publishing House.

Elward, B., & Davies, P. (2001). *US Navy F-4 Phantom II MiG Killers 1965-70, Part 1*. Oxford: Osprey.

Eugene Lawrence Self. (n.d.). Retrieved January 17, 2012, from The Virtual Wall: http://virtualwall.org/ds/SelfEL01a.htm

Fard, M. F. (n.d.). *Keeping a loved one's memory alive*. Retrieved January 13, 2012, from http://www.maggiefazelifard.com/2008/07/16/keeping-a-loved-ones-memory-alive/

Fields, L. (1968, May 30). Memorial Day: The Life and Death of Spec 4 Schmidt One of 798 Missourians Killed in Vietnam. *St. Louis Globe-Democrat*, pp. 1A, 18A.

Flight Nurse From Indiana Among Missing. (1975, April 8). *Valparaiso Vidette Messenger*, p. 14.

Flight Safety Foundation. (n.d.). *Criminal Occurrence description*. Retrieved May 9, 2012, from Aviation Safety Network: http://aviation-safety.net/database/record.php?id=19680306-1

Friends to Comfort Dead GI's Mother. (1966, December 24). *Chicago Sun-Times*.

Frisbie, A. (1969, May 30). The Best Flier Was More Than A Statistic. *Omaha World-Herald*.

Funeral for a Forgotten Veteran. (n.d.). Retrieved May 13, 2012, from American Gold Star Mothers, Inc.: http://www.goldstarmoms.com/Events/FuneralForAForgottenVeteran/FuneralForAForgottenVeteran.htm

Garnett, R. (1965, September 15). Letter to the Editor. *Harrisburg Patriot Evening News*.

Garnett, R. (1966, January 15). Letter to the Editor. *Harrisburg Patriot Evening News*, p. 6.

Grissom AFB Honors Parents of Dead Nurse. (1975, August 10). *Logansport Pharos Tribune and Press*, p. 13.

Hackworth, D. H., & Sherman, J. (1989). *About Face: The Odyssey of an American Warrior*. New York: Touchstone.

Hansen, J. (2000, November 28). Medal of Honor Winner now in Fit Grave. *The Birmingham News*. Retrieved April 23, 2012, from http://www.homeofheroes.com/news/archives/2000_0300_leonard.html

Harris, M. A. (2012, April 7). *In Memoriam*. Retrieved from Endless Journey: http://www.riverinesailor.com/RiverQueen.htm

Heck, C. P. (n.d.). Retrieved from Memoirs from Nam: http://memoirsfromnam.blogspot.com/

Helena Native Priest, U.S. Navy Chaplain Killed in Ship Fire. (1966, October 27). *Independent Record*.

Henry, B. (1969, July 20). The Dead of the 69th Brigade: Grief, Pride Mark Families. *The Wichita Eagle*, p. Section B.

Highway 11 in Greene County renamed for Matthew Leonard. (2011, 29 September). *Greene County Democrat*. Retrieved April 23, 2012, from http://greenecountydemocrat.com/?p=1945

HMCS Beacon Hill. (n.d.). Retrieved March 26, 2012, from CFB Esquimalt Naval & Military Museum: http://www.navalandmilitarymuseum.org/resource_pages/ships/beacon.html

Hocklander, S., & Bridges, A. (2012, Jan 4). *Vietnam Veterans Memorial Fund corrects spelling of soldier's name in online database*. Retrieved January 2012, 2012, from News-Leader.com: http://www.news-leader.com/article/20120104/NEWS01/201040391/stephen-phillips-name-misspelled

Kapps, L. (2010, June 12). Stained-glass window now memorial for soldier. *Utica Observer-Dispatch*. Retrieved May 22, 2012, from http://www.uticaod.com/news/x1057816990/Stained-glass-window-now-memorial-for-soldier

Karp, R. T. (2011, December 30). *Chesapeake Torah*. Retrieved from Parsha/ Torah Reading of Vayigash, Historic Personality: Rav Mordechai Tzvi ben Yechiel-Rabbi Morton Singer, martyred Vietnam chaplain who gave his life for Chanuka Part II, Halacha Topic: Self Defense and Physical Fitness: http://chesbaytorah.com/?p=876

Kelley, M. P. (2002). *Where We Were in Vietnam*. Central Point: Hellgate Press.

Kempf Fund to Aid Student. (1969, September 16). *The Coshocton Tribune*, p. 1.

Kempf is Medic. (1969, July 6). *The Coshocton Tribune*, p. 7.

Kempf Scholarship Fund is "Growing." (1969, October 4). *The Coshocton Tribune*, p. 1.

Kent, D. (1994). *The Vietnam War*. Berkeley Heights: Enslow Publishers, Inc.

Khe Sahn Veterans, Inc. (n.d.). *Casualties- 40 Years Ago This Month-March 1968*. Retrieved May 8, 2012, from Khe Sahn Veterans: http://www.khesanh.org/40th/march-68.html

Knox, R. P. (2002, May 24). Stories from the Veterans History Project. (J. Kent, Interviewer) Retrieved May 13, 2012, from http://lcweb2.loc.gov/diglib/vhp-stories/story/loc.natlib.afc2001001.01146/transcript?ID=sr0001

Lakeview H.S. Sets Memorial For Marine Killed in Vietnam. (n.d.). *Macomb Daily*.

Lamar Soldier Killed. (1969, September 21). *Joplin Globe*, p. 1.

Lamar Soldier Killed in S. Vietnam. (1967, March 8). *Joplin Globe*, p. 2.

Langguth, A. (2000). *Our Vietnam: The War 1954-1975*. New York: Touchstone.

Leary, W. M. (2008, June 27). *CIA Air Operations in Laos, 1955-1974*. Retrieved May 13, 2012, from Central Intelligence Agency: https://www.cia.gov/library/center-for-the-study-of-intelligence/csi-publications/csi-studies/studies/winter99-00/art7.html

Linderer, G. (1997). *Six Silent Men: Book Three*. New York: Ballantine Books.

Linderer, G. A. (1997). *Six Silent Men: 101st LRP/Rangers: Book Three*. New York: Ivy Books.

Local Youth Given Tour of Ft. Chafee; Prompts Career Interest. (1964, August 14). *Sequoyah County Times*, p. 6.

Longfellow, H. W. (1903). *The Courtship of Miles Standish*. Indianapolis: Bobbs-Merrill Company.

Manzanar, California. (2005). Retrieved May 14, 2012, from Japanese American Veterans Association: http://www.javadc.org/manzanar.htm

Martin, G. (n.d.). *Ultimate Bomb Truck: Vought's A-7 Corsair II*. Retrieved March 27, 2012, from Aircraft Information: http://www.aircraftinformation.info/art_A7.htm

Martini, P. (2002, August 4). *Father Urged Government Not to Write Off His Son*. Retrieved May 23, 2012, from Vietnam Veterans Memorial Fund: http://www.vvmf.org/thewall/anClip=225773

McDonald, S.S. (2002, April 4). *In Memoriam*. Retrieved May 21, 2012, from Vietnam Babylift: http://www.vietnambabylift.org/Memorial.html

Memorial For A Marine. (n.d.). *Macomb Daily*.

Miss Parrish is bride of Douglas Kempf. (1969, January 19). *The Coshocton Tribune*, p. 5.

Moore, H. G., & Galloway, J. L. (1992). *We Were Soldiers Once–and Young: Ia Drang, the Battle that Changed the War in Vietnam*. New York: Random House.

Mortar Explosion Aboard PCF 9. (2012, May 7). Retrieved May 9, 2012, from Coastal Squadron One Swift Boat Crew Directory: http://www.swiftboats.net/stories/pcf9mortar.htm

Muerto Capitan Del Ejercito De EE.UU. que Vivio en el Zulia. (1970, March 7). Panorama.

National Parks Service. (2012, April 10). *Japanese Americans at Manzanar*. Retrieved May 14, 2012, from Manzanar National Historic Site: http://www.nps.gov/manz/historyculture/japanese-americans-at-manzanar.htm

National Personal Records Center. (2012). *Military Personnel Records*. St. Louis: National Archives.

Nation's Highest Medal Awarded Abilene Marine. (1971, September 10). *Abilene Reporter News*, p. 34. Retrieved May 24, 2012, from http://newspaperarchive.com/

Newby, C. (2003). *It Took Heroes: A Cavalry Chaplain's Memoir of Vietnam*. Random House Digital.

NURSE WHO DIED IN VIETNAM REMEMBERED. (1987, November 15). *New York Times*. Retrieved January 13, 2012, from http://www.nytimes.com/1987/11/15/nyregion/nurse-who-died-in-vietnam-remembered.html

Olson, J. S., & Roberts, R. (1999). *Where the Domino Fell: America and Vietnam, 1945 to 1995*. St. James: Brandywine Press.

Parents accept 3 medals given to son posthumously. (1971, July 24). *Arizona Republic*, p. 59.

Parks, H. D. (n.d.). *Eleanor Grace Alexander*. Retrieved January 13, 2012, from New Jersey Vietnam Veterans Memorial: http://www.njvvmf.org/ELEANORALEXANDER-vetmemorial1402

Percy, S. (2001). On a Bittersweet Adventure at Sea. *Proceedings*, 96-101.

Percy, S. C. (2004). The Bracelet. *Proceedings*, 93.

Podgus, C. (2002, November). *Eight Names On The Wall Belong To Women*. Retrieved January 13, 2012, from The VVA Veteran: http://www.vva.org/archive/TheVeteran/2002_special/8women.htm

Prescott, R. M. (2011, October 26). *Letter from Rhona Prescott to Eleanor Grace Alexander*. Retrieved January 13, 2012, from Experiencing War: Stories from the Vietnam History Project: http://lcweb2.loc.gov/diglib/vhp-stories/story/loc.natlib.afc2001001.01146/letter?ID=tx0001

Prisoner of War bracelet 'part of my son' says mother. (n.d.). Retrieved January 19, 2012, from War Tales: http://donmooreswartales.com/2011/04/08/barton-creed/

Quinslek, D. (n.d.). Vietnam's fall painful for Gold Star mothers. *The Wichita Eagle*, pp. 1A, 10A.

Rabbi Mordechai Tzvi/Morton Singer(1936-1968) martyred Vietnam Chaplain and his brother Rabbi Norman Singer,YEhuda Yehonasson,Rav of Williamsport,Pa (1933-1995) Part III. (2012, January 7). Retrieved May 13, 2012, from American Historical Ethics: http://www.americanhistoricalethics.org/?p=307

Rendall, I. (1999). *Rolling Thunder: Jet Combat from World War II to the Gulf War*. New York: The Free Press.

Reuben Louis Garnett Jr. (n.d.). Retrieved May 4, 2012, from 101st Airborne, 327th Infantry Regiment: http://www.327infantry.org/327thmemorial/garnett.htm?phpMyAdmin=2a8cbab6008b35bc262dc17200499568

Rogers State University. (n.d.). *Oklahoma Military Academy*. Retrieved from Rogers State University: http://www.rsu.edu/oma/

Rogers, B. (n.d.). *History of the Abu Monster*. Retrieved from 32nd Infantry: http://www.327infantry.org/files/first/images/abu2.jpg?phpMyAdmin=2a8cbab6008b35bc262dc17200499568

Rubin, D. (2011, November 14). *Cantor honors father, friend at new chaplains' memorial*. Retrieved May 14, 2012, from New Jersey Jewish News: http://njjewishnews.com/article/7197/cantor-honors-father-friend-at-new-chaplains-memorial#.T7PQasXWfmB

Sadler, B., & Mahoney, T. (1967). *I'm a Lucky One*. McMillan.

Sanford, M. G. (1964, May 4). *Commencement Address*. Oklahoma Military Academy, Claremore, Oklahoma, United States.

Schlatter, J. (2011, November 27). *The Origin of the POW-MIA Bracelets*. Retrieved March 27, 2012, from MIA Facts Site: http://www.miafacts.org/bracelets.htm

Sister helps dedicate field for brother. (2010, May 23). Retrieved May 22, 2012, from WDRB.com: http://www.wdrb.com/story/12528489/sister-helps-dedicate-field-for-brother?clienttype=printable&redirected=true

Specialist 5 Doug Kempf Killed in Vietnam. (1969, September 11). *The Coshocton Tribune*, p. 1.

Swaim, C. (2009, July 17). *A Responsibility to the Living: Frances Turley and American Gold Star Mothers*. Retrieved February 9, 2012, from Americans in Wartime Museum: http://www.nmaw.org/a-responsibility-to-the-living-frances-turley-and-american-gold-star-mothers/

Task Force Omega. (n.d.). *CREED, BARTON SHELDON "BART"*. Retrieved January 19, 2012, from http://taskforceomegainc.org/c116.html

Teacher Recalls Keith's Big Grin. (1971, October 14). *Abilene Reporter News*, p. 34. Retrieved May 24, 2012, from http://newspaperarchive.com/

The Aeronca 11 Chief. (n.d.). Retrieved from Airliners.net: http://www.airliners.net/aircraft-data/stats.main?id=399

The Battle of Lo Giang. (2005, July 10). Retrieved May 14, 2012, from The Virtual Wall: http://www.virtualwall.org/units/logiang.htm

The Mitzva of Welcoming Guests:Starring Rabbi/Vietnam Chaplain Morton and Eva Singer. (2012, March 30). Retrieved May 15, 2012, from American Historical Ethics: http://www.americanhistoricalethics.org/?p=313

The U.S. National Archives & Records Administration. (2012). *Access to Archival Databases*. Retrieved from The National Archives & Records Administration: www.archies.gov

Toler, V. (1996, November). *The Coast Guard Reservist*. Retrieved May 24, 2012, from http://www.jacksjoint.com/cgvietnam.htm

Tonsetic, R. (2007). *Days of Valor*. Philadelphia: Casemate.

Too Wounded to walk, 2 Are Slain By Guerillas. (1962, April 11). *Pacific Stars and Stripes*.

Tucker, E. (2011, April 20). Bill aims to honor Jewish chaplains at Arlington. *Deseret News*. Retrieved May 15, 2012, from http://www.deseretnews.com/article/700128669/Bill-aims-to-honor-Jewish-chaplains-at-Arlington.html

Tucker, S. (1971, Octobr 14). Tribute Paid Slain Marine Who Won Medal of Honor. *Abilene Reporter News*, p. 34. Retrieved May 24, 2012, from http://newspaperarchive.com/

Tucker, S. C. (Ed.). (1998). *Encyclopedia of the Vietnam War*. Oxford: Oxford University Press.

United States Air Force. (n.d.). *History*. Retrieved May 22, 2012, from United States Air Force Thunderbirds: http://afthunderbirds.com/site/history/

United States Army. (2011, June 27). *Medal of Honor Recipients Vietnam A-L*. Retrieved 23 April, 2012, from http://www.history.army.mil/html/moh/vietnam-a-l.html

United States Coast Guard. (2012, February 29). *U.S. Coast Guard Lightships*. Retrieved May 24, 2012, from U.S. Coast Guard: http://www.uscg.mil/history/weblightships/Lightship_Station_Index.asp

United States Naval Academy. (1967). *Lucky Bag*.

USS Oriskany (USS-34). (n.d.). Retrieved April 11, 2012, from The Virtual Wall: http://www.virtualwall.org/units/oriskany.htm

Vietnam Veterans Memorial adds 5 more names; a Birmingham serviceman among them. (2011, May 8). Retrieved February 2012, 2012, from AL.com: http://blog.al.com/wire/2011/05/vietnam_veterans_memorial_adds.html

Vietnam War. (n.d.). Retrieved March 26, 2012, from The Canadian Encyclopedia: http://www.thecanadianencyclopedia.com/articles/vietnam-war

Wichitan, 19, is Victim of Viet Action. (1969, January 18). *The Wichita Eagle and Beacon*.

Wolf, R. (2009, December 16). *Royal Canadian Sea Cadets*. Retrieved March 26, 2012, from Canada Free Press: http://www.canadafreepress.com/index.php/article/21197

Young Flat River Man Killed In Vietnam . (1969, October 29). *THE LEAD BELT NEWS*. Retrieved May 13, 2012, from http://www.rootsweb.ancestry.com/~mostfran/military/franciscorter_killedvietnam.html

Young, M. B. (1991). *The Vietnam Wars 1945-1990*. New York: Harper Perennial.

Zippert, J. (2011, June 2). Memorial Day ceremony honors P/Sgt. Matthew Leonard. *Greene County Democrat*. Retrieved April 24, 2012, from http://greenecountydemocrat.com/?p=1338

In addition to the sources above, the following websites were consulted on a regular basis:

Ancestry (http://www.ancestry.com/)

Find a Grave (http://www.findagrave.com/index.html)

The National Archives Coffelt Database (http://aad.archives.gov/aad/index.jsp)

The Vietnam Veterans Memorial Fund (http://www.vvmf.org/)

The Vietnam Veterans Memorial (http://thewall-usa.com/)

The Virtual Wall (http://virtualwall.org/iAlpha.htm)

Artwork

Jungle Column (p. 58). Samuel Alexander, courtesy of Army Art Collection, U.S. Army.

Day in Nam (p. 129) and *Job Well Done, Brother* (p. 88). Roland Castanie, courtesy of Wild Texas Art.

Faces (p. 34); *Hot LZ* (p. 192) and *Price Tags, Vietnam* (p. 78).; Bernie Duff.

Point Man (p. 109). James A. Fairfax, courtesy of Janet Fikar and Janet Fikar Photography.

Illustration of F-4B (p. 12). Courtesy of Jim Laurer.

Not Forgotten (p. 4); *POW-MIA* (p. 7) and *War Dogs Sacrifice* (p. 66). Carolyn Marshall, courtesy of Carolyn Marshall and Living Life Photography.

Waiting to Lift Off (p. 72). James Pollack, courtesy of Army Art Collection, U.S. Army.

Heading Home (p. 96). John Stuart.

Gently, Ever So Gently (p. 65) and *Monsoon Initiative* (p. 87). Frank Thomas.

Gunner (p. 74) and *Leaving the Perimeter* (p. 9). Richard Yaco, courtesy of the National Museum of the Marine Corps, Art Collection, Triangle, Va.

Index

IFC – Inside Front Cover
IBC – Inside Back Cover

A

Abrams, V. 110
Adame, Arthur P. 3
Aderholt, Henry 104, 105, 106, Judy 105, 106, Lester 104, Margaret 104, 105
Adikai, Alvin, Jr. 101, 110, Alvin, Sr. 101
Adikai, Leon 101, Ralphina 101
Adkins, Marvin *IFC*
Aigeldinger, Eldridge C. *IFC*
Alden, John 73
Alderman, Winfred *IFC*
Alexander, Eleanor 53, Samuel 58, 117, Susanne 53
Alford, Michael L. *IFC*
Allen, Eddie James *IFC*, Lee 6, Lyle Ernest Jr. 2
Alonzo, Manuel B. 2
Alvarez, Victor 6, 32
Ammon, William R. 2
Anason, Kay 6
Anderson, James H. *IFC*, Richard 22
Andres, Stephen 6
Andrews, Richard 6, Robert P. *IFC*, Shirley 70
Angel, Tommie Ray 23
Antol, Anna 6, 19, David 19, 20, Patricia 19, Stephen 19
Apodaca, Victor Jr. 3
Appleton, John Burdette 3
Aragon, Henry T. 2
Arant, Dan 59
Arbogast, Adam 6
Archer, George 6, Richard C. 3
Arent, Kenneth Jacob *IFC*
Arnado, Fredrico *IFC*
Arthur, Dion 102, Ernest 102, Evangeline 102, John, Sr. 102, Judith Bekise 102, Ryndall 102
Arthur-Imel, Prisylla 6
Artis, Herbert John 2
Arvizu, Amado 48, Mary Lou 48, Terry 48, Xavier Amado 48
Ashley, Eugene Jr. *IFC*
Atchley, Brian 6
Atteridge, Leon Jr. 3
Austin, L. 110
Authur, Johnny 102
Autry, Gene 73

B

Baer, William C *IFC*
Bailey, Norm 6
Baker, Curtis R. *IFC*, Debby 6
Balai, Andres 2
Baldonado, Secundino *IFC*
Balters, Stephen A. Jr. *IFC*
Barbee, Patricia 6
Barden, Arnold Jr. 3
Bargatze, Landis 6
Barnes, Bud 6
Barthelmas, William 3
Bartholomew, Jay 70, 71, Laura 70, Lela 70, Lisa 70, 71, Roger 70, 71, Shirley 70, 71
Bazulto, Salvador *IFC*
Bekise, Judith 102
Belcher, Glenn *IBC*
Bell, Marquessa 83, Samuel Wayne 83, Susan Deck 83
Bennett, Ann 101, Donald Casper 2
Berger, S. 110
Bernal, Margie 6, 48
Beulow, Terry 57, 58
Bickford, Christy 76, Christy, Jr. 73, Judy 73, 74, Mary 73, 75, 76, Ralph 73, 74, 75, 76
Blackman, Alonzo 79, Alphonso 79, Fabian 79, Jeannette 79
Blavat, James Norbert 2
Bletsch, William P. *IFC*
Blinder, Richard B. *IFC*
Bogdan, J. 110
Boniface, R. 110
Bonnici 18, Robert 22
Boone, Dennis Clayton 2
Borowski, Raymond 19
Borowsky, Charles George *IFC*
Bradbury, Ray 8
Brancheau, Nanette 18
Brannon, David 22
Brett, Anastasia 60, Camille 103, Florence 103, Francis 60, Joseph 60, Melissa 103, Patrice Costello 103, Robert 60, Robert Arthur, Jr. 103, Robert Raymond 60, Robert, Sr. 103, Rosemary 60
Brian, Faye 85
Bridenbaker, Patrick *IFC*
Bridges, A. 112
Brillo, Albert, Jr. 2
Briscoe, Charles 2
Brock, James 22
Brockman, Verndean A. *IFC*
Brookens, Willard Jr. *IFC*
Broumas, Andre *IFC*
Brower, Ralph Wayne 2
Brown, David 22, Jerry E. 6, Vaughn Lee *IFC*
Bruggerman, Joe 58
Buckner, Anthony Eugene *IFC*
Budzinski, Lawrence Joseph 2
Buhan, Don 6
Bullock, Glen *IFC*
Bunch, William Lloyd *IFC*
Burnett, Sheldon *IFC*
Burns, Darrell Edward *IFC*
Burton, Paul 6
Busch, M. 110
Buskey, Orrie J. *IFC*
Byrne, Conal J. Jr. *IBC*
Byrnes, Robert S. *IBC*

C

Cabbagestalk, Eugene 2
Cahoon, Herman Curtis *IBC*
Cain, Cyndie 21
Calabrese, Andrea Stec 6
Callivas, Gust 2
Calloway, Ronald D. 2
Cameron, Virgil *IFC*
Campbell, Barbara 6, Clay 6, Keith *IFC*
Campestre, Albert J. 2
Campos, Jose 75
Canas, Roberto L. *IFC*
Carmody, Robert J. 2
Carricato, Steve 52
Carroll, Kathleen 14
Carter, David Edward 2
Casey 6
Casey, Bertha 93, 95, 96, Bivra 93, Bonnie 93, 96, Donald 93, Doris 93, John 93, Michael 93, 94, 95, 96
Castanie, Roland 29, 88, 117
Castro, Alfonso Roque 3
Caudillo, Joseph *IFC*
Cauley, J. R. 110
Cavender, Jim Ray *IFC*
Chamberlain, Robert F. 2
Chambliss, Roger 3
Chandler, Michael 6
Chaney, Larry W. *IFC*
Charbonneau, Tom 58
Chatmon, Nathan Eugene *IFC*
Chavez, Ram 6, 67, Ramiro 65
Chin, Alexander 60, 61
Choquette, Robert G. *IFC*
Chun, Reginald W. *IBC*
Clark 18, Grant 3, Jerry 22, Terry Richard *IFC*, Thomas Edward *IFC*
Clay, Darleynn Hacker 80, 81, 82
Clendenen, Richard *IFC*
Cochrane, John F. 2
Collette, Larry 6
Collier, James Allen 3
Collins, Mike 6, Vernel 3
Coltman, William 103
Combs, Sue 6, Thomas 6, 91
Cook, Lewis Collin *IFC*
Cooley 6, Annie 64, 67, Harvey 65, Harvey Lynn 64, Harvey Lynn, Jr. 65, John 67, John Carl 64, Millie 67
Cordero, Dorothy 14, Tony 6, 14, William E. 14
Cortor, Francis E., jr. 90
Cortor, Francis, Sr. 90
Costello, Patrice 103
Cote, Grace 6
Couch, Leslie *IFC*
Coven, Melissa Brett 6, 103
Cowart, David L. *IFC*
Craig, Edward J. 2
Creed, Barton Sheldon (Bart) 98, 99, 114, George, Jr. 98, 100 Judith Page 98, Page 100, Scott 6, 98, 99, 100, Susan 99, Verna 98, 100
Criser, T. 111, Thomas 44
Crockett, Davy 73
Cronin, Philip 6
Crotty, R. 111
Cruse, Michael L. *IFC*
Cryan, Kenneth M. *IBC*
Curttright, Larry Bre 2

D

Daily, Thomas *IBC*
Dalton, Theodore H. 2
Dark, Linda Pinegar 6
Davies, P. 111
Davis 18, James 20, 21, Lena 20, Richard S. Jr. *IFC*
Davison, David *IBC*
Dawson, John Robert *IBC*
Dayun, Li 12
Debernardo, Frank Jr. *IFC*
Deck, Susan 83
DeHaven, Thelma 6
Deitrick, George D. 3
Delgado, Christopher G. *IFC*
Demler, Robert 6
Derrickson, Thomas G. *IFC*
DeWitt, R. 111
Di Bartolomeo, Ronald 2
Dickinson, David 3
Dieboll, Kimberly 7
Dignan, Don 6
Dillard, John A. Jr. 3
Dillinder, Randy 22
Dilly, Ann 7, Erin 7, Heather 7
Dixon, James C. *IFC*, Lee C. *IFC*
Donovan, Edward (Ted) 68, Joyce 68, Pamela 68
Drazba, Carol 26, 27, Joanne 26, Joseph 6, 26, Marcella 26
Drzinski, Cailee 7
Duane, Lynn 6
Duff, Bernie 33, 117, Brian 58, Brian Francis 57, Francis 58, Therese 57, 58
Dyer, Jay Cee 23, Kimberly 100

E

Earick, James *IFC*
Early, Howard Lee 79, Jeannette 6, 79
Eby, Jodie 6, Judy 74, Mike 6
Eckle, Stephen John 3
Elford, Gary 2
Elizondo, David 2
Elkins, Jerome *IFC*
Ellison, Charlie Melvin 2
Elward, B. 111
Elwart, Paul 2, 22
Encina, Sebastián E. 13, 26, 27, 31, 35, 53, 54, 68, 69, 100
Engelbrecht, Richard 6

Ericson, William F. II *IFC*
Evans, Donald Ward Jr. 2
Eyring, Kenneth R. *IFC*

F

Faircloth, Henry F. 2
Fairfax, James A. 109, 117
Falcone, Larry 10
Faller, Ken 6
Fard, M. F. 111
Fayz, Alison 7, Lexi 7, Maddie 7
Fegan, Richard 6, 11, 12, 13, Ronald 11, 12, Tina 13, Velma 11, Walter 11
Felton, Duery 6
Ferraris, Susan 6
Fields, L. 111
Fikar, Janet 117
Fischer, Joseph 2
Fisher, Marianna 26
Flanigan, Dennis 6, 37
Fleming, James 22
Florence, Dexter B. 2
Flores, Raul *IFC*, Roy 6
Ford, Gerald 39, 108
Forman, Rich 6
Foxworth, Roger 22
Foy, Sidney 97
Francis, Durr 57
Freitag, Dieter K. 2
Friedman, Norm 6, 101
Fugett, Henry 22
Fuss, Robert E. *IFC*

G

Gabriel, Billie 6, 10, James, III 10, James, Jr. 10
Gage, Norman Glenn *IFC*
Galbreth, Bonnie 107, Brittany 107, Emmet Reid, II 107, Emmet, Sr. 107, Sandi 107
Gallagher, Patrick Joseph 2
Gallegos, Robert R. 97
Galloway, J. L. 113
Galloway, Joseph 70
Gamache, Joe 58
Gambotto 18, Larry *IFC*, 22
Gandolfo, Philip 2, 18, 22
Garcia, Pedro I. *IFC*, Richard 6
Garnett 113, Bertha 28, India 6, 28, R. 111, Reuben 28, Reuben, Jr. 28, 29, 113, Paul E. *IBC*
Garrison, Art 6, Margaret 19
Gause, Bernard Jr. 2
Gee, Gregory 2
Gentinne, Alan 6, Lori 6, Thomas 22, *IBC*
Genwright, Mckenzie W. *IBC*
Germany, Franklyn 23
Gerth, Peter H. 2
Giannelli, Giuseppe *IBC*
Gibbons, Ron 6
Gibson, Terrell *IBC*
Gillert, Laura Davis 6
Glover, Douglas J. *IFC*
Gmack, John R. *IFC*
Godwin, Harry 28
Goias, Everett William 2

Gooch, Bonnie 6
Goodman, Bob 107, James D. *IFC*
Goolsby, Robert 6, 102
Grace, Larry E. *IFC*
Gracida, Joaquin 6, 46
Graf, Tina Fegan 6
Graham, Annie R. 2, 69, Gilbert James *IFC*
Grano, Carol 6
Graves, Carter Lee *IFC*
Greene, Joseph 2
Green, Kenneth Leon *IFC*, Phillip W. Jr. *IFC*
Grice, Paul 6
Griffin, Harold Dexter 2
Griffis, William A. III *IFC*
Guy, Leonard A. *IBC*

H

Haan, Walter 53
Hacker, Darelynn 6, 82, Fred 80, Nancy 80, Ronald 80, 81
Hackworth, D. H. 111
Hahn, Fred 6
Hahn, Karen Yuhasz 6
Hankerson, Jimmie *IBC*
Hanley, Frederick 27
Hannon, John 6
Hanselman, Charles 22
Hansen, J. 111
Hansey, Mitchel *IBC*
Hanson, Lisa 6
Hanson, Lisa Bartholomew 70
Hargett, John Jr. *IFC*
Hargrove, James W. *IBC*, Joseph N. *IFC*, Sandy 6
Harmon, Daniel Lee 2
Harrell, Lenwood T. *IBC*
Harris, M. A. 111, Michael A. 6, Paul Winiford *IBC*, Samuel Gary 3
Hartwick, Floyd Jr. 2
Hath, James 22, *IBC*, Jamie 18
Hauser, Vincent Vanalstyne *IFC*
Hayes, George F. *IFC*
Hays, Gale 35
Healey, Chuck 6
Heck, Cathy Parrish Kempf 86, 88
Heck, CJ 86, 87, 88, C. P. 111
Heil, Jackie Phillip 2
Hendricks, Sterling Craig *IFC*
Henley, Darryl 6
Henry, B. 111
Hernandez, Ralphina 6, 101, Rolando *IFC*
Herring, Pedro 2
Higgins, William 6
Hill, Maurice R. *IFC*
Hintz, James 22
Hocklander, S. 112
Honour, Charles M. 27
Hood, Bobbette 42, Budd 42, Charles 42, Ronald 42, Valerie 42
Hoopengarner, Kim 6
Hopkins, Emmett 104
Hopkins, Karen 6, 104, 105, 106
Hosnedle, Alan 18, 22
Houston, Richard P. 2

Howett, Richard 6
Huard 6, Cyndie 21, James 21
Hubbard 21, Orville 18
Hurry, Samuel G. 2
Hutchinson, G. Calvin 6

J

Jaafar, Hassane 7
Jacklin, Sue 6
Jackymack, Rudolph 22
Johnson, Thomas W. 6
Johnson, Tom 27
Jones, Elizabeth 26, 27, George 27, Mabel 27
Juarez, John Richard *IFC*
Judy, David Lynn *IFC*
June, Beatrice 86, Elizabeth 6, Ron 6, 86
Justice, William Paul *IFC*

K

Kaiser, Don 6, 57, 58
Kampworth, Judy 40
Kapps, L. 112
Karp, R. T. 112
Karr, Charles 23
Katula, Joanne 6
Katzenberger, Raymond L. *IFC*
Kawamura, Terry Teruo *IFC*
Kearney, Charles D. *IFC*
Keedah, Ann 101
Keith 114, Miguel 97
Kelley, Harvey. 2, M. P. 112
Kelly, Frank 6, 57, 58, Sue 6, 57, 58
Kempf, Cathy Parrish 86, 87, 88, Dennis 6, Denny 86, Douglas 86, 87, 88, 113, 114, Gilbert (Gib) 86, Ortha 86, Terry 86
Kent, D. 112
Kerr, Michelle 7
Kiefer, Alena 4
Kincannon, Raymond *IFC*
King, Patrick Willmer *IFC*
Kiraly, Jack 7
Kirby, Christine 69
Klieman, Janet 6
Klinker, David 6, Mary Therese 108
Knox, R. P. 112
Koufax, Sandy 103
Kowitz, David 23
Kozai, Kenneth B. *IFC*
Kraft, Margaret 7
Kubowicz, Ron 6
Kurth, Jerry 60

L

Lambdin, Daniel Alvey *IFC*
Land, David 73, 74, 75, 76, Diane 73, 76, Ed 73, 74, 75, 76, E. H. 6, E. Homer 75, Elvert 73, Joe 6, 73, 74, 75, 76, Michael 73, 74, Peggy 73, 75
Lane, John 84, Kay 84, Sharon 84
Langguth, A. 112

Lark, Carol 7, Dennis 7, Edward 7, Lisa A. 1, 8
Larry, John D. Jr. *IBC*
Latham, Craig 6
Latoria, David J. *IBC*
Laurer, Jim 117
Laurier 12, Jim 6
Lawrence, Bobby J. *IBC*
Lawson, David 6, 64, Leroy 47, 91
Laws, Rena 7
Lawton, Michael E. *IBC*
Leal, Jennette Swartout 7
Leary, W. M 112
Leatherbury, Louis Anthony *IBC*
Lee, Jim 109, Roy Ronald *IBC*
LeGarie, Lou 6
Leonard, Lois 43, Matthew 43
Lerman, Alicia 7
Leslie, Emme Radcliffe 6
Likely, James T. *IBC*
Lilley, Joseph Emmett *IBC*
Lindbloom, Charles *IFC*
Linderer, G. 112
Linting, Jennifer 7
Lish, Gilbert R. *IBC*
Llamas, Jose *IBC*
Lloyd, Freddie G. *IBC*
Lockridge, Annie 32, Anthony 6, 32, Hui Cha 32, James 32, Raymond 32
Logan, Bradley J. 2
Long, Doris 6
Longfellow, Henry Wadsworth 73, H. W. 112, Wadsworth 76
Long, George Wendell *IFC*, Joe Wes 95
Love, Harry William *IBC*
Lukert, Edward *IFC*
Lundin, John *IBC*

M

Macellari, Lou 19
Machin, James 6
Maddock, George 56
Magri, William 6
Mahoney, T. 114
Maldonado, Tammy McClure 6
Mangan, Tom 6
Manual, Virginia 6
Manuguerra, Pete 6
Marchand, Wayne 10
Margle, Thomas Joseph *IFC*
Marshall, Carolyn 7, 117, Greg 6, H. 95
Martenis, John 58
Martin, G. 112
Martini, P. 112
Martin, Sandra 38, 39
Mason, John 56, Jon 6, Mary Louise 56, Robert 56
Masuda, Robert S. *IFC*
Matayoshi, Wallace K. 2
Matier, Curtis Owens *IBC*
Matthews, Larry 6
Maxson, Ronald 96
May, Del 6
Mayo, Dudley W. *IBC*

McCann, Cecil 23
McCorkle, John 6
McCosar, Bunnie 6, 62, Matthew 62, Matthew, Jr. 62, Nellie 62, Shirley 62, Victor 62, Winford 62
McCraney, James 88
McDade, Hayden 7
McDonald, S.S. 112, Susan Carol 108, William E. Jr. *IBC*
McGee, Colin 6, Robert L. Jr. 2
McHugh, Doc 6
McIlhenney, Jim 6
McIlroy, Douglas 23
McKenna, Robert 23
Mckenzie, Paul *IBC*
McNair, William *IBC*
McNown, John 6
Meek, Charles Edward (Chuck) 37, 38, 39, Ed 37, 38, 39, Gary 6, 39, James 6, June 37, Kristine 39, Mark 6, Sandy 37
Metoyer, Bryford *IBC*
Metz, Donald S. 111
Meute, Howard M. *IBC*
Miller, William 16
Mitchell, Galen 6, 28, 29, John E. *IBC*, Ralph *IBC*
Mitzel, Lonny *IBC*
Mock, Bivra 94
Mock, Rufus 94
Mollison, Ed 104
Monroe, Charles Caleb *IBC*
Montoya, Louie Gooch 102
Montz, Lorraine 84
Moody, Alfred J. *IBC*
Moore, Harold 70, H. G. 113, Hoyt Bruce, III 6, Jimmy Ray *IBC*, Joyce 6, Robin 10, Ronald A. 2
Mora, Emily 6, 48
Morimoto, Nobue 10
Morris, Bob 6
Morrow, James 23
Mueller, Ralph 23
Mulcare, Brian 6
Mullin, Gerald *IFC*
Munoz, Jose Jr. 2
Murphy 13, Terence 12, 13, Arthur 83
Murrell, Aaron Crusoe *IFC*
Myers, Betty 6, 40, 41, Diane 6, Frances 40, George Arthur 40, 41, George, Jr. 40, George, Sr. 40

N

Najar, Adam Serna *IBC*
Naughton, Thomas, Jr. 23
Neace, Bob 6
Nelson, David 85, Paul Arthur 2
Neumann, Pete 17
Nevarez, Alexandro 48, Mike 48, Vera 48
Nevins, Eldon E. *IBC*
Newby, C. 113
Newcombe, Andrew Jackson *IBC*

Niezgoda, Michael 23
Nigro, William 34
Nixon, Dale 63, Jeffie 63, Jerry 63, Laura 63, Ronald 63, Samuel 63
Noone, Lana 6
Northrop, James Leeroy *IBC*
Norton, Karen Thall 6
Nozewski 18, Robert 23

O

O'Brien, Clyde H. *IBC*
O'Connor, Anne 7, Steve 7
O'Flaherty, Page Creed 6
Oliver, Kimberly Spinks 7
Olmstead, Stanley *IBC*
Olson, J. S. 113
O'Mara, Kristine Meek 6, 37, 38, 39
Omstead, David K. 2
Orlowski, Hedwig Diane 54
Otani, Mary 50
Overacker, Earl John 2
Owen, Jan 6

P

Pack, Robert Van 3
Page, John 98, Susan 98
Painter, Faye 85, Michael Harris 85
Paprocki, Patricia 19
Parks, Harold David 53, H. D. 113, Joe 3
Parnell, Verna 44
Parrish 113
Paton, Richard 23
Patterson, James 23, Michael 23
Payne, Chuck 6
Pearce, William 23
Pellerin, Richard 6
Pena, Jesse J. *IBC*
Pennell, Wilbert 23
Percy, S. 113, Susan Creed 6, 98, 99
Perhogan, Nancy Santorum 6
Peters, George C. *IBC*
Peterson, Bill 6, 74, Kathleen 7
Phillips, Arlene 15, 16, Jack 15, 16, James Clifford *IBC*, Jeannie 16, 17, Nathaniel J. *IBC*, Neoma Jean 15, Opal 15, Shephen H. 15, Stephen 15, 165, 17, Steve 6, 15, 16, 17, Wood 15
Pietrzyk, Mark 23
Pinson, Cloyde Jr. *IBC*
Pittman, Robert Edward 3
Plise, Marilyn Wright 6, 52
Podgus, C. 113
Poisson, Collette 7
Pojani, George 6
Pollack, James 117
Pool, Ed 6
Prescott, Rhona 53
Prescott, R. M. 113
Pusillo, Michael 6
Pyle, Chris M. *IBC*

Q

Quinslek, D. 113

R

Rabacal, Patrick H. *IBC*
Ragle, Linda 6
Ramirez, Nelson *IBC*
Ramsey, Michael Wayne 2
Randolph, Seth E. *IBC*
Ravey, Major Guy 6
Raymond, Ron 6
Redding, Kit 18
Redinger, Harold 11
Reece, Jim 6
Reese, Dan 6
Rego, John H. *IBC*
Reid, Kenneth Wayne 2
Rendall, I. 113
Ribitsch, Eric 2
Riles, James C. 2
Riley, Howard G. *IBC*
Riordan, George William *IBC*
Ritchie, Glen Jr. *IBC*
Roane, Mildred 64
Robertson, Mark 18, 23, *IFC*
Roberts, R. 113
Rodriguez, Calixtro S. *IBC*, Israel 2
Roehler, George 18
Rogers, B 114, Peter 21, Roy 73
Ross, Stanley D. 2
Rouse, Edward 6, 60, 61
Rowell, Jennifer 6
Rowley 6, Donald 23, *IBC*
Rubin, D. 114
Rucker, Emmett Jr. *IBC*, John O'Neal *IBC*
Ruiz, Jose 2
Rupinski, Bernard F. *IBC*
Russell, John E. *IBC*
Ryder, Dan 6, 18

S

Sadler, B. 114
Sadler, Barry 10
Saegaert, Donald 2
Salazar, John *IBC*
Sampson, Gerald Hilbert *IBC*
Sandoval, Jerry 6, Joaquin 6
Sanford, M. G. 114, Teddy H., Jr. 6
Sankey, Bud 75
Saukaitis, Joseph S. 2
Saxon, Tomeka 6
Scavone, Dave 106
Schirra, Danielle 6
Schlatter, J. 114
Schmidt, John 40, 41, John George 40, 41, Mary 40, Theresa 40
Scoggins, Walter 6, 30, 31
Scruggs, Jan 6, 8
Seagroves, Michael Anthony 2
Self, Bernice 34, Eugene 34, 35, Mason 34, 35, Sue Jacklin 34, Susan 34, 35
Senick, Paul 58
Sexton, Richard II 2
Shane, Cameron 7
Shaw, Joe Carl 2
Shea, Thomas C. 2

Shepard, Clyde 104, Henry, Jr. 104, Henry Sr. 104
Sherman, J. 111
Shine, Colleen 6
Shook, Darelynn 80
Shorter, Nancy 52
Shorts, William Vincent *IBC*
Shue, Donald 2
Shugarts, Bill 6, 8
Siegwald, George 18
Sieting, Stanley *IFC*
Silberberg, Vera 6
Simpson, Douglas Edward 2
Sims, Clifford Chester 2
Singer, Eva 72, 114, Karina 72, Morton 72, 113, 114, Norman 72, 113, Vera 72
Skaron, Margie 48
Skeen, Richard 2
Skilling, Greg 6
Skocich, Frank *IBC*
Slane, William Llewellyn 2
Smith 18, David 23, Earl 18, 19, Hubert Ray 2, Leslie R. *IFC*, Phil 6, Ronald 23
Smyth, Doug 34, 35, Douglas 6
Snyder, Gerald A. 2
Sosnoski, Lindsay 7, Natalie 7
Spitzer, Howard Ray 2
Sprewell, John Spurgeon 2
Sprowls, Ruth 6
Stake, Kendall *IBC*
Stancroff, Dennis 18
Standish, Miles 73
Stanley, Gary 83
Stanton, Scott N. 2
Stasko, Thomas 27
Stec-Calabrese, Andrea 34
Steedly, Homer, Jr. 6
Stemac, Stephen Joseph 2
Stephenson, Diane 6
Stewart, Danny 6, 106, Peter *IBC*, Ulysses *IFC*
Stringer, Isaac 2
Stuart, John 96, 117
Stubblefield, James 23
Sulek, Kim 6
Sullivan, Brian 6, Joseph H. *IBC*
Sustersic, Louis *IBC*
Swaim, C. 114
Swanson, Jon Edward *IBC*
Swartout, Jennifer 7
Sweet, John Harlan *IBC*

T

Tadios, Leonard M. *IBC*
Tapp, Marshall Landis *IBC*
Tarango, Magdaleno 2
Tarrant, Jill 6
Tatnall, Clyde *IBC*
Tenorio, Sam *IBC*
Terry, Delton E. *IBC*, Janice 6
Terwilliger, David 23
Theresa, Meyers 40
Thomas, Frank 65, 85, 117
Thompson, Charles Michael *IFC*, Dennis Michael 2, Larry 17
Thoreson, Joel 6
Tillman, Craig 6

119

Toler, V. 114
Tonsetic, R. 114
Torello, Carl *IFC*
Traylor, Fred 30, 31, Glenda 30, 31, Howard 30, 31, Peggy 30, Velma 30, Wayne 30, 31
Treis, Robert 6, 98
Trescott, Charles 23
Troyan, Michael 18, 23
Tucker, E. 114, S. 114, Willie *IBC*
Tuck, Hubert, Jr. 35
Turley, Duke 90, Frances Cortor 6, 90, 91, Morvan Darrell *IFC*

U

Ulm, Donald 42
Underhill, David Joseph *IFC*
Unruh, Victor 6

V

Vasquez, Eddie 2
Vilonis, Victor 6

W

Wade, Mary 6, 40, 41
Wagner, Samantha 7
Waller, JoAnn 6
Walls, Diane 6, Kenneth Marion 2
Ward, Timmie *IBC*
Wardwell, Eric. *IBC*
Ware, Roger 6
Warren, Jeider Jackson *IBC*
Watanabe 6, Carol 51, Gordon 50, Goro 50, Hayako 50, James 51, Julia 50, 51
Waters, Samuel E. Jr. 2
Watson, William L. *IBC*
Weaver, George R. Jr. 3
Webb, Gregory *IBC*
Wehde, Gerald *IBC*
Wells, John 23
Wentworth, John V. *IBC*
Westmoreland, William 94
Wetzel, Jerry 6
Weyher, Celia 7
Whitaker, Rudolph *IBC*
White, Charles M. Sr. 2, Cordis 44, Donald Eugene 44, Lila 44, Lucille 44, Verna 44
Whitney, Bruce 102
Wiles, Geoffrey 6
Williams, Lester Lee 2
Williamson, Glenda 6, 31
Willis, William Sherrill *IFC*
Winters, Darryl Gordon 2
Witzig, Raymond 65, 67
Woddall, Leslie 104
Wojciak, Bob 6, Pat 6
Wolf, R. 115
Wolos, Cathy 6, 45, 46, 47, Margaret 45, 46, Michael 45, Nellie 45, 46, Paul 45, 46, Peter 6, 45, 46
Woodall 106, Frances 105, Judy 6, 104, 105, 106, Leslie 105
Wright, Claire 52, Clarence 52, Loretta 52, Marilyn 52, Nancy 52, Walter Clarence 52, William 52

Y

Yaco, Richard 9, 71, 117
Yamashita, Kenji Jerry *IBC*
Yee, Edward *IBC*
Yokom, Chip 6
Youngblood, Charles E. *IFC*
Young, M. B. 115

Z

Zippert, J. 115
Zwerlein, Robert 2

103. Lundin, John
104. Matier, Curtis Owens
105. McNair, William
106. Pyle, Chris M.
107. Moore, Jimmy Ray
108. Nevins, Eldon E.
109. Moody, Alfred J.
110. Stake, Kendall
111. Tenorio, Sam
112. Phillips, Nathaniel J.
113. Sweet, John Harlan
114. Tatnall, Clyde
115. Tapp, Marshall Landis
116. Daily, Thomas
117. Shorts, William Vincent
118. Sampson, Gerald Hilbert
119. Salazar, John
120. Ward, Timmie
121. Watson, William L.
122. Wehde, Gerald
123. Whitaker, Rudolph
124. Mayo, Dudley W.
125. Stewart, Peter
126. Mckenzie, Paul
127. Mitzel, Lonny
128. Najar, Adam Serna
129. Newcombe, Andrew Jackson
130. Rodriguez, Calixtro S.
131. O'Brien, Clyde H.
132. Pinson, Cloyde Jr.
133. Ramirez, Nelson
134. Rabacal, Patrick H.
135. Rupinski, Bernard F.
136. Sustersic, Louis
137. Sullivan, Joseph H.
138. Skocich, Frank

139. Yee, Edward
140. Yamashita, Kenji Jerry
141. Warren, Jeider Jackson
142. Webb, Gregory
143. Wentworth, John V.
144. McDonald, William E. Jr.
145. Monroe, Charles Caleb
146. Mitchell, Ralph
147. Metoyer, Bryford
148. Meute, Howard M.
149. Gentinne, Thomas
150. Northrop, James Leeroy
151. Terry, Delton E.
152. Wardwell, Eric
153. Tucker, Willie Jr.
154. Swanson, Jon Edward
155. Rowley, Donald A.
156. Davison, David
157. Love, Harry William
158. Rego, John H.
159. Riley, Howard G.
160. Riordan, George William
161. Rucker, Emmett Jr.
162. Mitchell, John E.
163. Guy, Leonard A.
164. Harrell, Lenwood T.
165. Hankerson, Jimmie
166. Phillips, James Clifford
167. Pena, Jesse J.
168. Lawrence, Bobby J.
169. Tadios, Leonard M.
170. Russell, John E.

171. Llamas, Jose
172. Hath, James S.
173. Harris, Paul Winiford
174. Lish, Gilbert R.
175. Larry, John D. Jr.
176. Latoria, David J.
177. Belcher, Glenn
178. Randolph, Seth E.
179. Lawton, Michael E.
180. Olmstead, Stanley
181. Garrett, Paul E.
182. Dawson, John Robert
183. Leatherbury, Louis Anthon
184. Peters, George C.
185. Lee, Roy Ronald
186. Cryan, Kenneth M.
187. Hansey, Mitchel
188. Ritchie, Glen Jr.
189. Lilley, Joseph Emmett
190. Lloyd, Freddie G.
191. Gibson, Terrell
192. Giannelli, Giuseppe